# Children
## of
## Dust

# CHILDREN OF DUST

## A Portrait of a Muslim as a Young Man

## Ali Eteraz

HarperOne
*An Imprint of HarperCollinsPublishers*

HarperOne

This is a work of creative nonfiction. All the events are true to the best of my recollection and subject to my interpretation at various points in my life. Some characters are composites, segmented, or transposed in various places along this narrative. Identities and locations have been changed to protect lives, reputations, and privacy.

FIRST HARPERCOLLINS PAPERBACK EDITION PUBLISHED IN 2011

Library of Congress Cataloging-in-Publication Data
    Eteraz, Ali.
    Children of dust : a portrait of a Muslim as a young man / by Ali Eteraz. — 1st ed.
        p.   cm.
    ISBN 978-0-06-162685-2
    1. Eteraz, Ali. 2. Muslims—Biography. 3. Radicalism—Religious aspects— Islam. 4. Islamic fundamentalism. 5. Religious awakening—Islam. I. Title.
BP80.E85C45 2010
297.092—dc22
    [B]                                                     2009009666

11 12 13 14 15 BV 10 9 8 7 6 5 4 3 2 1

*For my parents*
*and those who have been like parents*

*God said to the angels: Make obeisance to Adam;*
*they made obeisance, but Iblis [the satan], did it not.*
*He said: Shall I make obeisance to him*
*whom Thou hast created of dust?*

QURAN 17:61

# Contents

# Prologue

I n Mecca fathers become inclined to give up their sons.

In 1980, at the spot where the Prophet Ibrahim once sought to slaughter his son Ismail after receiving a revelation from God; at the same place where God gave a dream to Abdul Muttalib asking him to sacrifice his son Abdullah; my twenty-two-year-old father-to-be put his head to the floor and entered into a covenant with Allah Azzawajal, the Exalted.

"Ya Allah! If you should give me a son," he said, "I promise that he will become a great leader and servant of Islam!"

That accord, called a *mannat,* made before my birth, singularly and exclusively guided my life for three decades. It conditioned me to serve Islam and it made the service of Islam my condition. In fulfillment of that covenant I studied at *madrassa*s. I rejected the companionship of non-Muslims. I rose up against secularism. I struggled on behalf of oppressed Muslims. And, in the age of terrorism, I sought to become a reformer of Islam.

To say that I was enamored of Islam would be an understatement. I waved the banners of this faith from Asia to America. I studied Islamic scripture and scholarship from an early age. I aspired, perspired, and prayed to one day be lucky enough to rise to the apex of my religion. Over and over again I strove to be an Islamic activist—to become the embodiment of Muhammad's religion.

This book is about what happened when I loved Islam—with affection, with torment, with stupidity—more than anything else in this world. This book is about ardor bordering on obsession. This book is about a thoroughly Islamic childhood and about a boy's attempt not merely to know his identity, but to assert his sovereignty. (Some parts of it are about the girls he met along the way.)

Read! In the name of the God who taught man the use of the pen . . . and remember, you can't get a death *fatwa* for laughing.*

---

\* Probably.

# Book I

## The Promised—Abir ul Islam

*In which the author, as a child in Pakistan,
learns of his destiny and attends a madrassa*

# I

My mother, Ammi, had just returned from Koh-e-Qaf, where women went when they were annoyed with their husbands. It was far up in the heavens, far beyond the world of men, above the astral planes of the *jinn*s, and hidden even from the angels. Upon reaching Koh-e-Qaf a woman became a *parri* and congregated with others like her. Then all the *parri*s gathered upon rippling streams and rivers of celestial milk. They bathed and splashed and darted around on rich, creamy froth.

I was just a seven-year-old child living in a tiny apartment in Lahore, Pakistan. I couldn't get enough of Koh-e-Qaf.

"What happens there?" I asked Ammi. "Please tell me! Please!"

"It's a safe place where I can gather my thoughts," she said. "When women go there, we don't take our earthly concerns with us. We don't even need our earthly clothes. Allah restores to us the cuticle skin we had when He first created Hazrat Adam and his wife, Havva."

Ammi said that Koh-e-Qaf was created secretly at the time the universe was made. Allah had asked each one of His creations whether they would be willing to bear the burden of free will. He asked the mountains and they said no. He asked the skies and they refused. He asked the sun and the seas and the plants and the trees and the angels.

They all said no. But Adam, the first male—"who took too many risks just like your Pops"—accepted the burden. "And he didn't even ask his wife what he was getting into!" Upon hearing the news, a chagrined Havva went to Allah and told Him that men would make a big mess of things and "then take out their frustration on their wives." So, for all the wives of the world, Havva convinced Allah to create Koh-e-Qaf, a sanctuary for all time.

"Then she made Allah give long nails to women so they could remember their special place."

"That's not fair," I said, poking a finger through Ammi's curly black hair. "I don't have a special place to go to."

"You don't need a special place," she replied. "My little piece of the moon is more special than the whole world."

"You're just saying that."

"No, I'm not," she said. "Haven't you ever thought about what your name means?"

"Abir?"

"Your *full* name. Abir ul Islam."

"So what? It's just a name."

"Not just a name."

I shrugged. Compared to intergalactic travel and teleportation and heavenly drinks, my name didn't inspire much awe.

"Come on," Ammi said, taking my hand as if she could read the disappointment on my face. "You don't believe me? Let's go see Beyji. She will tell you that you are the most special."

Beyji was my maternal great-grandmother. She lived in a white marble bungalow in Lahore. She was a saint because she had forgiven the woman who used black *jadu* to kill Beyji's husband. Beyji regularly met with the Holy Prophet Muhammad in her dreams. One year, during the Night of Power in the month of Ramzan, she got chosen as one of Allah's elect and saw a glimpse of the Light.

Ammi led me past my grandfather's room, where he was busy listening to old Noor Jahan recordings, and toward Beyji's darkened quarters. We went inside and Ammi pushed me toward Beyji's bed. She wore a floral print *shalwar kameez*—loose trousers with a tunic top—

and had cast a gauzy blue *dupatta* over her head. Taking my wrist with one hand and holding my chin with the other, she gave me a smile. Her gummy mouth murmured a series of prayers.

"Beyji," Ammi said. "This one doesn't believe me when I tell him that he's special."

"The *most* special," Beyji corrected.

"I told him that his name is Abir ul Islam."

"Such a beautiful name, isn't it?"

"He doesn't think it's such a big deal."

"Is that right?" Beyji looked at me for confirmation.

I made my case. "Ammi flies around like a *parri* and goes to Koh-e-Qaf. I just sit here."

Beyji looked at me with compassion. She pulled a piece of dried orange out from under her pillow and handed it to me. "Come and sit with me," she invited. "Then ask your Ammi to tell you the story of your birth."

"What about it?"

"She'll tell you," Beyji said.

Ammi sat down on the other bed and rested a cup of *chai* on the palm of her hand. With two fingers she pinched the cream congealed on the surface.

"When I was pregnant with you," Ammi said, licking her fingers, "Pops moved to Saudi Arabia for work. When he was there, he went to the Ka'ba in Mecca and made a *mannat*. Do you know what a *mannat* is?"

"No."

"A *mannat* is like a covenant with Allah. You promise to do something if Allah grants one of your wishes."

"Like a *jinn* in a lamp!"

"Except God imposes conditions!" Beyji amended.

"Your father's *mannat* was that if his first child was a boy," Ammi continued, "he would be raised to become a leader and servant of Islam. Are you listening?"

"Yes," I said, orange sticking out of my mouth.

"Then *you* were born—a boy—which meant that the *mannat* must be fulfilled."

"Are you still listening?" Beyji prompted.

I nodded and adopted the serious expression that their intensity seemed to require.

"So we needed to give you a name that reflected your purpose in life," Ammi said. "There were many options, but Pops said that your name should be Abir. It means perfume. Full name: Abir ul Islam. Perfume of Islam. You were thus born to spread Islam as if it were a beautiful fragrance. Special, no?"

"It's just a name," I said skeptically.

"Ah, but that's not all," Beyji said, nudging me affectionately. "Keep listening."

"Then," Ammi continued, "right when you were born we moved to Saudi Arabia. When you were barely eleven months old, you and Pops and I went to do *hajj*—the pilgrimage to Mecca. I dressed you up like all the other pilgrims. You looked so cute wrapped in all white. You had been trying to walk for many weeks, but I swear as soon as we got to Mecca you began walking properly. It had to have been that holy sand. You really took to Mecca. Walking around. Greeting everyone. You even ran away from me in the middle of the night. We were frantic until you were discovered hours later with a pair of Bedouins. It was like you were meant to be there."

"Did the Bedouins have goats?" I asked, my attention momentarily derailed.

"I think they did," Ammi said. "Anyway. One night I went to circumambulate the Ka'ba and took you with me. The place wasn't as crowded at night. There was a long row of Africans walking with their elbows locked like a chain. I stayed behind them until they made their turn and I found myself right at the border of the Ka'ba . . ."

"The House of God," Beyji said, her eyes shining. "I've been there twice in my life. It's the most beautiful thing in the universe. Astronauts will tell you that the world sits right in the center of the universe, and that Mecca sits right in the middle of the world, and that the Ka'ba sits right in the middle of Mecca!"

"There's a semicircular wall around the Ka'ba," Ammi continued. "It was built by the Prophet Ibrahim thousands of years ago. I forget the name of that space, but it's said that if you pray there, it's as if you'd prayed inside the Ka'ba. It was peaceful there that night. No one else was in the area. Imagine: millions of people wearing the same thing and chanting the same thing—*Labbayk Allahumma Labbayk*—all around us, and a mother and son just all alone with the Ka'ba. It was beautiful."

Beyji interrupted again: "Don't forget! Mecca was founded by a mother and son, too. At Allah's instruction, Hajira and baby Ismail were left there by the Prophet Ibrahim. They had no water, so Hajira put Ismail down in the sand to go and find something to drink. While she was gone, little Ismail kicked his feet and the Zamzam spring sprouted from the desert sand. A town was built there when some nomads discovered the spring."

Ammi nodded and continued: "I had you stand next to me and we made a pair of *nafal* prayers together. I asked Allah to place Islamic knowledge in your heart and make you a true servant of Islam. Then I removed your clothes, lifted you up, and rubbed your bare chest against the ancient wall—back and forth a few times."

As I listened to the women, my heart beat fast and my face became warm. I felt connected to this distant place that I didn't remember. The reverence it elicited in my mother and great-grandmother poured into me.

"Then later, when I was resting," Ammi continued, "your Pops took you with him. He went to rub your chest against the heavenly Black Stone at one corner of the Ka'ba. He wasn't able to get to it because it's always so crowded with people trying to kiss it, but he pressed you against the bare walls of the Ka'ba itself. He made the same prayer I did, about you serving Islam."

"*Subhanallah*," Beyji said and put her hand on my heart. "One day you should go back to Mecca and kiss the Black Stone. It will absorb all your sins. But not yet. Go when you are older. Right now you are sinless."

I nodded eagerly.

"So," Ammi said. "Do you believe you are special now?"

I felt as if the entire universe was listening to my answer. God. The angels. Even the *parris*.

"Yes. I believe you. I believe that I'm special."

"By the way, did you know that when the Black Stone first came down from heaven it was white?" Ammi said.

"What happened to it?" I asked.

"People touched it and it became dirty," she said.

I imagined billions of hands touching a large, egg-shaped crystal over thousands of years and gradually making it black. Suddenly I pulled away from Beyji and stood up in the center of the room, feeling proud and powerful.

"I will take a towel and make it white again!"

Beyji kissed my hand and told me that I would be Islam's most glorious servant.

# 2

During the daytime, while Pops was off working at his clinic—he was a doctor—Ammi, my little brother Flim, and I often spent the daytime hours at Beyji's bungalow.

Beyji came from a long line of elevated people. Her father, an *imam* at a small mosque in a village in Punjab, had commanded a clan of *jinn*s that converted to Islam at his hand. The old man's piety was so great that when he died his fingers kept moving as if they were flipping *tasbih* beads in prayer.

Beyji prayed endlessly. When she wasn't praying, she murmured Allah's praises—*subhanallah* and *alhamdulillah* thirty-three times each, *allahu akbar* thirty-four times. Then she repeated the set. She kept count on the individual pads of her fingers, on black beans that were stored in a number of huge vats in her room, or on the *tasbih*, the wooden rosary.

Beyji had mysterious connections with the angels. In addition to having seen the Light that time in Ramzan, she seemed to know Jibrail, the leader of the angels, quite well. "He's the greatest angel," she said. "He brought the Holy Quran to the Prophet in the cave of Hira. He hugged the Messenger and imparted the Word."

"Have you seen him up close?"

"I have. He's beautiful. He has forty thousand wings, and each of his feathers is made of light. He can pick up the entire universe on one wing."

"How many angels are there?" I inquired.

"Millions."

"Did the Prophet meet all the angels?"

"There are too many for him to meet, but some of the angels used to come to him during his daily life. They came in the guise of men—beautiful men—and ate with him and asked him questions that prepared him to deal with his enemies in Mecca."

"Who's the most important angel?" I asked.

"They're all important. Mikail is pretty important because he maintains the history of the world in his big book. Israfil because he has the trumpet that—"

"Do you think I can meet an angel?"

"Of course you can," she said. "The Guardians are always with you. That's why when Muslims pray we say *Salam* to the right and the left shoulder. That's where they sit. It's very good to talk to your angels, but make sure you say only good things, because they have little notebooks and they write down everything you do."

"Everything?" I asked, horrified.

"Yes."

"Even what I do in the bathroom?"

"Yes."

"Gross."

Learning that angels were always with me made me want to learn more about them, so I went to Ammi. She told me that Guardians came in two shifts, one that lasted from dawn to afternoon and the other that covered late afternoon to morning.

"Why is the evening shift longer?" I asked. "That doesn't seem fair."

"Beats me. Ask Allah."

That day I laid a prayer rug and prayed for equality among the angels.

My sympathy for the angels receded, however, when one day I learned that they could be as frightening as they were beautiful.

There was the angel that killed you, said Ammi; another angel that blew the trumpet on the Last Day and destroyed the world. There were angels that worked in Dozakh, where the hellfire burned, and stirred the bodies of sinners in huge vats full of hot water; angels that put a black flag in your anus if you listened to music; angels that turned people into pillars of salt and flipped civilizations over and caused huge storms of fire. There were even angels that urinated in your mouth— "for forty days minimum"—if you used a swear word.

"Why are the angels so scary?" I asked Ammi.

"Sometimes Allah sends them out to punish the people that follow Iblis," Ammi said. "But you see, the angels are just doing their job. Most of the time they're very nice; they just stand around and sing Allah's praises. It's Iblis who is the scary one."

"Who is Iblis?"

"The worst: Shaytan. Mankind's mortal enemy."

Iblis was a *jinn* that, before the creation of mankind, had been raised up to heaven because he was pious, but then he disobeyed Allah and was cast out of the Garden and now sought revenge against mankind by leading people to falsehood. He did many evil things:

If you yawned and didn't cover your mouth, he slept under your tongue for the whole night and defecated in your throat, which gave you bad breath. If you didn't recite *bismillah*—"in the name of God"— before eating your food, he ate all of it so you remained hungry. He was the one who told you not to take a walk around the block after dinner so you would have gas in your stomach and break your *wazu,* your ablutions, by farting. He was the one who was responsible for pulling a donkey's tail and making it heehaw during prayers. He was the one who caused those scary shooting stars, because at night he tried to sneak into Paradise to topple the *kursi*—Allah's throne—and the angels fended him off by throwing meteorites at him.

"You must never follow Iblis," Ammi said. "You are Abir ul Islam, and Iblis wants to deceive Muslims."

"I won't. I promise. I am Abir ul Islam, and Iblis is my enemy."

I resolved to one day join the angels that fought Iblis, and in preparation for hurling meteorites I threw my tennis ball against the wall.

# 3

One day when he wasn't working, Pops took me for a long walk alongside the canal and told me the history of Islam and Pakistan.

He told me about the British taking over Mughal India; the fall of the Ottoman caliphate in 1924, which took away the protector of the Muslims; the circumstances around the creation of Pakistan, a state for Muslims who sought to avoid being dominated by the Hindus; the emergence of the Jamaat-e-Islami Party; the breakup of East and West Pakistan; the rise of Zulfiqar Ali Bhutto and his eventual hanging at the hands of General Zia ul Haq.

"I support him," Pops said about the general. "Because he's a pious Muslim and because he gives unwavering support to the *mujahideen* in Afghanistan attacked by the Soviets."

"Why did the Soviets attack Afghanistan?" I asked as we crossed a street full of sputtering blue and green motorized rickshaws.

"There are two reasons," Pops said, giving me his pinky to hold. "First, the Soviets persecute people who follow Islam. In their country Muslims have to hide their Qurans and pretend that they are non-Muslim. Second, the Soviet Union wants to capture Afghanistan so that it can then capture a part of Pakistan and gain our warm-water port at Gwadar. They need this to attack America by sea."

"And Zia ul Haq is helping the *mujahideen* fight the Soviet Union?"

"Yes. The *mujahideen* fight in the name of Islam, and even the world's greatest army cannot defeat them."

The *mujahideen* immediately inspired me. When Pops wasn't around I'd try to talk about them with Ammi, but she didn't listen to news and didn't have much to say about them. However, because I insisted on hearing about *jihad*, she told me stories about the famous battles waged by the Prophet and his Companions. There was the Battle of Badr, where the Prophet and his 313 Companions held off a polytheistic army far greater in number because the Muslims were joined by scimitar-wielding angels; there was the Battle of Uhud, where the Prophet suffered a wound in his side because of the treachery of the Hypocrites; and there was the Battle of Khandaq, where the Prophet dug a trench around Medina on the advice of his Persian friend Salman, who used to be a slave but was freed by Muslims.

Because I insisted on hearing even more about the *mujahideen*, one day Ammi took me to a bookstore and bought me a children's magazine that contained part of a serialized novella about a boy named Mahmud who lived in Kabul. His father fought against the Soviets while his mother tended to injured *mujahideen*. His little sister was mutilated when she picked up a land mine that the Soviets had disguised as a teddy bear. Mahmud wanted everyone to know that all around Afghanistan the Soviets had placed land mines that looked like toys and were causing all the little boys and girls in the country to lose appendages and eyes. He also described helicopter gunships that sprayed fire, and talked about how he dreamed of owning a missile that would allow him to take the gunships down. He wanted to liberate his land in the name of Islam. I wished I could help him.

When I was done reading that story, I desperately wanted to go and get the next part in the series, but whenever I appealed to Ammi to take me back to the bookstore, she said it was too far and there was no use getting *khajjal* in all the traffic. I went back to the story of Mahmud and read it over and over until I nearly had it memorized. Eventually I grew bored and started reading another action story in the magazine. It was about a black South African rebel living under apartheid. Whites spat on him and segregated his people and insulted his family so that eventually he had no choice but to stand up for his dignity and take matters into his own hands. One day the white governor, under whose rule the rebel lived, was throwing a party on a lake, and the rebel, having read about the pending event, decided that he would drive a boat laden with explosives into the governor's yacht. The story of his resistance ended with a blaze that consumed the yacht and the rebel and the governor. This story didn't interest me so much because it wasn't about Islam.

It was then that I discovered *Aakhri Chataan*—"The Last Mountain"—a long-running serial produced by Pakistani TV. The series was based on the novel of the same name by a Jamaat-e-Islami journalist, Naseem Hijazi. The drama, set between the years AD 1220 and 1226, at the height of Genghis Khan's invasions of Islamic Asia, and thirty years before the fall of the caliphate in Baghdad at the hands of Hulagu Khan, was lavish and star-studded.

The protagonist, the proverbial last mountain, was Sultan Jalaluddin Khwarezmi, a prince of Persia, bereft of his kingdom when his father was killed by the Mongols. He waged a long-standing series of battles against Genghis, raising armies and chasing him from Armenia and Azerbaijan to India and back again. The serial was a tragic-romantic recounting of the major military and political events in Khwarezmi's life, interwoven with the exploits of his allies.

In the final episode, one of Khwarezmi's cohorts gave a rousing speech to the leaders of Baghdad about making a call for *jihad*—which only the Caliph had the power to do—and sending troops to Khwarezmi's assistance. He told them to believe in Khwarezmi because he was the only Central Asian leader who had defeated the Mongols in open battle. The speech caused the leaders to break out in spirited debate, because they didn't want the Caliph to declare *jihad*. Meanwhile, the scene shifted to Khwarezmi, standing atop a cliff with his men near the front against the Mongols. At a distance he saw riders bearing Baghdad's colors. The sight of the riders prompted him to break into a monologue in which he thanked the heavens for Baghdad's support and lambasted the skeptics among his crew for doubting Baghdad's mettle: "I told you that Allah would hear our prayers and they would come."

Once the riders came closer, however, Khwarezmi realized that they were simply messengers carrying a letter of decline from Baghdad. The Caliph had shown his cowardice.

It was here that the tragic climax of the series occurred. Intermixed with scenes of dance, wine, and women—symbols of a Muslim warrior's failure—Khwarezmi engaged in a sequence of monologues. He bemoaned his castles of sand, complained of the way the soldier's blade melted before the enemy's wealth, and wept that his voice didn't reach the heavens. The series came to an end with *tasbih* beads falling ingloriously upon the ground as an anonymous old man cried, while Khwarezmi, no longer worthy of a horse, got atop an ass and rode off into the snow. The scene of his departure was followed by still paintings accompanied by melancholy music depicting Baghdad's eventual fall to Hulagu Khan in 1258, a story of great tragedy and humiliation that all Muslims know well.

The main character of the series turned out not to be Khwarezmi. It was Baghdad—its decadent elite, its political intrigue, its traitors, its emasculated Caliphs. It was the infiltration of pro-Mongol elements, and the monopoly of sniveling, pacifist, fatalist, out-of-touch clerics who simply wouldn't allow the Caliph to make an open call for *jihad* and go to Khwarezmi's assistance. To avoid being defeated as Baghdad was by the Mongols, Muslims had to be more like the Companions of the Prophet or the *mujahideen* of Afghanistan. They had to engage in *jihad*. That was the TV show's simple lesson.

I took a tennis racket, tied a rope around it, and slung it around my torso like a Kalashnikov. Then I went around declaring people Mongols and shooting them.

# 4

I learned of sin from a girl named Sina.

A few years older than my seven, she was a servant at Beyji's house. She had dark brown skin and her musk was musty. She bore the irrepressible smell of a kitchen drain clogged with stale vegetables. She owned just one outfit, a light pink floral *shalwar kameez*. Due to age and infinite washing it had become nearly see-through, so that when she went into a squat and swept the veranda in long, controlled, side-to-side sweeps of the *jharoo* I could see her sinewy thighs—dark pythons wearing gauzy veils. When she picked up my plates I could see the small areolas on her chest. Day after day I watched her, wanting only that she raise her downcast eyes and look at me. Yet she remained expressionless. She performed her chores with such blind commitment, such indifferent exactitude, that there was never any reason for anyone to speak to her. If out of all the other servant girls she was arbitrarily selected to sift a batch of peas or pick a tray of lentils, she moved to the assigned task, completed it, and merged back into the shadows of irrelevance. I didn't know how I could catch her interest.

Then Adina visited the house.

Adina was a rich girl from overseas who had recently moved to Lahore and was invited over to play with me. She had been well fed on romance novels and Indian films. The first day together she took me into a bedroom and had me act out various film scenes with her. In one, where I was a restaurant owner and she was the habitually late waitress, I was supposed to lower my sunglasses—our only prop—and give her a deep, stern, manly look, a look that she had me modify and tinker with until it fulfilled her vision. In response to the look she wiggled and squirmed in apology, softening up her boss with feminine pouts, befuddled sighs, delicate knee slaps of haplessness, and mildly sensual nail-biting. In another scene she scripted, she and I had just entered into an arranged marriage and now, after the reception, were meeting for the first time. We were supposed to do "dialogue" with each other, she instructed: she would say creative and adult things about how she resented her parents for not asking her consent before marriage, to which I was supposed to respond with dramatic pronouncements that proclaimed the inevitability of her love for me.

I took Adina's role-playing game to Sina.

Following her around for a day, I found that there was a moment in her daily routine when she stripped off her cloak of invisibility, a time when she wasn't a servant but became, for lack of a better word, a woman. It was in the evening, when it had become dark but was not yet late enough for dinner. During that interval Sina went to the shed in the backyard and took a shower in the partly open servants' enclosure. Then, hair dripping, she put her clothes back on and walked around the backyard, airing herself. Save for the lights seeping through the curtains, it was completely dark by the time she finished. It was there in the yard that I approached her.

"I want you to play with me," I ordered.

"You want to play now?"

The darkness made me bold. "Yes. We will play here. I will be the husband."

"I don't know . . . ," she said in a voice drenched with reluctance.

"It will be all right," I assured. I grabbed her by the hand and took her to the lawn. The moon, full and fourteenth, had broken out of the clouds, and her skin and eyes were glowing. "So, let's see," I said, stalling for time as I came up with a scenario. "How about we're at a picnic?" I clinked an imaginary glass with her. "Drink!"

She mimicked, but without any eagerness.

"Come on, show a little *joash*," I demanded. "You're out on a beautiful day with your powerful husband! Show some desire!"

She didn't respond. After sipping my imaginary drink for a little while, I became annoyed by the silence.

"I think we need more dialogue. How will you feel if I tell you that your beauty is like that of a Night Princess?"

"I don't know," she said, looking genuinely bewildered.

"Look," I said, becoming the director. "You have options when someone says that to you. You can do *nakhra,* like whine and complain, to convey that you're very shy. Or you can be my enemy who gets angry—"

"I'm ashamed," she interrupted.

"Don't be!"

I pulled her close, more from affection than perversity. As she struggled against me, I made her fright a part of our role-play. She became the damsel in distress and I was her protector. As I held her body against mine, her hair spilled droplets on my arms. Her clothes were damp and sticky. My mood suddenly turned.

"Take off your clothes," I instructed. Then I paused for a moment, hearing the swishing of the trees, checking for the sound of footsteps in the driveway, listening to the laughter of oblivious adults safely lodged deep inside the belly of the bungalow. "I want to see your girl things," I said. "I will show you my privates in return."

It was a command. She was a servant: she obeyed. She pulled her *shalwar* to her knees and lifted up her shirt to her neck. The blue light danced on her scrubbed nudity. I stood back on my knees and pulled down my shorts for a brief moment. Then just as quickly I pulled them back up but let her remain naked so that I could touch her stomach.

While stroking her skin I made melodramatic *filmi* comments about her body, the moonlight, and fragrant roses. Then my mouth sought her chest, stomach, and thighs. Because I was not yet familiar with the concept of kissing, my movements were just that, actions that represented affection.

Yet, for all my interest in maintaining the integrity of the game, I couldn't bear to keep my lips against her body. Her smell oozed out of her skin and burned my nose. It was the smell of her poverty and servitude; of her caste and lower station. It disgusted me. In a sudden move I pulled away from her and stemmed a wave of nausea by holding my breath.

My withdrawal was an act so savage and sudden that it cut through the conditioning that over the years had made her obedience personified. It sliced through her submission. She pulled her clothes into place and writhed away, turning violently like a stepped-on worm. One pink *chappal,* hanging off her foot as she pulled away, dragged against the white marble as she disappeared into the dark.

Then she went and told on me.

The next day I was playing in the backyard when the adults came to punish me.

"Good boys don't play games with girls," Ammi said. "It is *gunah* to play games with girls. Do you understand?"

I nodded.

"Have you become Shaytan?"

"No. I am Abir ul Islam."

"You sure aren't behaving like it."

"Put out your left hand," my aunt said.

I obeyed.

Upon it she placed a piece of paper and a pencil and told me to write the penitential sentence—"I ask Allah for forgiveness"—one hundred times in neat handwriting and then make a signature at the bottom.

"Do you know why you're getting this piece of paper in your *left* hand?" she asked.

"No."

"Because of Islam."

"What about Islam?"

"On the Day of Judgment, when Allah raises mankind from their graves and decides who goes to Paradise and who goes to hell, everyone will be gathered under the Throne. Then a quick breeze will blow and it will deliver a piece of paper into each person's hand. If the paper is in the right hand it means the person will be bound for Paradise. If the paper is in the left hand it means the person will be bound for hell. What hand is *your* paper in?"

"Left."

"Do you understand what that means?"

"Yes."

"Now go and write your punishment."

Until that moment I hadn't assigned any significance to what had happened with Sina. Now, with the introduction of Allah's judgment, with the introduction of penitence and forgiveness and apology, with the threat of hell hanging over me, the entire sequence of events took on a dark tinge. I could feel *gunah* creeping on my skin like a lizard on a hot summer wall. I had done something that Allah didn't like. He would find me impious and unvirtuous and punishable. He would lean forward upon the *kursi* and look at His angels and say, "That Abir ul Islam really wasn't worthy of his name!" The angels would agree. Then they would revoke my membership from among the meteor-hurlers. Suddenly I couldn't bear how full of *gunah* I was and began crying. Then I wrote each word individually down the sheet:

> I-I-I . . .
> ask-ask-ask . . .
> Allah-Allah-Allah . . .
> for-for-for . . .
> forgiveness-forgiveness-forgiveness . . .

As I finished my hundredth petition, I began loathing girls. Being nice to them upset Allah, and upsetting Allah's rules was not something becoming of Abir ul Islam.

# 5

My family had ended up in Lahore because we couldn't get into America.

When I was an infant, Pops was an instructor at a university in Saudi Arabia. It was a good job that allowed him to buy a Volvo and send money to his parents in the village. But Pops dreamed about being a true medical doctor—and not in Pakistan or Saudi Arabia, but in America, where his children could grow up and become *someone* without having to pay bribes. So Pops left that job and moved us all the way to the island nation of Dominican Republic, where he enrolled in medical school. People said it was easy to get into America from there.

We lived among hefty Dominicans, suave Lebanese émigrés, vacationing Castilians, and a small contingent of sweaty Pakistani students who were following the same path to America—the state of salvation. With his feet in many jobs and a bottle in my newborn brother's mouth, Pops graduated and started looking into moving to New York. But when he filed his papers, he learned that due to immigration quotas we couldn't get in. Ammi also filed for immigration—this time through her brother, who already had American citizenship—but she was told that it would be seven to ten years before her name would be called if she followed that channel.

Out of ideas and in search of a job, Pops sent the three of us back to
Pakistan. Then, with our last eight hundred dollars in his pocket, he
went to Italy, hoping to gain admission in a medical fellowship. Less
than forty-eight hours later he was conned of all his money by a Muslim.
He had to call back to relatives in Pakistan to have money wired to him
so he could buy a return ticket.

He joined us a week later.

We stayed with Beyji at her fine bungalow for a little while and then
moved to a tiny apartment on a noisy lower-income street choked by
smog and trash, with a thick carpet of dust lapping against our door.
Every day Pops would get on his bike and ride around the towns en-
circling Lahore, seeking a place to launch a medical practice. After a
while, a small-time feudal landlord who lived in a red *haveli*, a mansion
left over from colonial days, invited him to open up a clinic in one of his
buildings.

It was a tepid practice: the patients came rarely, and when they did
it was only to compare medical prescriptions with what the *pir*, the
homeopath, and various quacks were peddling. Day after day Pops
came home on his bedraggled Suzuki motorcycle, his face darkened
by smog, and vented the frustration of another profitless day. Never the
stereotypically bulky Punjabi, he had cheeks that were sunken in, the
skin leathery and dark, and his hair was both in a balding recession
and a state of disarray. His arms were thin. His head was an enormous
bobbing egg on a skeleton that was all clavicle, elbows, and knees. His
clothes, a mishmash of checkered shirts and gray pants, bore the dusty
residue of the streets.

When it became clear that the medical practice was not going to do
well, Ammi and Pops had fights and Ammi retreated to the bedroom to
cry. As she sat and sobbed, I touched the tears on her face and flicked
them away. Then, when she forced a smile between her tears, it was my
turn to cry and she wiped my face with her wrist.

"Don't cry," she said reassuringly. "We will pray and all will be
well."

"*Inshallah*," I said.

Then Ammi became devout. The *jai namaz*, her prayer rug, was
flung open and pointed toward Mecca. A little red copy of the *punj*

*surah,* which contained the five most important chapters of the Quran, kept perpetual presence in her hand. She went repeatedly to a neighbor's to make calls to Beyji to find out what type of *zikr,* or chants with Allah's various names, the saints recommended to improve one's fortune. She told me to turn off the cricket matches and sat me down regularly to teach me the Quran. She appealed to Pops to establish all five prayers at the prescribed times of day. She calculated whether we had paid out adequate amounts of *zakat* to care for the poor. She fasted with great earnestness during the daylight hours of Ramadan, waking up to make food well before the pre-dawn meal, *suhoor,* and preparing food for the post-sunset *iftar* way before evening.

Seeing Ammi's devotion, Pops was impelled to emulate it, albeit in his own way: his religiosity was communal and intellectual. He took me to Friday prayers at all the great mosques of Lahore, and we showed up early so we could listen to the entire sermon. We went to the house of one of the old Jamaat-e-Islami organizers at the university, and his daughter served us sherbet while he talked about how Islam was slowly changing the world. Pops found various religious scholars who held evening study circles at their mosques, and we tried them all out. He was particularly fond of one *shaykh* of the Deobandi movement—a revivalist branch of traditional Islam—who taught in a well-off residential area of Lahore. The lectures were long. The *shaykh* sat on the floor with a Quran supported on a *rehal* before him at the end of a long row of men. (The women listened from behind a partition.) Occasionally touching the skin of the Quran, the *shaykh* spoke evocatively about the importance of family life, the virtues of hard work, and how patience in the face of adversity was a form of worship, and then he tied all of these things together with events from the life of the Prophet and his Companions. He said that one had to put prayer and worship before everything else, and when that happened, success followed. As proof he'd point out that he used to be just a simple villager, but—Allah be praised—because he followed this method, Allah put him in a place where he was able to teach Islam in such a beautiful mosque to such wonderful people. Pops and I rode back home on the motorcycle after such evenings, and he often quizzed me to see if I had been paying attention.

One day Pops learned that my grandfather, Dada Abu, and my older uncle, Tau, who both lived in a town in the desert, were coming to Lahore to attend the Tablighi Jamaat convention at nearby Raiwand. They called ahead and asked Pops to meet them there.

Tablighi Jamaat, Pops told me, was a worldwide order numbering in the millions that had become disenchanted with the world. Its members—Tablighis—said that at some point in history Allah had become upset with Muslims and had taken away their glory, and now no material or worldly gain was possible for a Muslim unless the broken bridge between believer and Creator was first repaired. Tablighis were of the opinion that Muslims—each and every true Muslim—were facing failure in the world, and that indeed those in the world who happened to be successful were successful only because they had left Islam behind. The organization's specific goal was to go to these people and bring them back to true Islam, which belonged to the unsuccessful. To this end they organized themselves into cells, and every few evenings they went door to door to the homes of Muslims, encouraging them to give up their work and wives and take a *chilla,* a devotional trip that lasted forty days. Pops had never been on a *chilla,* but Dada Abu and Tau had been many times. During a *chilla* the Tablighi leaders forbade discussion of worldly things like jobs, politics, and education and focused on things that made one a good Muslim—things like what supplication to recite before washing one's posterior, whether Allah Azzawajal was the Lord of all the worlds (or if there was only *one* world which He owned in its entirety), and whether eternal damnation literally meant forever or whether eternity could be cut in half. Talking about these things, they asserted, would turn every failed Muslim into a success, would give Muslims financial prosperity, and would raise their status in society. The organization wasn't against money; it was just against non-Tablighis having it.

Every year the Tablighi Jamaat met in a virtual tent city on the marshy salt plain in Raiwand. After Mecca, it was the largest single gathering of Muslims in the world. It was called *Ijtema.*

"Get on the bike, *shabash,*" Pops said one morning. "We're going to Raiwand."

I sat on the motorcycle and wrapped a checkered scarf around my mouth to protect against the dust. On the Suzuki we sped past the slums that surrounded Lahore. Soon we were on a flat highway cutting through fields of barley. A multicolored bus with mirror-work and murals on its exterior passed by. Outside of a small town we stopped to help an old peasant with a donkey cart. His lord had heaped too much weight on the cart before sending the peasant off, and the donkey kept getting tipped into the air.

Nothing could have prepared me for Raiwand's immensity. There were thousands of tents on a burning-hot white plain. Countless men in *shalwar kameez* and beards, most carrying backpacks, walked around greeting one another. Vials of musk, *tasbih* beads, and tapes of religious instruction were on sale. I saw Mongolian men and Caucasian men and African men. There was considerable discussion among them about the possibility that Nawaz Sharif, General Zia ul Haq's favorite politician (and a future prime minister of Pakistan), would be coming in by helicopter.

I was marched endlessly around the plain as Pops searched for Dada Abu and Tau. He eventually found them standing around in a large circle of men who had also come up from Dada Abu's village, and there were loud introductions all around.

Dada Abu pinched my cheeks. Tau went to his stuff and pulled out one of the backpacks he had sewn at his workshop; he threw it around my shoulders.

Dada Abu and Pops stepped away from the group, me tagging at their heels, and discussed Pops's practice. Dada Abu was trying to convince Pops to forget Lahore and move back to the desert where he had grown up (and where Dada Abu still lived) and start afresh. They talked in hushed whispers for a little while; then Pops grabbed my wrist angrily and we rode back home. Pops was upset about something and drove so fast that we flew into a ditch. After that we had to limp home, pushing the motorcycle along.

Over dinner Pops told Ammi what Dada Abu had suggested, and she also dismissed the idea. Schools were better in Lahore, she pointed out, and there was more opportunity there even if expenses were greater. However, a few days later, Lahore made the decision for us. A local businessman who was friendly with Nawaz Sharif sent his thugs to our apartment building and informed the landlord that they were going to come back in a week's time and knock the building down. It would behoove the tenants to go quietly, they warned. By the time a gang of university students, Nawaz Sharif's supporters, came to the neighborhood and rocked the buildings until the structures collapsed with a groan, we had wrapped up our things in knotted bedsheets and were at the train station.

# 6

The Prophet Sulayman, son of Daud, King of the Jews, controlled the elements, spoke to animals, and commanded the *jinn*. He traveled across the world on a throne made from a diamond so flawless that before the Queen of Sheba stepped upon it, she hiked up her dress, thinking she was about to step in a pool of water. One day Sulayman's aerial adventures took him to a great mountain at the easternmost edge of the Iranian plateau. He looked across South Asia but found it covered in darkness; then he turned toward Jerusalem. That mountain where he stopped, later known as Takht-e-Sulayman, sits in what is now the arid desert of central Pakistan, west of the mighty Indus. In that desert, my father's family lived in Sehra Kush, a tired town surrounded by sand dunes.*

We had no throne. We took third-class rail to get there.

On the multi-day trip we occupied a window seat and a sleeping berth. We rode with migrant workers smelling of soil who slept with their turbans pulled over their eyes. Those who couldn't snare a seat were comfortable sleeping in front of the train's pungent latrine and in the aisles, apparently unconcerned about being stepped upon by barefoot passengers coming in from the muddy fields. Men brought

---

* Sehra Kush is a made-up name, to protect the people who live there.

aboard everything from bicycles, to a line of women in veils, to lambs and goats—along with a wide range of similar life essentials—minding them with a dismissive nonchalance. The atmosphere in the train was jovial. *Chai* flowed freely; roasted nuts, poured out into paper cups, were omnipresent. The predominantly good-natured conversation was punctuated by laughter, and there were many jokes about politicians and their corrupt *char so beesi*. There was occasional yelling as well, especially whenever a shepherd led his bearded goats onto the train track ahead of us and caused a delay. A delay was usually considered deplorable only if it was overnight, however; even then, if it was a precautionary stop in order to avoid an ambush by *dakooz,* it was shrugged off with a casual reference to Allah's ownership of the universe (followed by a stream of profanities about the incestuous anal activities of the armed degenerates). When there was a woman discovered to be traveling all by herself, she was shuttled off to some other part of the train, where a coterie of hefty matriarchs who had heard about "the poor creature" yelled at their men for not showing more initiative in bringing the vigorous *jawan* girl under their protective umbrella.

A few nights after leaving Lahore we came upon a deserted train station and switched to a midnight lorry that would take us over unpaved roads the rest of the way. Because we had a woman with us, Flim and I were put in the front, while numerous men—Pops among them—jammed themselves into the back.

I looked out the window at the station we'd left behind and in a cloud of dust saw a pair of men running at the moving lorry, holding their sacks with one hand and their falling *lungi*s—a traditional Punjabi sarong—with the other, cursing at the driver in a language I didn't understand.

They shone with a blue luminescence that made me wonder if they were angels.

Unlike Lahore, where the immensity of history forced hierarchy to become subtle in manifesting itself, Sehra Kush felt no qualms about segregation. The town was bisected by a highway that did the job.

The lower portion of the town, in the shape of a polygon, was for the administrators, judges, civil servants, and military men, all of whom lived in bungalows inside compounds marked by streets of the blackest asphalt, manicured lawns complete with imported trees, and an order epitomized by security guards and regular trash pickup (with refuse sometimes dumped onto empty plots on the other side of the city). The central institution of this section: the clubhouse; the popular mode of transport: unmarked car; the favored type of violence: against servants.

There was a larger upper portion of the city expanding like a heinous goiter. It belonged to *bazari*s with their stalls, traders, cart-*wala*s, *maulvi*s on their way to teach at the mosque, and mendicants. Most of these people lived in mud houses lined up haphazardly on streets of dust marked by trash, open sewage, and the furry green droppings of low-breed donkeys. The central institution of this section: the mosque; the popular mode of transportation: the horse-drawn *tanga;* the favorite type of violence: insult. This is where we were headed.

We arrived in Sehra Kush on a hazy morning and took two *tanga*s to Dada Abu's house. After clop-clopping on a highway for a while, we turned onto a badly paved road and passed an empty field full of trash where a pair of wide-horned black buffaloes—whose milk was sold to the neighboring families—swished their tails. We then took a turn into an unpaved alley, passing open gutters leaking witch blackness onto the street. Homes were on both sides of the alley, set off from the narrow street by a foot-wide gap for the *nali,* the open sewer, which flowed in a slow froth full of everything from stones, to phlegm, to animal dung, with light-brown dollops of human feces bobbing to the surface. Each house had a thick wooden plank that bridged the *nali*. The doors on the houses were all flung open, although there was a heavy curtain in each doorway that assured privacy for the women within.

When our *tanga*s made their way into the alley, children ran toward us from each side. They yelled greetings and stuck sticks into the churning spokes, picking up another stick whenever a grinding wheel snapped a spear and nearly took a child's hand along with it. Soon we came to a dilapidated Land Rover from the mid-1950s that was parked in the middle of the alley. (We later learned that it belonged to the Balochi neighbors.) The *tanga* drivers, clicking their tongues at their horses as they reversed, cursed at the ungainly car for blocking the thoroughfare. The horses took short, unsteady steps backward during this process, and the heads of the animals swayed from side to side as if they were intoxicated mystics.

Dada Abu's house, constructed from a mixture of mud, hay, rope, and wooden beams, was airy but not big. He lived there with Dadi Ma and four of my uncles and their families. The house had a courtyard, a kitchen, a cemented area for the hand-operated *nalka* that supplied the water, a tiny latrine with an unpaved hole in the ground, a sitting room, two bedrooms with shuttered windows, and an open staircase going to the roof. On warm nights people slept on the roof; on cooler nights in the courtyard. In the desert it never got cold enough to require sleeping inside.

As this host of relatives greeted my brother and me with pats on the head and pinches to the cheeks, I took a look at the cramped quarters and realized that we had moved in as well.

# 7

W hy bother? I'm just ugly and old!"
Dadi Ma was fond of saying this to people who told her to
cover her face when she went for her great walks around town. She was
a small woman with a gold tooth, thin hennaed hair, and a loud voice.
Although the women of Sehra Kush, when they left their compound,
always wore the *niqab,* a full veil that covered the face, when Dadi Ma
went out she preferred the comfort of a loose garment called the *chador,*
which draped over her head and shoulders but was open at the face; she
typically tied it with a ribbon under her chin.

During the days, I spent a lot of time in Dadi Ma's vicinity. She
usually sat near the kitchen on a small *charpai,* or cot, giving instructions to Ammi and the aunts about what to cook for dinner, how many
pinches of salt should go in the cookpot, and why the milkman needed
to be thrashed for adding water and skimming the cream.

She also told tall tales. How sleeping under a tree caused you to die
from asphyxiation because the *jinns* that lived in the branches sucked
up all the oxygen; how the scary backward-footed *churayl*s were actually fallen souls seeking forgiveness for some crime they had committed; how going to a particular saint's grave and spreading a ceremonial
*chador* over it would lead to the expiation of one's sins. Most of the

aunts and children had already heard the stories and never asked Dadi Ma any questions, but Ammi enjoyed talking to old people and often probed her, to my great delight.

One day they began talking about the Partition of India and Pakistan in 1947, and Dadi Ma started telling *really* scary stories.

"Five of them," she announced, making her hand into a claw. "Five girls. Count them. One, two, three, four, five. Five girls jumped into a well. Into the same well. Just to protect their honor. This was in 1947, back when we lived in Indian Punjab. All because that Mountbatten switched the borders on the founders of our country and put us in India when we would've been in Pakistan."

"Who were the girls?" Ammi asked.

"*Our* girls! They were just girls. The virgin ones. My cousins-in-law. All single. No husbands. No children. Their whole life lay before them. What a waste! They just went in, one after another after another. Into that well. And what for? This country—Pakistan! What did this country give us? Refugee camps and then a war where they dropped a bomb—splat—on our house. Well, at least the poor girls are martyrs. Straight to Paradise."

"Why did they have to jump?" Ammi asked—the very question that had been in my mind.

"The animals, Hindus and Sikhs, were kidnapping the women. Just picking them up and running off with them—just because the girls were Muslim!"

"Did they come after *you*?" Ammi asked.

"Of course not. They didn't want married women. They just wanted the virgins. They had standards—even as animals."

"Do you think maybe the girls were pulled out of the well? Maybe they're still alive?"

"I don't know. Those were Muslim girls. If they were pulled out? God knows. *I* don't know."

"Did anyone go back to find out what happened?"

"Our men went. Before he died, may Allah bless him, my older brother-in-law went back to the old house. To find out about the girls. To see if the treasure was still there."

"What treasure?" Ammi asked, as perplexed as I was.

"Our things! Jewelry belonging to hundreds of years of women. Coins. Gold. Silver. Money. Deeds to land. Receipts for cattle. All of it. Before they fled, my father-in-law put it all in one big cauldron and buried it in the frontyard. Said he would go back when things were safe and retrieve it. You know, we all thought that this India-Pakistan thing was going to be temporary."

"Did they get it?" Ammi asked.

"What do you think? It wasn't there. The maid they'd had back then must have seen them dig the hole. She was a smart little Hindu girl. She dug the treasure up and disappeared, or so we think. She went to some big city. Maybe Bombay. Maybe Delhi. She's gone. No use crying over what's lost. We gave it up for Islam. That's how it is."

"The Holy Prophet and the Emigrants to Medina gave up everything also," Ammi said. "All for Islam."

"There you go," Dadi Ma replied. "You live; you worship. That's what this life is for. Rewards are in the next life. Riches are in the next life. Did you hear that, Abir? Pray. Pray and pray and you will have your entire existence to recline on beds of gold in Paradise."

"I just want a regular bed," I said. "And a ring for my pinky."

"Whatever you want," said Dadi Ma. "You should still pray. It will take you to Paradise. Now someone bring me my fan. At least it won't be hot in Paradise. Too hot here in this desert. Imagine! To go from the cool breeze off the foothills of Kashmir to this desert, where the breeze—. No, this isn't breeze, it's furnace blasts; it's what hell will be like. Well, what can you say? Everything has been written."

"*Kismet*," Ammi said.

"*Kismet*." Dadi Ma took her fan, leaned back against the wall, and drew her *dupatta* over her head to form a makeshift tent against the flies. "Anyway, forget it. Send someone to get the *naan*. Put aside some curry in that pot over there. The boys from the *madrassa* are coming tonight to ask for food. I'm going to sleep. Wake me up when my husband comes home to bother us all."

Unlike his wife, I couldn't wait till Dada Abu came home. I liked him more than anyone else. He was a stylish old man who wore a glittering watch and suits made of *boski* thread cotton. He drove an apple-red Kawasaki motorcycle and often gave me a ride. He usually arrived shortly before the *maghrib* prayer at sunset, made *wazu,* went to the mosque, and then came back for dinner, which he ate quietly with his hands. Then he drank three glasses of cool water from the clay *matka*—squatting on the ground for each chug as per the example of the Prophet—and left the house to go up the street and sit with his brothers. As he left the house, he often took me along with him and joked with me.

"Who is this strange boy next to me?"

"It's me!" I said.

"What is that voice I hear?"

"It's me," I repeated. "It's Abir ul Islam!"

"Oh! It's the fragrance of Islam that I smell on my nose."

"Yes!" I said, grabbing his pinky. "I'm coming with you."

"My father, may Allah bless him, said your name should be Alauddin," Dada Abu said. " 'The heights of the faith.' But I think your name should be Naughty Boy."

"You can't change my name," I protested. "I am Abir ul Islam. Do you want me to change *your* name, big man?"

"No, no, big boss," he said, laughing. "You keep your name and I will keep mine. You serve Islam and I will serve you. How does that sound?"

"Sounds good to me."

Dada Abu was the youngest of all his brothers, and when in the evenings they sat together it was his job to maintain the *hooka,* or waterpipe. He often passed this assignment to me.

"Take this chamber and go to Mateen's house. Tell him to fill it up with tobacco," he instructed. "And hurry back. Don't start playing with those cows."

I picked up the head of the *hooka* and ran over to a neighboring home. It belonged to a Gujjur family. Their entire existence revolved around their four black buffaloes. They milked them. They sold the calves. They piled dung and made patties, which when crisped in the sun they sold for fuel. They hitched the buffaloes to carts and took the patties to the market. While there they rented their cart out to those not fortunate enough to have a beast of burden. To supplement this meager livelihood, they also refilled *hooka*s with bitter tobacco for the old men in the neighborhood.

With the embers like liquid gold, I brought the head back and placed it atop the *hooka* while Dada Abu patted me on the head. Then I quietly sat down in a corner, observing the four brothers with beards and turbans sitting cross-legged on low wooden beds, whispering smoky kisses to the desert—their wives either dead or irrelevant; their business troubles forgotten; their conflicts resolved through the placid acceptance of everything. When there was an occasional splatter of disagreement, a political confrontation perhaps, it resulted in one brother opening his mouth and then just as quickly closing it, because ultimately they knew that nothing had changed over the past forty years: they still considered everyone a crook and every leader a fool. We—the youth, the children—were the only ones to bring any disorder into their lives. But to counter the dissonance that we caused, they had perfected many methods of mollification. A son with troubled finances was given a room in the house. A boy rebelling too much was indoctrinated with Islam. A wife nagging too much was sent to her parents for a little while, where she started to feel guilty for being a burden and came begging back. A daughter getting too high-minded got married off to a humble man. Disobedient cattle got eaten. All such decisions were sacralized without speaking in that nightly circle around the *hooka*.

When I sat among the four old brothers, I felt assured of the continuity of the world. When the nostril-burning secondhand smoke gave me a buzz, the four brothers turned into white pillars of permanence. I felt immortal. One of the angels of Allah. Given the familiarity with which the brothers talked about the Prophets, I figured they were ageless. They must have walked with Ibrahim and crossed the Red Sea with Musa; surely they had walked with Isa and ridden with Muhammad. They were above and beyond history, beyond Shia and Sunni, beyond India and Pakistan, beyond Muslim and not. There was a God; His name was Allah; He was represented by the act of pointing an index finger to the sky. There were the sons that Allah blessed you with. There was a *hooka* to be smoked at night. A prayer called *isha* preceded the little sleep. When the big sleep came, others offered a prayer on your behalf; then you were dormant till the Day of Judgment, when you were raised and whatever Allah had determined for you was given to you.

When the melodic words of the *azan* for *isha* rang out in the evening, the brothers' conference of silence would come to an end.

"Big boss," Dada Abu would ask. "What should we do now?"

"Abir ul Islam says it's time to pray."

# 8

Under Dadi Ma's tutelage, Ammi became an inveterate storyteller. When she was in the kitchen, squatting on her green straw *chowki,* grinding *masala* in the stone *chukki,* kneading dough in the steel *praat,* tinkering with the kerosene *choola,* and wiping her nose on her shoulder, she spoke and spoke and spoke until her speech became narration, her sentences bedizened with similes and metaphors, and my cousins and I were treated to epics. It was as if her imagination were composed of a never-ending series of photographs for which, some time long ago, at the primordial gathering of mothers, she had been given the most appropriate, perfectly descriptive words to use.

All her stories related to Islam.

There was the one about the People of the Cave—the Seven Sleepers of Ephesus—who were so disappointed by the idolatry of the society they lived in that they withdrew to a cave, where they were put into a miraculously deep sleep by Allah, and when they woke up, they were in a better age.

Then there was the story of King Zulqurnain, whose name meant two-horned one, a monotheistic ruler who believed in the afterlife and traveled to the east, west, and a third direction, dispensing wisdom and justice.

"He saw the sun setting in the water, which is the west," Ammi told me. "Then he visited a place where the people had no cover from the sun, which is the east."

"Then where did he go?" I asked.

"He went to a valley; we don't know where," Ammi said, lowering her voice. "The people were being killed by Yajuj and Majuj!"

"Who were they?" I asked.

"Absolute monsters!" Ammi said, making claws with her hands. "There were two tribes of them, and they were raiding the people of the valley, so the people begged King Zulqurnain to save them. He instructed the people to mine lead and iron and copper and brass, and he melted all those things in a huge furnace and poured the molten ore onto a wall, strengthening it to separate the people from the monsters."

"But Yajuj and Majuj are going to get through the wall, aren't they?"

"Well, each day Yajuj and Majuj try to break through the wall by licking it. They lick it all day, and each day they can almost see the other side, but then they get tired and go to sleep, and at night Allah thickens the wall again."

"What if they get through one day?"

"Oh, that day will come," Ammi said morosely. "Yajuj and Majuj are one of the promised *azab*s that will afflict the Muslims before the end of the world. When they lick their way through that copper wall, they'll come out into the land and eat everyone—all except those people who hide in mosques. That's why I keep telling you to go to the *masjid*. If you are in the habit of going, when the panic of Yajuj and Majuj strikes you'll instinctively go to a *masjid* and save yourself."

"I hope they come during Friday prayer. I'm in the *masjid* at that time for sure!" I said, feeling reassured.

"Well, whenever they come, we'll know," she said. "And we'll know that the end-times are near."

This made me nervous. "We can't kill the Yajuj and Majuj? Not even with a gun?"

"Afraid not. From what I've heard, they're supposed to take the Muslim world to the brink of extinction, and when they've done that, Dajjal will appear!"

Dajjal was the Islamic equivalent of the Antichrist.

"What does Dajjal look like?"

"He'll be a regular man who will have one eye. Across his forehead the word KAFIR, or 'unbeliever,' will be written in black. He will be riding a donkey. He will come to the people and encourage them to abandon Allah. Those who listen to him will be given a Paradise on earth. To those who reject him, he will say, 'I will make the world a hell for you.' But righteous Muslims will reject him, seeking refuge from him in mosques, because he cannot enter a place where prayer is made. The Jews and Christians will become bound by his spell and because of submitting to him find glory in this world. Dajjal will be on their side. He will be their God, and he will tell them that he can make the sun rise from the west and they will believe him."

The idea of a simple man, a man among us—riding a donkey, no less—dispensing the sort of justice I associated with Allah Azzawajal, filled me with terror. The tangibility and nearness of Dajjal's presence—I imagined him offering me his earthly Paradise at the roundabout nearby—made me so nervous that I cannibalized my cuticles. But I couldn't simply dismiss Dajjal to the distant future, because Ammi made it sound as if the arrival of Dajjal was imminent, if not already under way.

"If you look around the world, you'll see that the Jews and Christians are glorious and powerful, while Muslims are persecuted and killed just for being Muslim."

I reflected on her assessment, and it seemed to be based in reality. I had seen *Full House* and *Sesame Street* and *Star Trek* and *Airwolf* and *Knight Rider* on TV. Everything about the world of those people—those Christians—smacked of luxury. Ice cream whenever they wanted it; houses with air-conditioning; lights that never went out; cars that talked. The difference between them and us was evident: they were rich and had many possessions, while we were deprived. There was no way to explain this difference except to believe that they had given obeisance to Dajjal.

"Dajjal will rule the world for forty years," Ammi continued. "Then there will be hope for Muslims. A man from Hijaz, whose name will be Muhammad, whose mother's name will be Amina, and whose father's name will be Abdullah—"

"Those were the names of the Prophet's parents!" I shouted.

"Yes," Ammi continued. "At the age of forty, which was the age at which the Prophet began receiving revelations of the Quran, this man will be leading a prayer at the Grand Mosque in Damascus. Suddenly the sky will split open. There will be a beam of light that touches the dome. In that beam, the Christian Prophet, Isa, will descend, wearing all white."

"Isa is alive?" I exclaimed. "I thought he was crucified!"

"Yes, alive! He wasn't crucified. Allah put Isa's face over someone else, over a traitor, while he raised Isa to the fourth heaven," Ammi clarified. "So Isa will come and stand before the congregation, and he will say, 'I am Isa, son of Maryam, Prophet of God, and I am a Muslim. This man here is Muhammad, the *mahdi,* and you must follow him.'"

"The messiah!" I pumped my fist.

"The *mahdi* will step back and let Isa lead the prayer," Ammi said. "But Isa will push him back to the front and say that he himself has come only to serve as a general and will fall in line behind the *mahdi.* They will finish the prayer and go east. Then they will start liberating the world. Isa will tell the Jews and Christians to believe in Islam, and many people will convert, but the stranglehold of Dajjal will be too strong for most people, and they will refuse. Isa will kill all of these nonbelievers. He will destroy them. If they hide behind a stone, the stones will bear witness against them and reveal them to Isa. If they hide behind a tree, the trees will bear witness against them and reveal them to Isa."

"What about Dajjal?"

"Isa will battle him and kill him with his sword," Ammi said somberly. "Then Isa will die a natural death and finally be buried as a Muslim, and the *mahdi* will continue liberating the world. His reign will be forty years."

"What will that world be like?"

By this time, Ammi had become tired, so she sped up the narrative. "In those forty years Muslims will thrive, but then they will lose all their gains and face utter humiliation, bringing a forty-year reign by their enemies. That's when the Day of Judgment will finally come. The mountains will blow away like puffs of wool. Humanity will be gathered naked underneath the Great Throne for the Day of Reckoning."

Then, shivering from fear and guilt, Ammi asked Allah for forgiveness and announced that it was time for prayer. I hastened to make *wazu*.

Prayer was the only protection against the apocalypse that was already here.

Upon hearing Ammi's story, I began to train myself to go to the mosque more faithfully. I prayed all five prayers there most days, and my preparations for attending each prayer were meticulous.

I took Ammi's heavy iron, applied gobs of *kalaf*, and starched my clothes until they were cardboard-hard. I found in Pops's closet a checkered red-and-white *kafiya* that I learned to tie as a turban, though most of the time I simply draped it on my shoulders with the corners hanging forward on my chest, as the Quran reciters did on TV. I also had a hand-stitched *topi*, snow-white and delicate as gossamer, to grace my head.

There were many old men at the mosque, all of whom were regulars, and they loved to hobnob with me. One of them told me to give up using a toothbrush and opt for a wooden *miswak* like the one the Holy Prophet had used. Another one saw me using the pads on my fingers to count the *zikr* and gave me a wooden *tasbih* to use instead. "Now instead of counting in fifteens," he said, "you can count in hundreds."

I noticed that many worshippers had calluses on their foreheads and ankles from a lifetime of prostration and sitting on folded feet. Those were marks of piety that I wanted to develop as well. Thus, instead of praying on the carpet inside, I took to praying in the courtyard of the mosque, on straw matting that was hot and rough. During prostration I rubbed my forehead on the mat until it became raw.

I figured that if Yajuj and Majuj came and saw that I had marks of piety, they would know not to lay a hand on me.

# 9

The mysterious Balochi neighbors who owned the Land Rover blocking the alley, as well as the largest house and compound in the *mohalla,* inspired a lot of curiosity. Unlike everyone else, they kept their door closed. Their children never played outside. They didn't try to initiate conversation with anyone. They didn't send anyone to the mosque.

They were arms traders, as it turned out.

One early morning Ammi saw various men come out of the house and unload a fruit truck full of crated weapons. When she went and told Pops, he praised them for "being able to fabricate any weapon without ever going to school." He also commended their business plan, explaining that the Afghan War had produced a surplus of weapons that now got sold all around the country. The Balochis were "just like sugarcane juicers," according to Pops, "except they sell bullets and *bandook*s."

Occasionally my cousins and I went to our roof and tried to peer across through their windows. We wanted to see a Stinger missile or a stash of Kalashnikovs. Sometimes late at night, while we were sleeping on the rooftop, I heard the Land Rover roar to life and drive out of the alley, rattling bricks and causing propped-up *charpai*s to fall. By the time I woke up again the next morning, the Jeep would have returned, dusty and muddy.

For all their secrecy, the Balochis had a mole: the matriarch. She came regularly to sit with Dadi Ma, who attracted all the beleaguered housewives from nearby *mohalla*s. They came to sit at her feet and complain about their husbands, and in turn she handed them lentils to sift.

The Balochi wife was named Sabra. She had given her husband many boys, but now, as she grew old, according to Balochi custom she had been moved to the children's room and her husband had brought in a new wife. Sabra came to complain about that supplanter. Specifically, "about how black-skinned that one is, *astaghfirullah*!" Everyone came to know the villainous second wife as Black Baloch.

Sabra wanted to see Black Baloch's downfall and asked Dadi Ma whether there was any dark magic she could use.

"No!" Dadi Ma said vehemently. "No black magic. We have to think about the afterlife!"

"If you're thinking about the afterlife," Ammi countered, "then we shouldn't backbite the woman either. Those who do *gheebat* will be made to eat their sister's flesh in hell."

That reminder about the severe punishment that Allah would mete out to backbiters was thrown out any time gossip-mongering occurred—which was often. The comment was usually made by the woman who, at that particular moment, felt most guilty about the discussion. The other women, equally guilty of the crime overall if not at that moment, lowered their heads and picked at their trays with a forefinger and thumb, flicking the desiderata that dirtied the lentils. Then, because gossip was a major industry—one that couldn't be shut down even under threat from Allah—the conversation resumed.

Ultimately, Dadi Ma didn't need to resolve the tension between Sabra and Black Baloch, because their husband did it for them. He went to Balochistan and brought home wife number three. When he threw Black Baloch out of the bedroom, the ignominy caused Sabra and Black Baloch to immediately enter into an alliance. They often came over to our house, together as friends now, to ask about possible black magic, though Dadi Ma constantly rebuffed them.

One day, late in the afternoon while the men were at work—my father at the small clinic that he was trying rather unsuccessfully to establish—Ammi, Dadi Ma, and the aunts were sitting on the veranda. Suddenly the curtain was swept open by Black Baloch, who rushed in alone. She had a panicked looked in her eye, and her face was white. She was wearing neither a *niqab* nor anything on her feet, as though she had run out of the house unexpectedly. Dadi Ma summoned a glass of water and told Black Baloch to sit down.

"What is it?" she asked in a calming voice.

"Unbelievable! It's Sabra! Oh, the end has come!"

"Tell already!" said one of the aunts.

"Everyone is going to find out now! What will happen to the reputation of our men!"

I was on the rooftop, rolling marbles with my cousins, but we all headed downstairs to listen when it became clear that there was drama in the making. By the time we reached the ground floor, the women were wrapping up in *chador*s and shawls to cross the alley and head into the Balochi fortress.

"We have to do condolence," Ammi explained to us.

"This is really unbelievable," said one of the aunts. "I don't understand how this could happen."

"That poor creature!" Dadi Ma said, reciting a prayer.

Black Baloch led the caravan of condolence across the street. My cousins and I followed, pleased that finally there was a way into the mysterious Balochi house.

As the yellow door into the courtyard swung open, a rooster scuttled and squawked and several of the countless hens clucked. A small goat scurried past with an awkward limp, making a go at the exit, but one of the boys grabbed its rope. In a corner of the courtyard sat Sabra, rocking back and forth on her straw *chowki*.

"Evil men!" said my older aunt.

"Poor creature!" said Dadi Ma. "Look at how uncomfortable it looks!"

"Which one was it?" Ammi asked, looking around the courtyard.

"Evil men!"

"Just *did* her? Just like that?" Dadi Ma asked Sabra.

She wiped tears and nodded.

"You know, Ammi *ji*," Black Baloch said to Dadi Ma, "it *is* kind of funny."

Dadi Ma looked at her sternly, and then her expression softened. "It is *somewhat* amusing, yes."

Suddenly a chuckle erupted from Black Baloch. Then all the women started cackling.

"Which goat was it?" Ammi asked.

Sabra pointed to the limping goat whose rope was held by one of the boys.

"It was your son, Sabra?"

She nodded. "My oldest."

"Evil men!" said my older aunt again, still aghast.

"Oh my," Ammi said. "Look at the poor goat's expression."

"Bring it here, boy; we have to soothe it," Dadi Ma said. She read a *surah* from the Quran and then put her hand on the violated goat's head to bless it.

"He didn't even care that it was so young," Black Baloch said.

"How awful!" said Ammi. "I don't know if it will survive."

Then the women began discussing whether the goat's meat had become un-Islamic. It was resolved that the animal should be slaughtered and its meat distributed to charity. As for the culprit, it was apparent that he needed to be married.

Before the marriage could happen, however, the Balochis fixed up their Land Rover, outfitted it with a machine gun, and left town.

Pops said that they probably moved to Karachi. He claimed that they had become rich enough to become one of the elites of Pakistan.

# 10

Ammi became pregnant with my brother Zain at a time when Pops had few patients and we had no money, so everyone in the compound at Sehra Kush worried how we would manage our finances. In fact, Ammi had to go stay with her relatives in Lahore for the delivery. However, when she brought Zain back, all the earlier concerns were forgotten. The baby had the ability to elicit smiles from everyone. As he grew up, his favorite activity was to bash Flim and me on the head with his favorite spoon.

One day, while Ammi was cooking in the courtyard, she saw that Zain was looking up at the rooftop. Inching along in his walker, he approached the staircase, pointing and cooing. She followed him, and as she drew near she began screaming: someone dark and menacing seemed to be staring down at mother and son. A few days later she heard pigeons congregating in the same staircase, but when she went to check there was nothing there. Then finally, at all hours of the day, she began to hear the sounds of *jinns* whispering from the darkness of the staircase, calling for Zain. The sinister presence on the roof lasted seven days all told.

On the seventh day Zain was playing with another infant as Ammi and Dadi Ma sat and gossiped. I was outside, tossing a ball with my cousins. Suddenly screams went up inside.

When I ran to the bedroom, Ammi was holding Zain upside down, shaking him as if he had swallowed something, while Dadi Ma shouted, "He's not breathing! He's stopped breathing!"

Ammi remained calm but she couldn't get a reaction from Zain, whose body had gone limp. She tried CPR and the Heimlich maneuver, but still he didn't respond. Suddenly, one of my uncles burst through the curtain, swooped Zain into his arms, and ran toward Pops's clinic, approximately a mile away. By this time, Ammi was wailing too, and both she and Dadi Ma ran into the alley without a *chador* or *niqab*.

Inside the house, speculation began as to what had prompted Zain to stop breathing. Someone noticed peanut shells on the floor and concluded that he had choked on their contents. Ammi, when she came back in to await news from the clinic, said that she feared it was the mysterious presence she'd been feeling for a week that had strangled Zain. Dadi Ma pulled out a copy of the Quran and recited loudly, rocking back and forth aggressively as if the momentum of her body might affect the direction of destiny.

At the clinic, Pops performed a tracheotomy on Zain, but it was fruitless. A little before the *azan* for the evening prayer rang out, Zain was pronounced dead. Pops wrapped the body in a little sheet taken from the storage room of his barren clinic and walked his dead son back to Ammi.

Even before Pops arrived, word of Zain's death had reached Ammi via the children shuttling back and forth between house and clinic. She screamed and then cried, her body alternately doubling and straightening in agony.

I had little idea of what to do. I stuffed my tennis ball in my pocket and went to the bedroom upon some adult's instructions, but I still listened intently to all the goings-on and watched what I could. I heard Ammi trying to get outside and "go to my Zain." Her curly hair flew wildly as the other women restrained her.

By this time ladies from across the *mohalla* were streaming into the house. They lined up against the wall, standing stoically, neither joining in the fray nor commenting to one another. With blank expressions on their faces, they murmured verses from the Quran.

Zain's body was brought into the house and passed from uncle to uncle until Tau and Dada Abu took the body and put it through the ritual washing at the *nalka*. Pops, masking his emotion with activity, left to make arrangements for the funeral prayer. Ammi, meanwhile, refused to accept that Zain was gone and kept trying to snatch him away from those washing him. Despite her pleas, she was held far away, twisting and writhing at a distance because women weren't allowed to give a corpse its ritual washing.

Zain was wrapped in a white shroud and his body was placed on a little bed set atop a large box in the center of the courtyard. As the gathered crowd picked up copies of the Quran, they sat down in a circle around the platform and began reading *surah Yasin*.

It still hadn't really sunk in for me that my brother was dead. I was too caught up in watching Ammi's mourning. Gradually, though, the death was brought home to me. A woman thrust a Quran in my hand and told me that the departing soul would be comforted if the words of *surah Yasin* went along with it. I looked at Zain's body and at the dark evening sky, searching for a column of light in which the angels taking Zain's soul could be traveling. Another woman said that reciting the Quran would cure my grief.

Wanting the comfort of my mother, I went to the room where Ammi was being held. Numerous women rubbed and massaged various parts of her body, all the while exhorting her to give in to the balming effect of the Quran. Dadi Ma and other elderly women whispered how the Prophet Ibrahim lives with the dead children in the seventh heaven, and how a child that dies before the age of two is considered to have died during *jihad* and is thus considered a *shaheed,* or religious martyr, meaning that he can take his parents to Paradise on the Day of Judgment. This didn't comfort Ammi.

Eventually I fell asleep in the midst of all the wailing.

By the time I woke up in the morning, Zain had been buried, Ammi had collapsed from exhaustion, and Pops was nowhere to be found. One of my recently arrived aunts hugged me and then informed me that I should head off to the mosque to pray and participate in the *qurankhani,* a communal gathering during the period of mourning at which the Quran was recited.

I walked through the house and looked for a *chador* because it was cold. Suddenly I was aware of everything. Here was the place where my brother had taken his first steps just a few days ago. Here was the place where my brother had choked. Here was the place my mother had wept. Here was the place my brother was given his last rites. Here was the place where his dead body had lain. Yet now, a few meager hours later, the entire house dripped with indifference. There was nothing to suggest that Zain had ever been there. The alley, which the day before had been filled with people, was empty. The housewives expressing concern had gone home, having fulfilled their social obligation and recited the requisite amount of *Yasin*.

I left the house and wandered for a time. When I came upon the square where the donkey was parked, my eyes fell upon the mosque. Bathed in the soft blue of early morning, the building's architectural simplicity—a minaret, a dome, and an archway—left a deep impression upon me. It was the one place that welcomed my sorrow.

Before prayer, I sat on a straw mat in the cold courtyard, inhaling the dusty gloom. I pulled the edge of my *chador* across my face as Ammi had done and drew the other end like a hood. Then, thinking of the night long ago when Zain had hit me on the head with a spoon, I cried for my brother.

In the subsequent days, an investigation into the cause of death was launched. The peanut shells were suspected, but an X-ray Pops had hastily taken didn't support that thesis. Lack of scientific certainty opened the door for muted conversations about black magic. A prime culprit with witchlike tendencies was necessary, and one such person was found in the figure of Gina, my Uncle Saroor's wife.

From the first day their marriage had been tainted by something mysterious. Uncle Saroor was a well-built, attractive, and lively man in his twenties who dressed like the gangsters from Punjabi films and kept his mustache in meticulous condition. His wife was nearly forty years old, her skin leathered and pock-marked. It was rumored that he had married her for her wealth, an idea corroborated by an argument that broke out when she didn't bring a fridge as part of her dowry. Others claimed that she had used black magic to trap him. In any case, they didn't get along well, and this made the family wary of her.

On Uncle Saroor and Gina's wedding night, all the couples in the family pretended it was their wedding night too and acted accordingly. Within a few months it was revealed that four women in the family were pregnant—one of whom was Ammi, with Zain. Three of the four pregnancies were successful: all but Gina's. This meant that not only was she a rich, aged spinster who had managed to get herself a young man, but she was also completely useless, since she couldn't produce sons like the others. Naturally, given this background, the blame for Zain's death fell upon her.

The first shot was fired by my dad's older brother, Tau, who on the night of the death claimed that Gina had something to do with it. Due to the intensity of the moment, his comment had been forgotten. After the three-day mourning period, however, sources began to reveal strange occurrences involving Gina.

"I was in the latrine," Dadi Ma whispered, leaning into Ammi. "I saw something burned. I don't know what! Allah knows what it was! But that Gina, she definitely looked at Zain with envy!"

"You're suggesting it was *jadu*?" Ammi blanched, at the mention of black magic.

Dadi Ma stayed silent and nodded. Then she consulted with Tau. Being a member of the Tablighi Jamaat, he was the most religiously inclined in the family. Holding his henna-tinged beard in his hand, he mulled the possibility of *jadu* for a minute and then whispered that he knew a *jadu tornay walay ka alim*—a religious man who could break hexes.

A preliminary visit was initiated by the two women with the *alim*. Since he was very close to Allah, he instructed Ammi and Dadi Ma to wear *niqab* in his presence; further, he refused to look in their direction. (Women had the propensity to tempt him and potentially lead him to think sinful thoughts.) After listening to the problem, the *alim* instructed Ammi to return in a few days, bringing with her a shirt that contained her "musk."

This time taking Pops along, Ammi and Dadi Ma went back with the shirt. The *alim* smelled it and then instructed Ammi to walk around in front of him. Then he gave her a plain piece of paper, read something over it, and said, "If you now concentrate, you will see the picture of the person who did this."

Dadi Ma pressed up close, expecting to see Gina.

"I see someone!" said Ammi.

"Gina?" Dadi Ma asked. "You see her?"

"No," Ammi said in confusion. "I see a man. The dark man from the roof."

The *alim* told Ammi to ignore what she saw and suggested to her that she should see a woman—a description that fit Gina. Ammi concentrated harder but didn't see anything. The *alim* then gave Ammi seven pieces of folded paper and instructed her to take a bath every day with one piece mixed in the water. He advised her to be especially thorough with washing her hair. Then he gave a prescription to Pops.

It was unclear whether the *alim* had broken the hex, but a few days later Dadi Ma noted that Gina was being excessively sweet toward Ammi. "Now that she knows your child ended up the same as hers, she's happy," said Dadi Ma.

The hex-breaker's ineptitude had the effect of redirecting discussion about the causes of death back to science. A doctor from the United States with whom Pops consulted after the *alim* made a persuasive case that Zain had died as a result of a strange version of sudden infant death syndrome.

# II

To try to find a better life for us, Pops went to Iran. Having heard a rumor that Tehran had a shortage of doctors, he decided to see whether he could line up more patients there than at his struggling clinic in Sehra Kush. Ammi didn't want him to go—she'd just lost Zain and didn't want to lose Pops as well—but our financial insecurity convinced her.

Pops took a midnight train that took him to Quetta, from which point he would enter Iran by bus. I went to the train station to see him off. I imagined Iran as a distant place made of legends and stories involving forty thieves.

"Bring me back a flute," I told Pops as he stuck his head out of the window and waved. I figured an Iranian flute would let me conjure a *jinn* to whom I could make three wishes. One of those wishes would be that we could have all the money in the world so that Pops wouldn't have to go away again.

To make the trip Pops took all our savings. Ammi had assumed that she'd be able to ask Dadi Ma for help with the day-to-day costs while he was gone, but Dadi Ma wouldn't hear of it; she told Ammi that each family in the house had to pay for their own food. Ammi explained that she had only five rupees on her, which amounted to one American cent, but Dadi Ma was unbending.

Ammi didn't want the other women in the kitchen—the women who had food—to think that she was in need of charity, so she picked up her kerosene stove and took it into our bedroom. Rummaging through our luggage, she found a few packets of lentils and set them to boil. The thick smoke gathered inside the room, seeping into our clothes, our hair, our pillows. The smoke blackened Flim's tongue, and he ran around sticking it out at me and frightening Ammi.

Through the power of Islam, Ammi made those five rupees last a month. She made rice and lentils every day, the concoction becoming more watery each time. As the food bubbled on the stove before each meal, I would see her put her hand over it and recite something under her breath.

"What are you reading?" I asked her.

"I'm saying a prayer," she said. "There's a prayer that increases the amount of food."

"How can that be?" I asked.

"One time the Prophet Muhammad was a guest at someone's house, and the hosts were worried about what to offer him to eat: they had only a sick old goat, and she wasn't producing any milk. So the Prophet, recognizing their dilemma, called for the goat and spoke this very prayer over her, and the little thing's udders became full of milk, not just for himself, but for everyone. It didn't run out all night long."

I nodded happily at the idea of never running out of food and asked to learn the prayer.

Ammi's prayers, while sufficient to keep food on the table, weren't enough to address the constant hunger in my belly, so I turned into a scavenger.

If the children from the other families in our house were eating, I went to their tray and joined in with them. If I heard that someone in the neighborhood had ordered bread from the *tandoor*, I went up the street and parked myself next to the outdoor bakery, waiting for the baker to turn his head and reach into the clay oven to flip out a toasty piece of *naan* onto his stack. While his back was turned, I would grab a chunk off the bottom-most piece of bread. By the time he was done heaping the twenty or so pieces onto his stack, I would have fully consumed the bottom-most one and disappeared. One time, however, I stayed till the very end of his shift, wondering if he'd have any dough left over at the end.

My mouth watered a little when I saw that he did. "Are you going to throw that away?"

"What are you talking about?" he asked, gathering his *lungi* to keep it out of the way while he cleaned the oven.

"The dough," I said. "Let me have it, please. I want to make little toys from it."

"Suit yourself." He shrugged and handed it to me.

I didn't want him to think that I was *bhooka*—a derogatory word that implied greed—so I pretended to play with the dough, modeling it into little cars and balls and touching it nonchalantly, as if it were completely meaningless to me. Then, just as the baker was about to shut down the oven, I flattened the dough with my head and handed it to him.

"Stick it in there, will you?" I pleaded.

He sighed, flattened the dough further, and stuck it into the oven. Within moments a little piece of piping hot bread was ready—just for me. I took it in my hands, marveling over its thick edge, its crispy center, and then nibbled on it all the way back home.

A couple of months later, after Ammi had made many prayers for his return, Pops came back safe and sound, dejectedly explaining that there were no jobs to be had in Iran. He would reopen his clinic in Sehra Kush and hope for the best.

Instead of a flute that would summon a *jinn,* he brought me back a jacket.

# 12

As Pops began looking for a place to send me to school, people wondered why I wasn't becoming a *hafiz-e-Quran*—someone who memorized the Holy Book.

"It's the highest form of learning," Dadi Ma declared.

"First you memorize the Quran," said Tau, whose two sons, Tariq and Muaz, were enrolled in the *madrassa*. "Then comes everything else."

Being a *hafiz* was considered the apex of knowledge because of the revered status of the Quran—a status reflected in the names we gave it: the *Lawhul Mahfuz,* or Preserved Tablet, and the Uncreated Word of Allah. The Quran existed jointly with God. Timeless, immutable, perfect, the Quran was all Allah (though not all of Allah was the Quran). Allah had poured it through the mouth of Muhammad, and as it existed on paper now was how Allah intended for the Quran to look, taste, and sound. The Quran was the Islamic equivalent of Christ. The act of repeating the Arabic words, as they passed through the mouth and throat and echoed in the chest, was a form of transubstantiation: a way of making what was divine enter the human body. Christians took a piece of bread and a touch of wine and thought that they had taken of the body of their God; Muslims passed God in textual form in and out of their larynxes.

Most important, when Allah chose to impart his final, clearest message, he chose to convey it in the literary language of the Bedouin poets. Human translations of that message were not considered to be the Quran because they were not in Arabic, and thus not in the language of God. In fact, a Quran that was not in Arabic couldn't even be referred to as a Quran. The language of Arabic had a divinity of its own: the simple act of opening one's mouth and spouting Quranic Arabic was enough to endow the speaker with blessings. It was for this reason that a Muslim didn't really care whether or not he understood the Quran. It mattered only that he could pronounce the Arabic words situated between the covers—or, as Ammi put it in easy-to-understand theological economics, "Each Arabic letter in the Quran is worth ten blessings. Just saying three letters—*alif, lam, mim*—that's thirty blessings, creditable on the Day of Judgment!" In other words, the Quran was code, a sequence of 77,701 Arabic words, composed of 323,671 letters, which, at ten a pop, amounted to more than three million blessings. This is why rote memorization of the entire Quran was such big business. With the gazillions of blessings that a *hafiz* racked up in his life, he would be assured of entrance to Paradise. And that was the point: the afterlife was the most important thing in life.

Beyond being guaranteed heaven, there was another benefit to being a *hafiz*, one that extended to everyone around the Quran memorizer. On the Day of Judgment a *hafiz* would be allowed to save seventy-two people from hellfire in Dozakh. By having a few *hafizes* in every generation, entire families would be spared that suffering. The only other type of person that Allah would allow to intercede on behalf of seventy-two people was a martyr; but obviously to become *that* one had to die, a far more painful task. Since many boys in Sehra Kush were studying to become *hafiz*es, Pops decided to send me to a *madrassa* as well.

"It will sharpen your memory," Pops concluded. "Besides, I made a covenant with Allah that you would serve Islam, and it is because I wasn't fulfilling it that Zain died."

\*   \*   \*

I was awakened at dawn the next morning. "You're going with your cousins to their *madrassa*," Dadi Ma said. Then she ordered the other women away from her kerosene stove and made me a butter-fried egg with the flatbread we called *paratha*.

The *madrassa* that Tariq and Muaz attended was on the *bazar* side of town. Ammi was nervous about letting me go alone, but everyone reassured her and she relented. When I'd finished breakfast, she plopped a *topi* on my head and handed me a frayed little blue lesson book containing Arabic.

I walked up the alley with the boys, eager to see my new school. As we entered a square, we came upon a donkey tied to a big nail that was driven into the ground. Tariq threw a rock at the donkey, and the animal's grizzled gray felt quivered.

"Go pull its tail," he instructed me.

"Why?"

"When the devil pulls its tail, it brays."

"I am *not* the devil," I replied. "I am Abir ul Islam."

Tariq shrugged and we kept walking.

We soon passed a parked donkey cart. Tipping it over, we tried using it as a slide, with only limited success. As we continued our walk, we passed a pair of dolorous cows and tried to stick hay into their big nostrils, but we were chased away by a couple of barefoot girls with gooey hands and feet who had been piling cow dung into buckets. Muaz told them that they were ugly hags with backward feet, and they told him that his head was squelched in his father's anal sphincter.

Rather than taking the most direct route to the *madrassa,* we ducked in and out of people's houses, asking if this boy and that was awake. Then we abandoned the streets altogether: we entered a cement house and, without asking its owners—who sat on the floor of the courtyard eating breakfast—climbed the stairs to its roof and roof-hopped all the way to the end of the block. When we descended the stairs in another house, we chased a few hens around the veranda and discussed stealing an egg so that we could raise our own little chicken.

Eventually, we came onto a large paved road. Here there were a few rickshaws and numerous horse-drawn *tanga*s, along with fruit and vegetable vendors on donkey carts, as well as boys urging goats and bullocks toward the canals.

We crossed that street and entered a part of town even less developed than ours. Not only were the dusty alleys unpaved and run down, but sewage from the *nali*s spilled out onto the street, creating wide black pools infested with mosquitoes. In the pools of sludge some good Samaritan had laid a row of rocks upon which pedestrians could step. However, they were laid down for adult-length footsteps, so we youngsters had to hop from one to the next with both feet.

As we went forward, there were more emaciated cows, more donkeys, and even a big bull with lowered horns living a life of surrender.

"Look!" Muaz said suddenly. "Naked nincompoops!"

Looking where he pointed, we saw a row of naked boys—brothers, by the look of them—coming out of one of the houses. They had rich brown skins, bellies unnaturally rotund from tapeworm infestation, and dark navels. In a line, as if choreographed, they squatted quite near us with a wide stance over the *nali* and relieved themselves. In their sleepy state they didn't even bother to wave at the flies coming to sit at the corner of their eyes. Even from where we stood, we could see that the anuses of some, red and round, protruded a few inches out of their holes.

"Why does it look like that?" I asked.

"They're experts at shitting," Tariq said authoritatively.

"Does mine do that?"

"Want me to check?" he offered.

"Mine does," Muaz said with a grin.

Before I could laugh, the naked boys finished their business and started up a loud chant directed at their mother inside the house:

*Ammi, pitthi*
*tho thay tho thay*
*paani la dey pitthi tho thay*
*aaja Ammi pithi tho thay.*


*Mother, ass*
*wash it wash it*

*bring the water, wash it wash it*
*come on, Mother, wash it wash it.*

Getting no response, they repeated the chant many times. For a while the three of us chanted along with them. Then, having reached our destination, we climbed the steps to the *madrassa* and placed our slippers in wooden boxes on a shelf just inside.

The *madrassa* was packed with boys and filled with the drone of Quranic recitation. All other sounds—the naked boys outside, the whirring fans, the running taps—were subsumed under the recitation.

At the front of the hall there was a long wooden bench. Five *qari*s with beards, turbans, and sticks sat on one side, and an assembly line of students passed before them. Each student held a little *sipara* in his hand. When he got to the bench, he flattened it out and began rocking back and forth as he pronounced the words. Once a boy finished his lesson, the *qari* either dismissed him with a wave of his hand or, if the boy had flubbed the reading, hit him on the hand with the fat stick. The boys that were hit took the punishment stoically, for the most part, though when they'd gotten some distance away they let their faces contort in pain and they pressed their hands into their armpits and cried. There was a reason the boys took the punishment to the hands without wincing: those who broke down while being hit on their hands were pulled around the bench by their wrists, and as they twisted and turned they were beaten on their back and stomach.

The students not currently involved in a lesson ran around the hall. They played hide-and-seek behind the columns, enjoyed a game of tag, or threw the mosque's straw skullcaps at one another like Frisbees. An impromptu game of soccer—with two cloth *topi*s stuffed with straw skullcaps serving as the ball—broke out as I watched, with twenty or more students to each team.

Tariq told me to take out my book and get in line with him and Muaz. "When you get to the *qari*, just tell him that you're new and he'll tell you what to do."

"Will he hit me?"

"They always hit."

I looked at my hands and then toward the fat stick leaning against the wall. I started shaking. The hall suddenly felt deathly cold. With each step that took me closer to the *qari*s, little daggers of chilly fear jolted my body.

Suddenly, I heard something like a crack of lightning and looked up at the dome, thinking that perhaps it had cracked. Loud wailing and screaming ensued.

I soon realized that one of the *qari*s had become fed up with all the playing and was taking the stick to any child that he came upon. His preferred method was to grab a boy from behind by the hair or the collar and, in the act of yanking him, hit him on the back, the thighs, or the calves. If the *qari* caught a boy from the front, he almost always smashed the stick against the student's shins. That was what had created the unearthly cracking noise. As the *qari* rampaged, going one from one boy to another, there was a mad, chaotic scramble. I began running as well. One of the boys next to me was plucked by his shirt collar and yanked back. I had no way of checking whether Tariq and Muaz made it or not. I was concerned only with my own escape. I grabbed my shoes as I ran past the shelf, threw them down, and stepped into them while running toward home. I didn't stop until I got there.

When I told Ammi and Pops about the anarchy at the *madrassa,* they said that they were going to look into private tutoring.

P ops thought it would be better if I received religious instruction at home. He arranged that an educated man named Qari Adil would make regular house visits. Since he would be coming to our home and we would pay him a lot, Pops asked him to teach me about Islam beyond just memorizing the Quran.

Qari Adil was a dark, squat man with a silver beard tinged with henna. He had a gleaming smile and wore nothing but immaculate white clothes, with matching white turban. He was articulate and cheerful, and to my vast relief he didn't believe in punishment. He was the head of a popular mosque attended by many important men.

The first day that Qari Adil came to tutor, the atmosphere in the house was expectant and serious. Ammi made the sitting room spotless and the house smelled good. Food—*paratha*s and eggs for the *qari,* along with a glass of milk—was set forth. A brand new Quran sat on a new wooden holder, and there were Arabic textbooks and two copies of Abu Ala al-Mawdudi's exegesis. Normally one didn't study exegesis at a *madrassa,* but normally a *madrassa* didn't have teachers like this one.

Qari Adil rang the bell on his bike as he arrived, and I went to greet him. It was a gleaming silver Sohrab.

His comportment was unlike that of any other religious figure I'd seen in Sehra Kush. He was graceful, sparkling clean, and had an obvious sense of fashion. Riding in the sun made him sweat profusely, so that droplets fell from his forehead. When he arrived, he dabbed the end of his turban against his face and shook his shirt. Even with me—a kid—he had a nervousness that made me like him. When he finally sat down each day, he began by making small talk with me in a gregarious manner.

On most days, after I read the Quran with him we would read Mawdudi's *tafsir,* starting from the first *surah,* "The Opening," and move quickly into the dense material of the longest chapters in the Quran: "The Cow" and "The Family of Imran."

We talked about Jews a lot, because the story of Moses and his people takes up a large part of the two longest chapters of the Quran. The reference to the cow in the chapter by that name comes from a story involving a special cow that the Jews were asked by God to slaughter, but which they refused to kill on account of its lactic productivity. Qari Adil told me many stories about the Jews, such as the one about Jewish fishermen who were told to stop fishing on Saturday but wouldn't, because on Saturday, to test them, God would fill the lakes with fish, "and greedy people would become tempted to disobey God." He told me of the way the Jewish people compelled Moses to tell God how to show Himself on Sinai—and then refused to accept Moses's recounting of the event. He told me how the Jews in exile had started to starve, so Moses had God bring huge, heaping plates of *mann-o-salwa* from Paradise. After a period of eating such rich heavenly food, the Jews demanded lean legumes and shrubs and vegetables instead.

All of these stories of Jewish "disobedience and decadence" finally reached a climax when Qari Adil announced that the Jews had been turned into apes. In a gleeful narration he described in careful detail—a mixture of his own speculation and Mawdudi's imagination—how the actual transformation of a man into a monkey occurred.

Allah turning people into monkeys bothered me. If I were turned into a monkey, I'd eat lice and be unable to fly kites or spin tops. Being able to flip myself from branch to branch using just my tail wouldn't make up for the fact that I would be ugly, hairy, and loud. Besides, there was something strange about the punishment. It wasn't like the other divine punishments: floods, storms of sulfur, civilizations flipped upside down. Monkey-making seemed to be designed solely for amusement and mockery, things I hadn't associated with Allah. The possibility that Allah was a naughty boy in heaven who rolled around in the clouds making people into animals made me nervous. I came to fear God, but not just that: I became wary of Him as one does of a bully.

Only a few weeks into our study, it was revealed that Qari Adil was using the lessons as an occasion to flirt with Ammi, by writing love letters to her. When Ammi told Pops, the house visits stopped and Mawdudi's books were put away.

There were a few other books besides the Quran that evoked respect in my household. The foremost among these was an old leather-bound volume of Muhammad Iqbal's collection of poems, called *Baang-e-Dra* ("Call of the Caravan"). Pops often sat around on the veranda bellowing the first verse from the most famous poem:

*Ya rabb dil e Muslim ko*
*woh zinda tamanna de*
*jo qalb ko garma de*
*jo ruh ko tarpa de!*

*O Almighty, give to the Muslim*
*that spark of vitality*

*which enflames the heart*
*which enlivens the soul!*

Ammi also held Iqbal in great esteem, but for different reasons. She was impressed by his piety. "Iqbal recited *zikr* thirty million times in his life. You can't go wrong if you do the same."

"What invocation did he recite?"

"The *durood*."

"All of it?"

"Yes," she said. "*Allahumma sallay ala Muhammad wa ala aal-e-Muhammad kma sallayta wa ala aal-e-Ibrahim innaka hameedun majeed.*"

"That's long!"

"Read that thirty million times and *you* can become the next Iqbal, the founder of a Muslim nation. Don't you remember how you were taken to Mecca and had your heart rubbed upon the Ka'ba?"

"How could I forget?" I'd heard that story a hundred times.

The other household book was one I read was in English; it was called *The 100: A Ranking of the Most Influential Persons in History,* by Michael Hart. We owned it for one simple reason: the Holy Prophet was number one.

Hart explained his reasoning as follows: "My choice of Muhammad to lead the list of the world's most influential persons may surprise some readers and may be questioned by others, but he was the only man in history who was supremely successful on both the religious and secular levels."

I took great pride in the fact that someone from the West—a leader of science and education—recognized the Prophet Muhammad's influence.

The third book we had was a children's book in Urdu called *Lives of the Prophets.* This book explained that while every messenger of God before Muhammad had brought earlier versions of Islam, with Muhammad that religion reached its culmination. *Lives of the Prophets* contained the story of Adam and Havva's fall from the Garden; the story of Nuh's wife seeing the water in her oven and warning Nuh about the Flood so he could launch his ark; the story of Ibrahim destroying the town's idols when he was just a child; the story of Musa challenging the Pharaoh's wizards by casting his staff on the ground and having it turn into a cobra; the story of Yunus, who was eaten by a whale; Yusuf, who rose from a prisoner of the Pharaoh to one of his officials; and Isa, born to a virgin mother. I liked reading this book before I went to sleep.

One night the stars were out as we prepared to sleep on the roof. I had forgotten *Lives* downstairs. I couldn't get to sleep without it, but I was too scared to go get it in the dark. So I turned to Ammi.

"Tell me a story," I pleaded.

"About what?"

"Tell me a Prophet story."

"Pick a Prophet."

"All 124,000 of them," I suggested, smiling in the dark.

"How about just one?" she countered, fluffing her pillow and putting her glasses under it.

There were just too many options. "*You* pick," I said.

"All right," she agreed. "I will tell you about Yusuf. Did you know that when he was a little boy he had a dream in which the sun and the moon and the twelve stars were bowing to him?"

"Why did they bow to him?" I asked.

"Because Yusuf was so beautiful. Out of the ten parts of beauty in the universe, Allah gave nine to Yusuf."

"That doesn't leave a lot for the rest of us."

"Don't talk like that," she chided. "His beauty was a burden upon him. Women schemed and connived in order to try to seduce him. Things are always difficult for people who serve God. Take our Holy Prophet, for example. He had to struggle."

"Like how?"

"The people of Taif threw stones at him until his shoes were filled with blood. He was insulted and attacked in Mecca. Instead of calling him Muhammad, they called him Mudhammam, which was a bad insult. A woman used to throw garbage on his head every day that he passed by her house. The Quraysh—the tribe from which he came—tried to kill him, so he had to flee for Medina. Even then they didn't leave him alone; they sent armies after him so that he had to fight in battles and lose many of his friends."

"Why did God allow such things to happen?" I asked.

"God didn't *allow* them. God *commanded* them. He did it so that Muhammad would be prepared to deal with even greater challenges. Do you remember all the suffering Muhammad went through when he was a child? First his father died before he was born. Then his mother died when he was five. Then his grandfather died when he was eleven. Then his dearest uncle died when he was seventeen. When he grew up, all four of his sons died, each one shortly after being born. Why do you think all *these* things happened?"

"Why?"

"In preparation for his service to God. He was meant to do something great."

"Which was . . . ?"

"Serving Islam, of course. Just like you're going to do."

Although Ammi smiled at me with pride, I felt a shiver run through me. "Does this mean bad things are going to happen to me too?" I asked.

# 13

Combustible and explosive *jinn*s inhabited the kerosene stoves of Pakistan. These creatures were especially prone to heeding the incendiary commands of angry mothers-in-law, husbands dissatisfied by dowry size, and honor-obsessed brothers. At their behest, these *jinn*s spat a shower of oily fire on a housewife's body and then ignited, melting the skin of women all over the country. When the fire had been put out, the victim was usually taken to a hospital, where the entire episode was chalked up to an accident or attempted suicide.

One evening when I was trying to use my tennis ball to kill the flies resting on the wall, a frail old *masi,* a woman recognized as an elder of the *mohalla,* leathered by time and wearing a *lungi,* entered the house and hurriedly gathered the women. I could hear the word *afsos*—meaning, in this context, How tragic!—over and over.

"She was wearing polyester!" exclaimed the *masi*.

"Oh, she was done for then," said Dadi Ma. "That stuff melts and sticks to the skin!"

"They say it was an accident," said the *masi*.

"Oh, please!" scoffed Ammi. "Stove explodes and it's an accident? That's a cover-up! They always call it accident; that's what they *always* say! It has to be the mother-in-law!"

"Oh, how can you accuse her?" Dadi Ma—herself a mother-in-law—said defensively. "I'm sure it wasn't—"

"Poor girl!" Ammi continued. "It sounds like third-degree burns. Is she at the hospital now?"

"Yes, and her baby is at home!" offered the *masi*.

"I pray for Allah's mercy," said my older aunt.

"Me too—but it was *definitely* the mother-in-law!" Ammi said.

"You! Stop saying such horrible things!" Dadi Ma said reproachfully.

"Such things are common," the *masi* said. "What can you say? *Kismet* had bad things in store for the poor girl."

I followed the conversation avidly. However, within a few minutes of hearing about the incident I forgot about it, the image of a burn victim replaced by dead flies.

A few hours later I went to the kitchen and noticed Ammi sitting in front of the stove, turning a *roti* with her fingertips. When the bread puffed up, she pulled me over. "Look how it's filling up. It's Allah's way of telling us that the person who is going to eat this *roti* is very hungry."

As I glanced at the *roti*, it occurred to me that Ammi was using a kerosene stove—the sort of stove that had blown up in that woman's face. I imagined this stove blowing up in Ammi's face. Her curly hair going crisp. Her face melting off her bones. Her screams echoing in the empty alley. I threw my arms around Ammi and buried my face in her neck.

"Ammi," I asked, "is your stove going to blow up?"

"God forbid," she said, slapping me on the shoulder. "Mine is fine." Then, in a louder voice so that Dadi Ma could hear, she added, "And my mother-in-law doesn't want to hurt me."

"Then why did *that* woman catch fire?"

"Look here," Ammi said, opening up a second stove sitting near her. "The girl's stove, to explode like that, must have been tampered with. See, a stove has three parts. The bottom bowl is for the oil, and there's a shell that protects these twelve cotton strands"—she gestured at them—"that suck the oil to the top. When the stove burns, it's actually these strands that are burning. But if just one or two strands fall down, or if they're removed by a malicious person, that creates a vacuum in the system, and during cooking the fire travels down the shell and into the bowl of oil, causing it to explode and splashing the cook with scalding oil. Then you have third-degree burns."

An image of the burned girl started to form in my head, a pristine image, the face of an innocent and happy mother, someone like my own mother. I decided that I would go and find her.

I waited until late afternoon and slipped out of the house. The *azan* for dusk prayer—the commonly accepted time when a child must be back home—was about to occur, and I had never stayed out past that before. I was nervous. While I knew the block where the woman lived, I didn't know which house she was in.

Standing at the end of the block, not sure which house to go to, I acted on intuition, making my way to a small brick house with a thick brown curtain in the doorway. I chose it because the house seemed silent, there was no smoke signifying suppertime activity, and none of the lights were on. Because the curtain was hung improperly, there was a small sliver at the left side that I could see through as I approached. The inside of the house appeared dark as well, and there was no activity on the veranda, an odd thing for a house that still had its door open.

"*Allahu akbar! Allahu akbar!*" came the sudden call to prayer from the mosque.

As the first verse of the *azan* went up, I panicked. I had to get home before it finished. Something drew me closer to the curtain, however, and I stepped across the *nali* and put my eye to the gap, hoping to perhaps see signs of an exploded stove.

Without warning, the heavy curtain, rippling with dust, was flung outward, its thick edge smacking me across the face. I lost my footing, and one of my feet went directly into the *nali*, plunging down until my toes felt the sludge running between them. The sewage felt surprisingly cold. The man who had just emerged from the house—it was his exit that had sent the curtain flying—stopped in the act of wrapping his turban and turned to look at me. His eyes were dark and his teeth shone with a menacing whiteness. I had never been more frightened. I felt weak. Using my toes to secure my shoe before it floated away, I pulled my foot out of the *nali*—it came free with a sucking sound—and ran back home.

At the *nalka* I scrubbed my filthy leg and my spattered clothes as thoroughly as I could. I used some dust that had gathered on the stairs as makeshift soap. It had the effect of muting some of the smell clinging to me.

Despondent that I hadn't gotten a chance to catch a glimpse of the burned girl, I hurried to the mosque, accompanied by the last few verses of the *azan*. As I prayed, the smell of *nali,* foul and acrid, wafted up off me. When no one was looking, I leaned down and breathed it in. The more it made me disgusted, the more I inhaled it.

Then I fell ill.

When I got typhoid, I became a *jinn,* my body enveloped by a 105-degree fire. *Jinn* smoke filled me up, and I vomited until there was no more liquid inside. My body went limp and my eyes closed shut. I felt myself raised into the air, elongated, compressed, and then stretched out again. Flesh gave way to vapor. A shriek escaped my lips and left cracks in the walls. My hair curled up, cringed in pain, and ran off my body. My tongue started to shrivel. There wasn't a lick of saliva. "Ammi!" I cried. "Ammi!"

That night my body became a balloon and floated up to the ceiling. When Ammi entered the bedroom, she beheld my body jerking and twitching eleven feet in the air. She took a running start and leaped up to retrieve me. Unable to touch me, she ran out for tools and came back with a reel of kite string. She took a heavy lock from one of the trunks, attached it to a length of kite string with a sturdy knot, and then threw the lock up to me. I put it in my pocket as she instructed, and she pulled me down. But when she took the lock out of my pocket, I floated upward again; a draft came from the veranda and my ascent became wobbly. Jumping up, Ammi grabbed hold of my pants and dragged me to the bed. This time she used a bedsheet to tie me down. The other end of it she tied to the doorknob.

"You're moored now," she said.

"I'm so very hot," I said.

She went to the kitchen and returned carrying a huge steel bucket, filled to the brim with water. Little cubes of ice occasionally showed their sweaty bald heads at the surface. When Ammi dunked my feet, the *jinn* inside me, made of so much fire, shrieked loudly. The bucket soon steamed and became a bubbling cauldron. Ammi unbuttoned my shirt and ripped it off. She then wrapped a turban around my head, with cubes of ice lodged like diamonds in the gaps. Her attack alarmed the vaporous *jinn* and it rebelled, rocking back and forth, trying to float upward to safety. This time the whole bed lifted off the floor as the *jinn* pulled up on me, but the knot on the doorknob held me in place. Ammi, meanwhile, finished off my new outfit by giving me wristbands of chilled gauze, which regulated my pulse and kept cool the blood in my body's irrigation system. I slept then, but fitfully.

For that entire summer, every day became for Ammi a race to procure more cold water and more cubes of ice, and to tie the jeweled turban before the morning sunlight empowered the *jinn* inside. Still I became more and more frail. When my brother fell to a lesser *jinn,* her attention was momentarily diverted and she took to procuring other types of treatments. There were tablespoons of honey kissed with hope. Cool yellow rice chilled with desperation. Iced teas and custards refrigerated with a mother's love.

Nothing worked. My skin darkened. The *jinn* inside me, so eager to take me to heaven, had started to disfigure me, turning me into a shadow right here on earth.

With squeals of pain Ammi watched the splotches on my body expand. By the time the last of my hair fell out in clumps, she was broken. She gave in to exhaustion and fell asleep, forgetting to wrap the straitjacket of ice around me. She also forgot to set my feet in a bucket of water, so the *jinn* smoke rushed into my ankles and I began aspiring upward, to Allah Mian. Soon I was flipped upside down, my hair scraping the floor like a broom and the soles of my feet rubbing against the hot skin of the lightbulb.

I closed my eyes. I was cooked. That's what Dadi Ma said—and that's certainly what it felt like.

Then, right then, Ammi put her hand on my forehead and started reciting a teleportation spell. It sounded just like Quranic verses.

When I opened my eyes I saw that I was flying—not Superman style, but held under each armpit by Ammi, who flew above me. Transformed into a *parri,* she was covered with a lustrous, light-colored cuticle, and her wings dripped with light. As her long hair flowed free, she carried me through the vague fog.

"Where are we?" I asked, my voice echoing as if through a thousand invisible hallways.

"We're in the seven heavens," she replied.

"What level are we on?"

"Fifth."

"Who lives here?"

"Humans live on the first world," she said, "*jinn*s on the second and third, the Prophets on the fourth, the *parri*s on the fifth, and the angels on the sixth."

"Allah is on the seventh?"

"Yes," she agreed.

"Why can't I see into the other heavens?"

Ammi explained that the architecture of the seven heavens obeyed the laws of hierarchy. Imagine a house with seven stories, she said, each story separated from another by a pane of glass, and each pane of glass a one-way mirror, with the various mirrors arranged in such a way that the individual looking down from the seventh floor could see all the way to the bottom, but one couldn't see anything looking from the bottom up.

"So what are we doing here?" I asked.

"We're looking for a cure," she said.

"A medicine for me?" I asked.

"A magical fruit," she replied. "And look at your luck! There it is!" She pointed to a man carrying a paper bag.

Pops entered the room carrying the season's first batch of plums.

"*Aloo bukhara!*" he said. Literally translated: the fever potato. He shoved plums down my throat and for days didn't stop.

Over each piece of fruit, Ammi and Dadi Ma read *surah Yasin* from the Quran.

Within days the typhus *jinn* left my body. The hallucinations ended as well. The Quran had saved my life.

Soon after I was cured, I was enrolled at another *madrassa*. My illness had been a case of God reminding us of the covenant—which we had to fulfill.

# 14

The red brick *madrassa* where I was enrolled sat on a muddy canal where buffaloes and bare-backed boys swam. The juicer up the street broke sugarcane spines and pushed them through his eight-armed machine, secreting juice into a glass, which he mixed with salt, ginger, and lemon. Nearby, a billiards hall and a restaurant catered to truck drivers passing through the desert town. Behind the *madrassa* was an open field used for Eid prayer, though it was infested with scorpions. On the other side of the field was an abandoned mental hospital.

Wearing a light-blue *shalwar kameez* and *topi,* during my first day of class I found myself sitting in front of my new teacher, Qari Jamil. A heavyset man with fleshy pink hands and black skin, he wore an undershirt called a *bunyan* with a *lungi* that reached past mid-calf. A tan stick was propped close to him. The expression on his face—bemused irritation—suggested that he wouldn't be averse to using the stick. We sat face-to-face in the center of the room as all the other students rocked in front of their Qurans. He appraised me with a supercilious look that asserted the totality of his authority.

"What's your name?"

"Abir ul Islam."

"Incorrect."

I looked at him in confusion, frightened by the way he'd dismissed my name.

"But it *is* Abir ul Islam. It means—"

"That's *not* how you say your name."

"Then how?" I asked.

"You are pronouncing it as if it begins with an *alif*. In fact, your name begins with an *ein*. It is an Arabic word, and thus you must pronounce it in the Arabic way. Harden the *ein*. From your throat. Not from the front of your mouth like a housewife. Now say it again."

"Abir."

He reached forward with his stick and jabbed its blunt end into the small of my neck. "Pull it out from here," he commanded.

"Abir."

"No." He jabbed harder. "Say it again."

"Abir."

He lifted up his stick and crashed it on the bench between us. "Wrong!" he exclaimed. "Say it again. Say it *correctly* this time—from the back of your throat like a man."

I tried. I added a guttural growl to the first letter, but it came out sounding feeble and meek. I looked down in shame. Apparently reflecting on one's failure was not permitted, because he thumped the bench again.

"Say it again. Say it loudly. Let everyone hear."

"Abir," I said. "Abir, Abir, Abir, Abir . . ." until my voice became hoarse. Incrementally the class moved to laughter, and eventually Qari Jamil joined them.

"We'll work on it," he said. Then he turned to a short boy with oiled and parted hair. "Jugnu. You, Jugnu. Come here for a minute."

"Yes, Qari Saab?" said the boy in a voice so obedient that it made me pity him.

"Show Abir ul Islam here how to sit."

"Like this, Qari Saab," Jugnu said, adjusting himself. I couldn't get past how deeply reverent Jugnu was toward Qari Jamil. It was intimidating. Ammi and Pops had always told me that in Islam teachers were like parents—there was a *hadith* that said so—but I didn't treat even my parents with such submission.

Qari Jamil looked at me. "Do you see how Jugnu is sitting? Copy him. His back is erect. Both of his feet are tucked under him. His left ankle is turned under his seat and is parallel to the floor. His right foot is propped on the ground. This is how you must sit."

With a couple of false starts, I did my best to mimic Jugnu.

"Good," said Qari Jamil. "Just like that. This is how you will sit when reading the Quran. Do you understand?"

I nodded yes even as a sharp pain shot through the arch of one foot. Pops had always told me that I had flat feet and couldn't bend them the same way other people could. However, telling that to the *qari* didn't seem like a particularly good idea.

"Now take out your *qaida*," he said. "Let's start."

I produced the instruction manual, placed it on the bench, and opened it to the first page, where the alphabet was written. Meanwhile, my ankle stiffened and hurt.

"The reason that you cannot pronounce your own name is because you know only the Urdu alphabet," Qari Jamil said. "The Quran is in Arabic, so I am going to teach you the Arabic alphabet and its correct pronunciation. This way is different than how the housewives of Punjab pronounce things. This way is the *correct* way. It is the way of Islam. Do you understand?"

The Arabic way was the Islamic way, I told myself, and nodded. The *qari* then began to teach me how to gutturally pronounce the three Arabic letters most difficult for a Pakistani to master: the *ein,* the *ha,* and the *qaf.* After half an hour of lessons, I was instructed to go sit near the wall and practice saying those three letters for the remaining eight hours of the schoolday. From time to time as the hours passed, Qari Jamil, with laughter in his voice, said my name loudly to the class.

Abir ul Islam.

Like it was a joke.

U rine caused tremendous concern to all Islamic worshippers and was an object of great disdain at the *madrassa.* In fact, after I learned the pronunciation of the Arabic alphabet, my second major lesson had been about liquid excrement.

The first principle of urine was that you couldn't ever let a single drop get on your clothes, because that would immediately render them impure and you wouldn't be able to make prayer without changing clothes.

The second principle of urine was that you couldn't ever let a single drop get on your skin, because every part of your body that urine had touched would have to be burned in hellfire before you could regain purity.

The third principle of urine was that you had to recite a certain prayer before going to the bathroom, because if you didn't, you allowed *jinn*s to take over your spirit. This happened because *jinn*s were particularly active, and your defenses were particularly weak, when urine was flowing. The prayer read: *Allahumma inni aoozo bika min al khubusi wal khabais:* "O Allah, I seek refuge with you from all evil and evildoers." There was also a prayer for when you finished urinating. I was required to memorize that as well.

The fourth principle of urine was that you could touch your penis only with your left hand, because it was the devil's hand.

The fifth principle of urine was that you had to wash up with water afterwards, an act called *istunja*.

The final principle of urine was that you couldn't urinate standing up, because that increased the likelihood of the first and second principles being violated. The proper way to urinate—the way I was taught at the *madrassa*—involved getting down in a squat, spreading your legs, keeping your *shalwar* out of the way with your right hand, and directing your stream by holding your penis with the left. Then you used your right hand to pour water on your organ as you rubbed it clean with your left. Afterwards you washed your hands, saying a shorter prayer as you scrubbed: "O Allah, I seek refuge with you from the devil."

When I began at the *madrassa*, I heard and practiced the lessons about urine with great fervor, making a dedicated effort to avoid getting even a single drop on my clothes or skin. I drank as much water as I could so that I could practice the squatting technique.

Mastering the art of urination wasn't easy, but it was the way of Islam and therefore I had to know it.

Back in class we learned about a method for memorizing the Quran based on the architecture of the Holy Book.

Each of the Quran's thirty *juz*—volumes—were split into fourths. The first fourth was called *arba;* the second fourth was called *nisf;* the third fourth was called *salasa*. Each fourth was composed of four sections called *ruku*s.

A student began memorizing the thirtieth *juz* first, because it contained the shortest verses. Then he went to the twenty-ninth *juz,* where the verses were a little longer. After a student had perfectly memorized the last two *juz*es, he began memorizing from the first *juz* onward. Memorizing the entire Quran in little quadratic sections like this could take anywhere from two to eight years. The average was around five.

My class was split between part-time and full-time students. Full-timers studied from dawn till night with breaks for prayer and food. Part-timers like me came in after the noon prayer, and we all sat together.

"Make sure that you rock back and forth as you read," Qari Jamil said, extending his stick to pat my shoulder. "Rocking makes it easy." I looked around and saw that all the other students were rocking quickly.

After I had spent a whole day on my assigned *ruku,* Qari Jamil called me up along with two other students. We started reciting simultaneously from disparate places in the Quran while he closed his eyes and listened. If any of us made a mistake, the *qari* simply stated the correction; then the *talib,* or student, reversed mid-sentence and carried on as before. Most students made at least a few errors each time. If a student persisted in the same error, however—or if there were too many errors sprinkled in a recitation—Qari Jamil sent the offending *talib* out of the group and back to his place. This wasn't seen as particularly embarrassing, and Qari Jamil usually gave the student an opportunity to reclaim his spot later in the day. However, if the errors continued, it was likely that the student would be beaten. The severity of punishment depended on the *qari*'s mood, the student's previous performance, and the student's reputation for either laziness or diligence. Once a student got a bad reputation, beatings became progressively worse; and one's reputation couldn't be reclaimed except through an intervention by the student's family.

I completed my first lesson without getting beaten.

# 15

Before I became a regular student at the *madrassa*, though I did occasionally play with Flim, I didn't have any real friends. With so many of the boys from the *mohalla* in school, I had to play with girls. They particularly liked to play wedding. They took turns being bride, drafted me to be groom, sang songs in Siraiki and Punjabi and Balochi, fed me and my bride sweetmeats (which were really rocks), and saw off the happy couple with rose petals (which were really tiny pieces of cow dung). Sometimes I played house with a pair of girls named Bina and Samia and married both of them simultaneously. Up on the roof they lived in two separate "houses" that I constructed for them out of turned-over *charpai*s covered with sheets, and I took turns spending time with each. This continued until I was caught by a stone-faced Pathan widow while running my hands over my wives' bodies. Fearing that she would report me to Dada Abu, I regretfully gave up this activity.

At the *madrassa* I became friends with Marjan and Ittefaq. They were also part-timers. Marjan was mild and mellow—a short guy with a white *topi*. Ittefaq was aggressive and rambunctious—a taller guy in loose *shalwar kameez*. He was older than Marjan and me and was the leader of our little crew.

During school breaks and on Fridays we played cricket at the Old Hospital or looked for soccer games near the dusty roundabout.

Marjan told me that his older uncle had a spot in one of their family homes from which they could look into other people's houses and see naked housewives. We did that for a little while, but the women were old.

One time we stole adult bicycles and scissor-kicked them—with our legs through the frame—all the way into the military part of town, turning back when some soldiers in a Jeep glared us away.

Another time just Ittefaq and I went for a long excursion in the afternoon on the dusty streets heading out of town. We passed withered, turbaned men walking with their bullocks; wooden carts tilted back from the vast amounts of weight on them; women in the bright-hued scarves that Gypsies wore. Eventually we came upon a clearing amidst a collection of dunes where a carnival was underway. There was a tent with freaks of nature which we wanted desperately to enter, but we were too afraid to go near because we'd heard there was a backward-footed *churayl* inside, and Dadi Ma had warned me against those. Beyond that tent there was a merry-go-round, a massive seesaw, and many stalls selling food. After wandering among those, we made our way to one of the main attractions at the festival.

It was a hollow wooden tower made of large, curved planks screwed together. It rose up nearly three stories high, with a diameter of about thirty feet, like a bloated parapet from the Crusades. Attached to its exterior was a latticework of rickety wooden staircases that took the audience up to the rim, which was guarded by a railing. From the rim we could see into the pit below, where a Suzuki sedan, stripped of color and doors, and two denuded motorcycles were parked. Suddenly a small, shutterlike door snapped open at the bottom, and the audience—knowing what was to come—cheered loudly. Two men in jeans and collared shirts came out and waved. They kickstarted their bikes, the sawed-off mufflers coughing and roaring, and then rode around in circles, kicking up dust, picking up speed. Suddenly, with the assistance of a little ramp and centrifugal force, the bikes leaped up against the wall of the tower, going around in circles, still gaining in speed until they were going around perpendicular to the floor. Like cream coming to a boil the bikers rose ever higher, and I was afraid they would reach the very top and fly off into the crowd. Just when I thought things couldn't get any more exciting, the car below came alive with a roar. It turned on its headlights and made preliminary circles on the ground before it too jumped onto the wall. The weight of the car caused the entire tower to creak and groan. It strained against itself as if it were a mighty *jinn* trying to hold down a bad meal. The bikers crisscrossed in front of the car, teasing it, forcing it to follow them higher. Sometimes the bikers rode opposite from each other, giving salutes in our direction. Sometimes they were one in front of the other, the tires threatening to touch, evoking gasps from the audience. The drivers were men of momentum, artists of inertia, fearless and intrepid gamblers who put their lives in the palm of their hand. Their unbuttoned shirts fluttered like capes. They wore numerous taweezes of protection around their necks. They were desert superheroes blessed by the Quran.

Marjan, Ittefaq, and I also played *joda-mitti,* team tag, with other boys from the *madrassa.* Two people were "it." Everyone else had a partner, and those pairs held hands. As long as you were holding someone's hand, you couldn't be "it." Meanwhile, the "it" pair carried out a countdown. When it ended, everyone let go of their partner and tried to get a new one without getting tagged by the "it" pair. One day as we played *joda-mitti* I jumped from a raised porch into an empty lot and stepped barefoot on a shattered cola bottle. Blood ran everywhere, and the pain was fierce.

"You're it!" Ittefaq said.

"I'm bleeding!" I objected, using my hand to stanch the flow.

"Doesn't matter! Hazrat Ali's arm was cut in battle, hanging only by a tendon. He stepped on it and pulled it off himself so that he could keep fighting."

"Be a warrior," Marjan told me.

With a deep breath, I let go of my bleeding foot and started chasing the boys. Dirt and gravel pushed into my wounds. I shook off the blackness that threatened to curtain my eyes. I had to be tough like my friends. It was the only way to survive.

# 16

Beatings were a regular occurrence at the *madrassa*. The first good beating I saw involved a boy who hadn't washed his feet properly before prayer. Someone pointed out this oversight to Qari Jamil, and even though the student pointed to his wet footprints in the courtyard as proof of good intentions, he was made to bend over and was hit on the posterior.

My first beating came soon thereafter.

I had been doing so well with my lessons that when I finished memorizing my required *ruku* for the day, I usually flipped through the Quran for something more to memorize. Just to prove how good I was, I memorized some of the better known passages and quietly tested myself while waiting for my turn to recite. This project backfired.

As I was reciting one of my assigned lessons for the *qari* one day, I inadvertently began connecting that recitation to a verse from an entirely different part of the Quran.

Grabbing his stick, Qari Jamil interrupted me.

"How did you get all the way over there?" he asked. "That's not even part of your lesson."

"Mistake," I said, retreating back to my study spot to review my lesson, trying to forget the extra verses.

After some review I returned to my place at the bench and began rocking and reciting. Unfortunately, I persisted in the error.

"You aren't paying attention!" Qari Jamil exclaimed, fed up with my mistakes. "Come over here."

I bit my lip. I knew what was coming. His fat hand hung in the air and drew me close. I thought if I just apologized he might let me go. "I'm very sorry," I said, feeling as abject as I sounded. "I'll get it right after more review."

My apology didn't cut it. I had to be beaten to assure the perfection of the Quran.

Qari Jamil pulled me by my ear and then slapped my head with his right hand, my eyes rattling from the blow. Other students who were hit sometimes developed red splotches in the whites of their eyes, and I wondered if the same would happen to me.

"On the floor!" he instructed. "Become the rooster."

The rooster was the preferred punitive position at the *madrassa*. It was so named because of the way you bent your anatomy in order to comply. I leaned forward and crouched into a squat, bending my head down until it was almost on the floor. I hitched my arms behind my knees and brought them forward to hold the lobes of my ears.

My posterior went up. Qari Jamil's cane reeled back and came down. The bones accepted their walloping, though my thighs quivered from sustaining the squat. I constricted my rectum because I'd heard that some *qari*s shoved their stick into the anus. The pain of each blow required me to take a squatting shuffle forward.

After I finished crying, I went back to recite my lesson.

After I'd been there several months, the *madrassa* hired a new teacher named Qari Asim. He was in his twenties, with sleek black hair, a chiseled face, and a kempt beard. He dressed in the finest white cotton, crisped with *kalaf*. His checkered red-and-white *kafiya* was new, neatly folded on his shoulders, and it smelled of Medinan musk. His sandals were black and polished. He rode a red Kawasaki

70cc and sported black-market Ray-Bans. Now the class was split into two. Marjan ended up in his section, though I stayed with Qari Jamil.

Within hours of Qari Asim's arrival, news of his severity spread among the students. We gathered around the boys in his section before the evening prayer and looked at the signs of the *qari's* violence upon his students. Many had had their ears yanked and twisted so that they turned blue and purple. A couple had received full-handed slaps on the face, the red imprints still radiating heat. Some had been beaten with sticks, either on their backs or on their shins.

Marjan didn't say anything. He was one of the few who had managed to avoid getting called for a face-to-face encounter with the *qari*. But he had a guarded look about him: he knew his time was coming.

One day, on my way to the *madrassa* later than unusual, I detoured through Marjan's neighborhood to see if he was still home and wanted to walk together. As I approached his house I heard loud wailing punctuated by cursing inside.

I flipped open the jute curtain to the house and went inside, where I found his mother shrieking hysterically, chased around the veranda by her husband, who was trying to gather his *lungi* into a knot.

"Bring my son to me!" she commanded.

"Sit down, woman. Sit down! It'll be fine. We'll go get him right now!"

"Bring my son! Allah curse the *qari*!"

Marjan's grandfather and an uncle, who had been standing to one side when I entered, conferred with one another and walked into the alley, concern on their faces. Meanwhile, Marjan's mother made a beeline for the door, only to have a chorus of people remind her that her face was uncovered so she couldn't leave the house. An old *masi* that cleaned their latrine, her sludge-tipped sweeper dripping slime on the floor, stood immobile, taken aback by the entropy in the house. Another one of Marjan's uncles sat in the shade of a toy-fabrication machine. I recognized him. He had suffered near-electrocution a few weeks earlier when the machine had malfunctioned, and he'd come to Pops's clinic for treatment. He sat in a stoic squat with his back to the wall; partially fabricated cars, tops, and plastic animals littered the floor near him, awaiting his final touches once he was fully healed.

Unable to leave for school in the face of all this drama, I waited, unnoticed, in the courtyard. Marjan's grandfather and uncle soon came back, carrying Marjan in their arms. He was comatose. His pants were rolled up to his thighs, and his legs hung limply. The length of each leg was covered in blue and black bruises. There was blood dribbling from various blows to the shin. The beaten calves looked clumpy, protruding in some areas, deflated in others. His legs were clearly destroyed.

"Qari Asim!" said the uncle who helped bring him in. "He started beating him and wouldn't stop. Wouldn't stop."

"His legs are broken," the grandfather declared somberly. "Set him down. Ya Allah mercy. Ya Allah health." He then instructed someone to go find my father. Meanwhile, Marjan's aunts began mixing butter with brown sugar and glycerin, then heated the confection to rub as ointment. Marjan's father was more composed than his mother, but he looked like a beaten mule, excusing himself to the walls into which he crashed. After a few minutes, though, the entire house was quiet, lost in prayer.

Suddenly a powerful human conflagration erupted in the house. It was the uncle who had received the electric shock, enraged after learning of Marjan's beating. "Who is this Qari Asim?" he shouted, his face dangerously red. "Sister-fucking Qari Asim! If I don't get him back, I have no honor! If I don't get him back, my name is no longer Farrukh the Stud!"

Grabbing up an old mop he marched around the house, breaking pottery right and left. By this time a number of neighbors had streamed into the house. Having seen Marjan and heard Farrukh's vows, they became excited at the prospect of a beat-down. This kind of righteous violence was appreciated among us because there were no losers: an avenging relative, a beaten *qari,* and a satisfied audience vicariously unleashing their latent resentment against the masters of the *madrassa.* Uncle Farrukh exited the house head aloft, stick held like a broadsword, mouth streaming profanities about Asim's incestuous anal activities. Children followed him up the street, making rhymes about the forthcoming beating that had already become legendary. I followed.

At the *madrassa* Uncle Farrukh bellowed a challenge for Qari Asim to come and get his. Students loyal to the *qari* ran and told him his death was here. In fear, the *qari* ran out of class, hopped on his

Kawasaki, and rode away in a cloud of dust. Uncle Farrukh, upset that he wasn't able to unleash his wrath, made a great show of strength, shattering the benches, Quran-holders, and pulpits, threatening and intimidating the student body. He made it indelibly clear to Qari Jamil that Asim was not welcome back. Qari Jamil, looking more than a little anxious himself, put up his hands and apologized.

A few hours later word came that Asim had been spotted at the *bazar*. Uncle Farrukh rushed home, picked up a bicycle, and went in pursuit, spending most of the night chasing the violent *qari* around various parts of the city, smashing merchandise, hurling rocks.

Marjan was out of the coma by the time Uncle Farrukh returned from his retaliatory spree, but it took him many weeks to recuperate.

O ne evening after coming home from the *madrassa* I sat on the rooftop looking at the courtyard below. Ammi was moving a pot of black lentils off the stove. Tai, my older aunt, was bending over the drain, pouring the water out of a big pot of *basmati* rice. My other aunt was stirring the spiced yogurt in a steel tray with a wooden spoon. Suddenly there was a powerful banging on the doorframe and all three women dropped their pots.

"Ittefaq!" shouted a man from the street. "Ittefaq! Is my son Ittefaq in there?"

Normally someone would have simply shouted no in response, but not when a boy's father was out looking for him. That meant something was wrong. A pair of my uncles went out to greet the old man. I ran to the edge of the roof overlooking the alley and looked down.

"He hasn't come home from the *madrassa*," explained Ittefaq's father, a grizzled old man who owned a small shop in the *bazar*. "If he comes here, will you send him home?"

My uncles came inside and informed the women that Ittefaq was missing.

"That boy has been trouble for his family since day one," Dadi Ma observed.

"What do you mean?" Ammi asked.

"You think this is the first time that man has come looking for the boy with fear in his voice?"

During the evening we kept receiving updates about Ittefaq's absence. A neighborhood manhunt was launched, and people from his side of town kept coming over to our house, thinking he might be with me. As evening became night, people started wondering if Ittefaq hadn't run away but had been abducted.

I didn't think much of it. I ate dinner and went to sleep. I figured Ittefaq would turn up at the *madrassa* the next day. But when I went for my lesson he wasn't there. He also didn't come the day after. When I asked Ammi if he had been found, she told me she hadn't heard anything positive.

Two days later, Ammi was gossiping with the women and learned that Ittefaq had been recovered. Apparently one morning at dawn one of the women from his house went down from the roof, where everyone was sleeping, to wash up for the morning prayer. When she was down there she heard what seemed to be a cat scratching at the front door. She pushed the door ajar to check what was happening and saw Ittefaq lying prone, scratching the paint with his nails. He was mewling and whimpering. She screamed and pulled him in, and he was put under his parents' supervision.

It turned out that he had spent three nights hiding in an open grave at the cemetery.

"What in the world would make a little boy go running to live in a grave?" my aunt asked.

"He was too ashamed to come home," Dadi Ma said, avoiding discussing the difficult topic directly.

"He was raped," said Ammi bluntly. "Taken on the way home from the *madrassa* and raped."

"*Hai hai!*" Dadi Ma exclaimed. "Why would you say something like that?"

"Someone has to say it."

"*Know* it, yes. Don't *announce* it."

Ittefaq's parents had eventually heard from Ittefaq what had happened, but instead of blaming the *madrassa,* from which he had been taken, they blamed their son. They said that he had become a disciplinary headache and that neither they nor Qari Jamil's *madrassa* could set him straight. A young *qari* from another *madrassa* far north arrived at Ittefaq's house, encouraging his parents to allow him to take the boy away. The smart-talking stranger made it seem that his institution was a discipline-oriented place.

Through my parents I also came to hear of this more efficient northern *madrassa*—because they were considering sending me there—though in the end they decided to wait and see how Ittefaq's experience turned out.

I went to Ittefaq's neighborhood the day he was leaving. A *tanga* pulled up in the street. The recruiter sat in the front with the driver. Ittefaq was put in the back, looking dazed, carrying his things in a knotted bedsheet. With a click of the driver's tongue, the horse clopped away. There was a vacant look on Ittefaq's face. His eyes were glued to a faraway place.

As the horse clopped forward I followed my departing friend and ran after the *tanga,* suddenly desperate to keep Ittefaq from going. Running as fast as I could, I grabbed at the footstep on the back of the carriage, hoping to stop the horse and *tanga*. I wasn't strong enough. My fingers slipped and I fell on the street.

Ittefaq was gone so long that I forgot we were ever friends.

A few months later, however, I learned from Ammi that Ittefaq had recently reappeared like a dusty apparition in the heart of the night, his face covered with soot, his clothes dirty and torn. The vaunted *madrassa* had turned out to be less concerned with religious education and more with breaking the will of the students. Children, brought in from far-flung places on the promise of a disciplinarian institution, were brutalized under the gaze of young angry *maulvi*s, who were really soldiers coming back from Afghanistan—men who were far angrier than the rotund and aged Qari Jamil. Food wasn't a right at that *madrassa,* but a reward. Students were kept chained to the walls all day long, shackled, beaten, and broken. Ittefaq had tried to escape repeatedly, only to be caught and jailed and punished, until one day he snuck into a truck and convinced the truck driver to take him back to the desert.

The existence of the demonic *madrassa* that was recruiting boys all over the country was big news for a little while. But after making a striking impression, it was just as quickly forgotten. No one in Sehra Kush could conceive of industrial *madrassa*s like that.

I couldn't forget about it, though. I stayed awake many nights wondering what I would have done had I ended up at a place like that. Would I have been able to run away? I knew the answer was no. I would have been too afraid to try to leave. I then imagined all the pain that Ittefaq had put up with while he was there, and it made me sad. I stared at the sky and wondered why Allah wasn't nice to some people. I wondered if perhaps it was the case that Allah singled out some people for happiness and some people for suffering.

At night on the rooftop of the house, I stared at the stars. They were little specks, scattered like gravel across the sky. Where there was a cluster of stars, I imagined that it was an angel, resting. Where there was a shooting star, I imagined that it was the angels firing at Iblis, trying to keep him from coming too close to heaven. I imagined the angels looking at me. Did they see me and think, "Look, there's a speck of dust?" What about Allah? Why couldn't I penetrate this blackness He kept between Him and me? What would He say when I asked Him why he was so willing to let people be beaten?

Eventually I turned over and went to sleep. Allah was Light. What did little specks of dust matter to Him?

The angels must have heard my doubts, because they soon paid me a visit.

# 17

When he was a child, the Holy Prophet once found himself alone with a number of angels. They took him out into the desert one night, cut open his chest, drew forth his heart, and then—with a bottle full of milk from Paradise—washed all the blackness from it, and that is why Muhammad was the most pious and honest human being ever.

I wasn't the Prophet, so my angels were punitive.

Some afternoons I used to sneak out to a house near the *madrassa* where some of the students and older kids from other neighborhoods went to hang out. The owners, whose son was a ringleader in the group, tended to go off and visit their neighbors, leaving the whole house to us. It felt like a sort of playground. We sailed paper boats into the *nali,* shot *buntaz* with precise finger strikes, played games of seven stones, and even sometimes went to the roof and flew kites.

One day I noticed that there was a room in the back of the house whose shutters were closed. It looked as if it was locked from the inside, but there was a strange glow coming from within that drew me to the room. I went over and started banging against the door.

"What do you want?" said a voice.

"Let me in."

"No!"

"Let me in or I'll get everyone else and we'll break down the door."

"Everyone can't play this game!"

"Then just let *me* in. I won't tell anyone about it."

The door opened and I passed through. Once inside, I locked the door. Except for a sliver of light that slipped through the top window, the room was dark. A copy of the Quran wrapped in pink cloth was sitting atop a dresser. There was a prayer rug, a corner of it rumpled as if someone had slipped on it. The room smelled musty, of feathers and wet dust.

As my eyes adjusted, I noticed an area of intense brightness in the center of the room. I rubbed my eyes with my palms and then blinked rapidly. Before me were two golden youth, luminescent and shiny, nearly translucent, with wings of light from whose tips milklike *nur* dripped to the floor. One of the youth was standing while the other was on his knees.

Squinting harder, I realized that I was seeing something I had never seen before: angels.

"Do it the right way, Mikail," said the youth who was standing, his enormous wings expanding and retracting.

"I'm doing it like you said, Jibrail."

"Do you know better, or me?"

"*You* do. Definitely you."

Mikail was kissing a curving feather on Jibrail's body. It was of a pale golden color and it looked like an unearthly writing utensil. It was long and smooth.

"You," Jibrail said, turning to me suddenly. "Come here and show us yours." His eyes were piercing and powerful. There was no mercy in his voice.

"We'll show you ours," said Mikail with a suggestive smile.

Unable to resist their authority, I went close to the angels. They separated from one another and enfolded me in their wings. I felt pressure on my shoulders as I was pushed down to the floor. Before long I had Jibrail's feather in my mouth. He gave officious instructions that echoed ponderously in my head.

After a little while, Mikail pulled me up and stood behind me. I could hear his breath full of conspiracies. As he spoke, his wings wrapped around me and got caught on my clothes, tugging at them. "I must dip my feather into you," he told me. I could neither agree nor disagree. It wasn't my place to talk. As Mikail slid the curved feather into my body, it caused me to wobble forward, which in turn made him take quick little steps and follow me around the room.

I felt neither pain nor fear. My eyes turned to the singular slant of light cutting a corner of the room, and I became lost in observing the little particles floating aimlessly. I could see each little atom, tumbling on its axis in the sunlight, doing headstands and cartwheels, dancing in place, tiny, so tiny—as if the motes weren't dust, but children of dust.

Jibrail, meanwhile, stood back and watched. He had his head tilted and bore a curious expression on his face. When he saw me looking at him, he began laughing—a laughter that increased in volume until it was booming and loud, transforming into banging on the door, urgent and insistent. Someone else wanted in. I moved away from the angels to open the door. As soon as I ripped through the door, the unearthly visitors shrieked and hissed and then disappeared.

When I went outside, all the boys wanted to know what was happening inside, but I told them there was nothing to see, nothing to do. I went for a long walk up the canal where the buffaloes grazed. I didn't know how to describe the feelings in my stomach. All I could come up with were analogies. I thought of the hollow feeling of forgetting my lessons and getting my hands beaten with a baton. I thought of the feeling of sickness that came with tripping and ending up with one foot in the cold *nali*. I thought of the feeling of feverish panic that had come over me when I had misplaced my new tennis ball and had searched for it haplessly for hours. That last memory came closest to my current mental state, so I went inside that memory to see if I could find a clue to what I should do now.

Ammi's face shone through the haze of memory. "When you lose something," she had said to me while I'd been looking for my lost ball, "recite, *Inna lillahi wa inna ilayhi rajioon.* "To God we belong and to Him we shall return."

Sitting up next to the canal, clutching my knees against my chest, rocking back and forth, I began reciting:

*Inna lillahi wa inna ilayhi rajioon*
*inna lillahi wa inna ilayhi rajioon*
*inna lillahi wa inna ilayhi rajioon*

That was also the prayer a Muslim made when someone died.

# 18

After my meeting with the angels, I wanted to escape. One hot day I resolved to run away.

The city was hardboiled; the streets were deserted; a camel driver rested in the shade. Our cooler, the poor man's air conditioner—a box-looking fan lined with roots and filled with water—rumbled loudly, producing a jet of damp air that felt like Paradise itself. On that terribly hot afternoon, I didn't want to give up the company of the cooler.

"I'm not going to the *madrassa* anymore," I informed the household in a loud voice.

Ammi and Pops reclined behind me on a *charpai,* nodding limply in the noontime lull. When I made my announcement they didn't say anything, and this raised my hopes. But then, just as I turned onto my side to stretch out and sleep, Pops got up, grabbed me by the arm to yank me to my feet, and pushed me out of the room. "You aren't welcome back until you've gone to the *madrassa,*" he said coldly.

I stood and stared at the closed door. Then, before the sun-heated floor could burn my feet, I located an old pair of *chappals* and went to the bathroom to wash up. Because we got our water from a tank located on the roof—which heated up during the daytime—the water was boiling hot. With the hot afternoon *loo* blowing in from the dunes, the water felt even worse. Gargling with it almost made me throw up.

As soon as I finished, I heard a trilling bicycle bell outside. Opening the door, I saw that it was Bilal, a young orderly whom Pops sometimes hired on the hottest days to give me a ride to the *madrassa*. Feeling resigned, I swung my leg over and positioned myself on the crossbar of his Sohrab bicycle. As he leaned forward and pushed off, I felt his chest against my back. He smelled of sweat, adolescent cologne, and talcum powder. I knew that last smell well: expert carrom board players reeked of it. I knew that Bilal spent most of the hot days, days like this one, in the back of his father's shop playing long games of carrom. He had invited me to play with him once, and I enjoyed using his donut-shaped striker to knock the little round disks into the four-holed game board. I knew that after he dropped me off he was going to go back and play—something I wanted to do as well—and the thought filled me with a mixture of hate and despair. Part of me wanted to cry and the other part wanted to hit him.

As we rode to the *madrassa,* Bilal saw something interesting and pulled up his bike at the curb.

"What's happening?" I asked.

"Take a look."

Coming up the street toward us was a bearded Gypsy in puffy clothes, with an assortment of red, blue, and green scarves wrapped around his body. He carried a stick upon which were bells, shakers, and drums. He held a chain in his other hand, and attached to it was a large black bear. The animal's skin and face were scarred, making it look ferocious. A withered brown dog walked behind the handler and his bear, aimlessly following scent trails. The odd trio walked past us into the dusty ground within the *gol daira*. There the bear sat down on its haunches underneath a tree, while the dog lapped at crusty mud, searching for water.

I couldn't get past the contrast between the two animals. The dog was small and meek; the bear was big and black.

"Why are they here?" I asked.

"There's going to be a fight," Bilal replied. "Bear versus dog."

"Isn't such a fight unfair?"

"You have to understand," Bilal said. "At one point the Gypsy prob-ably owned three dogs to fight the bear at once. But I imagine that in each fight the bear must have killed one dog, so now only this one is left. This one is probably going to get killed too. It's supply and demand, after all."

"I don't know," I said with a measure of hope. "This dog seems different."

Bilal laughed. "You just *think* it's different. Dogs lose; that's just the way it is. It's their *kismet* to be killed by the bear."

We had hoped to stick around for the fight, but then we learned that the Gypsy was putting it off till later in the evening, when it would be cooler and more people would be around to make donations. "We don't have time to wait," Bilal said. He picked up his bike and we hit the road to the *madrassa*.

As I thought about the dog, my earlier sense of rebelliousness came rushing back to me. If that poor little dog, all alone, could stand up to a monster like the black bear, then I could stand up against Qari Jamil.

By the time we reached the *madrassa,* I was so empowered that I could think of a million other things I'd rather be doing. I could sit in front of the cooler. I could go and swim with buffaloes, or watch Indian films, or drink glasses of sugarcane juice spiced with ginger and lemon, or get a case of mangoes and soften each mango until it became *popla* and I could suck the juice out of it.

What I *didn't* want to do was to recite the Quran in a room with no fans in the stale sleepiness of late afternoon. Nor did I want to be bent over in the rooster position and beaten. I missed the life I had before I was enrolled at the *madrassa.* The days of playing catch against my bedroom wall, dreaming of becoming an Iblis-fighting angel. The afternoons when I propped *charpai*s on their side and made a fort and called myself Saladin the Liberator, spilling oil onto the Crusaders' armies, withstanding a siege by Richard the Lionheart, and then doing diplomacy with him during which I met with his sister and impressed her with my warrior prowess by throwing her scarf high in the air and cutting it in two perfect halves with my scimitar. I wanted to live in my imagination—not as a spindly-legged spider in the Quranic cryptograms. I didn't want to be a droning echo, stuck chanting a book in a language I didn't understand. I liked the Quran at night, when Ammi told me stories from it—stories about the Prophets. I didn't like the Quran forced into my mouth on the authority of Qari Jamil's big brown stick—a Quran to be chewed and vomited.

"Hey, Bilal," I said suddenly. "Do you know what time the lorry to Peshawar passes by?"

"Before *maghrib* prayer," he said as the shadow of the minaret fell across his face. "Why, *babu*? Are you planning on taking a trip?"

"Yes, I am. A long one."

"Don't bother," he replied. "A lorry would never stop for a little one like you."

"Not even if I stood in front of it?"

"That sounds serious!" he said, referring to my resolve. "You trying to run away or something?"

"Yes, I am."

"Now?"

"No. Take me home first. I want to tell my parents why I'm leaving."

When I got home the electricity was gone, as was often the case at midday, and so the cooler was off and everyone was in a bad mood. Pops lay in bed while Ammi fanned him. They had just finished eating mangoes; a tray of emptied plates sat near them. Two steel glasses filled with *lassi,* a yogurt drink, sat tilted in a clump of sheets. The fact that they had eaten mangoes without me made me think they were decadent, and that upset me even more.

They looked up, surprised to see me at home when I should have been in school. "I'm not going to go to the *madrassa* anymore," I announced, trying to sound even more definitive this time. "If you make me go, I'll run away to Peshawar. I've learned where the lorry leaves." I sat down and began drinking the leftover *lassi.* Even though it was warm and salty, it felt good going down. I felt in charge.

When I'd finished and had burped loudly, a slap hit the back of my head and sent me hurtling toward the door.

"I told you," Pops said. "You cannot come home until you've been to the *madrassa.*" He wasn't messing around.

Normally I would have cried and made a scene and ended up in Ammi's arms, but this wasn't a time for empathy. I had to up the ante.

"Well, that seals the deal," I said, standing up. "I'm going to run away from home. I'm going to take the lorry that goes to Peshawar. Then I'm going to join the *mujahideen* and go into battle. That means you'll never see me again. This is what you reap for sending me to that *madrassa. Khuda hafiz,*" I added in farewell.

"Come on, Abir," Ammi said. "There's no reason to run away. Just be a good boy and go to the *madrassa.*"

"No deal."

Pops stayed quiet for a while. Then he spoke up rigidly: "All right. Run away, then. We won't stop you."

"You don't believe me, do you? All right. Forget running away. Instead of getting in the lorry, I'll just let it run me over. Do you still want me to go to the *madrassa*?"

"Yes," Pops said. "Do it."

"You don't care if I die?" I shouted. "Fine! I'll kill myself right here. In this house. So that my blood is on your hands. I'm going to suffocate myself in the bathroom."

I went to the bathroom and slammed the door, thinking that if the door stayed closed for some time I would run out of air. While inside I realized that the bathroom had a big window that was always open, so the chances of suffocation were zilch. I also realized that going back outside to retrieve a tool with which to kill myself would take the fire out of my revolt.

"This bathroom will be my grave!" I shouted in a last-ditch effort.

Much to my satisfaction, I heard Ammi right outside the door. "No, my son," she urged. "Don't say such things!"

"You know what? Why should I wait till I'm suffocated to die? I'll just drink this shampoo here and make it quick." Just to show that I was serious I spilled some of it underneath the door.

Now Ammi banged on the door loudly. "I know I'm a horrible mother, but even horrible mothers don't deserve to lose their children. Come out of there, my son!"

I was not hearing her. During the patriotic holidays, among the videos that Pakistani TV used to play to commemorate its military heroes was one about an Air Force pilot, Rashid Minhas, who flew his plane into the ground rather than let it be commandeered by an Indian. In the movie he recited the Throne Verse from the Quran before his crash. That scene was burned in my head. This, my last breath on this world, my rebellion against the institution of the *madrassa,* seemed like a dramatic moment just like that of Minhas's last breath, and I began reciting the Throne Verse loudly. It made for a good soundtrack to suicide.

"Allah," I sang, "there is no God but He. The living. The self-subsisting. The eternal. No slumber can seize him, nor sleep. His are all the things on heaven and on earth—"

Just as I reached the middle of the verse, Pops broke down the door and fell against me. After knocking the shampoo from my hand, he handed me off to Ammi, who wiped away my tears. Despite the rescue, Pops glared at me. "Something is wrong with him," Pops said. "Fix him up and personally take him to the *madrassa.* Let's get this matter resolved."

Ammi went to the closet and put on her *niqab.* Then she took me by the hand and led me downstairs. When she saw Bilal hanging around— he'd stayed to enjoy the showdown, I guess—she told him to ride ahead and tell the *qari* that she wanted to schedule an emergency meeting.

Walking in silence, with Ammi holding my hand firmly, we went to Qari Jamil's private quarters. As soon as we were admitted, Ammi began talking about my "depression" to Qari Jamil's wife, of all people, as she served us *iskanjwi* made from stale lemons. In the background his daughter, Sameena, snickered at descriptions of me crying, cursing, and threatening death. I was embarrassed.

When the *qari* finally joined us, Ammi pulled her *niqab* over her face and repeated the story about my depression. She wondered if there was something "the learned *qari*" could do to cure me. As she spoke, the *qari* first smirked and then laughed outright, though there was no humor in the bloodshot eyes that speared into me. The more serious Ammi made my tantrum seem, the more sardonic became his grin.

"I will be sure not to let him take his life," he assured Ammi. Then he draped an arm across my shoulders and took me for a walk around the grounds, massaging my neck with his thumb and forefinger. I turned to look at Ammi, but she had fluttered out of the house as soon as she was sure that I was in safe hands.

"So, you want to go off to Peshawar, eh?" Qari Jamil said. "You're going to get on the lorry and fight the Soviets? That is very brave of you. Are you going to feed them bottles of shampoo and kill all of them?"

His sarcasm made me angry. "Yes," I said, "but the ticket to Peshawar is eight rupees and I have only four. Why don't you lend me the rest?"

He pretended that he didn't hear my retort. "All so you don't have to come here? Seems like you don't like learning Allah's book, my young friend. That's not a very good Muslim, is it?" He stroked my head while his other hand snaked to his pocket. "Well, you know what? You don't have to read the Quran when you come here. How does that sound?"

"Sounds good to me!"

He produced a set of keys, sorting through until he found an appropriate one. Then he unlocked the padlock at the storage room with the bars on the windows and pushed me inside.

I was incarcerated.

H ours passed. By now the courtyard of the *madrassa* was empty. The dusty, hot *loo* blowing off the desert broke its head against the bars. At a distance I could hear the noise from the people witnessing the fight between the bear and the dog.

With each roar of the distant crowd, I grew more unsettled. I yanked ineffectually at the bars. I kicked the door. I used a little wooden stick from the rubbish in the corner to poke at the cracking cement wall. I sat back and imagined what it would be like if I could just manage to escape.

A satisfying scene formed in my mind.

Me outside. Everyone else still in class. A warm breeze. The jubilation of emancipation. The dusty scent of evening sand. The noise of rambunctious children. A hefty truck painted with murals rumbling past me on the highway. Me trotting like I was on an imaginary horse. The feeling that I could do anything. Me creeping to the edge of the *madrassa*. Me pulling down my *shalwar*. Me drawing out my member— with my right hand, of course. Me urinating upon the bricks. Me doing it standing up. Me peeing on the *madrassa*.

It was such a fluid and well-drawn image that it left me smiling. But then I realized that in order to fulfill my vision, I actually needed to escape from the room. So ensued another round of pushing and tugging on the bars. Another round of kicking the door and boring tiny holes in the wall. Another round of frenzy.

It was all for naught.

As I sat, alone and lonesome, the shadows elongated further. The walls screamed and leaned over me. Standing again, I clung to the bars, not daring to look behind, thinking that at any moment a hand made of smoke might grab me by the neck and pull me into Dozakh. I looked to see if there was a lightbulb inside the room, but there wasn't.

Soon I could see no light outside the room either. When the call for the evening prayer went up and night descended upon the desert, I was plunged into blackness. The rest of the town fell quiet. I felt as if I hadn't seen a human in ages. I remembered Anar Kali, a legendary courtesan who had been buried alive in a wall. I channeled the specter of her death, her futile and frivolous death, and it filled me with despair. She had been foolish for loving a prince, just as I had been foolish for rebelling against the *madrassa*.

I stood back against the wall and realized that since I couldn't hear the roaring crowd anymore, the dog must have been martyred.

I sat down in a squat and started crying. I put my face into one corner of the room where the walls met one another and smelled the cement. I licked the salty surface to distract myself. As I tasted the rough wall, I felt a desert centipede crawl across my mouth, over my lips and toward my neck. My insides turned to mush. I stood up and maniacally beat myself with my *topi,* but that only made the creature drop down into my shirt. I hopped around in a frenzy, hoping it would fall to the floor. In the dark it wasn't possible to tell whether the centipede had fallen out or not; perhaps it was just hanging on and waiting. I began to run in small circles in the room, shimmying as I ran in an effort to get away from the beast and pressing my belly button with one index finger in case the vile creature tried to enter my body. Out of fear of the centipede, I urinated a little bit in my clothes.

I felt disgusted with my own cowardice. That new emotion stopped me in my tracks, and I forgot all about the centipede.

As I thought about it, I felt as if I deserved to feel disgusting. By my refusal to uphold the norms of the *madrassa*—a place where the Book of God was taught—I had behaved like the most reprehensible of people. Spurning Qari Jamil as well as Ammi and Pops, I had violated the *hadith* that said teachers were just like parents. What I had done with my tantrum was nothing short of sin. I had engaged in *gunah*. It was like what I had done with Sina, but many times worse because I had known exactly what I was doing. I was a sinner. And what was the lot of the sinner except pain, cauldrons of pus, and torture?

Torture within the grave. Torture before Judgment Day. Torture on Judgment Day. Torture after Judgment Day. Torture for an eternity. Torture would start at the moment of death. I would be placed in my grave, and then two angels would come to ask me a series of questions about my faith and deeds. I would answer them to the best of my ability, but the entire interrogation would be rigged: Allah would have instructed my tongue to give testimony against me so that I wouldn't be able to lie to escape the impending torture. Once I unwittingly admitted all my errors—and there were many, as I was realizing—the pain would commence. My soul would be sucked into Israfil's trumpet in a most torturous way. Then maggots would consume my body from the left and worms would consume it from the right. All the pain of decomposition would be felt by my soul—in fact, the pain of being eaten, my flesh being consumed in the grave, would be felt all the way till the Day of Judgment. This was the recompense of sinners. This was the fate of those who declared rebellion against the things that exalted God.

Squatting down again, I rocked in the dark and told myself that I should have expected being entombed like this. Hadn't I read the story of the Prophet Yunus in *The Lives of the Prophets*? He had been a Prophet of God, but when he told the Almighty that he wasn't going to spread the Word anymore—that he was giving up, quitting, that he was "not going to do it anymore" just as *I* had said—God caused Yunus to be cast overboard during a storm. As further punishment, Yunus was then swallowed up by a whale, and he had to live in the belly of that beast in complete darkness, in utter and desolate darkness—a darkness that was probably considerably worse than the darkness of this room. If God could punish his chosen—a Prophet!—for his rebellion, why wouldn't he punish me? In fact, my punishment would have to be worse, as my sin had been.

I leaned back against the wall and sighed. Then I traced back through my thoughts to determine where my mischief had started. The answer was easy: it had all begun when I started getting beaten. That was when I had first strayed from the path of obedience. As I thought it over now, getting beaten seemed like such a silly thing to have risked Allah's displeasure over. Rooster, donkey, tied; stick, slap, kicks. I could take it in all the positions, in all the variations. Ultimately the body wasn't mine. *Main hoon Allah Mian ka.* I belonged to Allah.

How could I have been so foolish? I wasn't beaten because it was bad for me. I was beaten now because I was meant to serve Allah in a greater capacity later. That was the same reason that the angels Jibrail and Mikail had visited me. They had prepared me for the pain I would feel later in life. This was the same thing the *qari* was doing with his various punishments.

The fact that I was Abir ul Islam—chest rubbed upon the walls of the Ka'ba, promised to God before I was born, delivered to Muslims with the express purpose of serving Islam—only meant that God demanded more from me, just as he had from his Prophets. Every ordeal was a stepping stone in the service of Islam.

All these thoughts—my transition from terror to acceptance—had passed through my mind in mere seconds. As I stood up in the darkness, I heard footsteps. It was Qari Jamil, on his way to lead the congregation in prayer. Entering the room, he had me stick out my hands, and laced my palms with a few powerful shots. Lines of ice went to my shoulder. The base of my hands turned blue. I accepted the punishment without flinching. Then he let me go.

Once I was let out of jail I went and joined the prayer, thanking God for keeping me on the straight path, the *sirat ul mustaqim,* the way of obedience, the way of His servants.

# Book II

## The American—Amir

*In which the author leaves Pakistan and arrives in the United States, where, living in the Bible Belt, he attempts to navigate life in high school while dealing with his parents, who are conservative Muslims*

# I

By 1991, when I was ten years old, we left Sehra Kush and moved to an agrarian town in Eastern Punjab. It was a place where pushing heroin addicts off porches was considered a form of entertainment, and planting rice and raising cattle were the primary means of livelihood. Pops was able to establish a successful clinic there, and we were even able to purchase a car, one of the few in the area. One day my family received a letter that prompted much jubilation. It was from the U.S. consulate in Lahore. The immigration application that Ammi and Pops had filed for us many years earlier had finally come through. We could become legal residents of the United States. We immediately sold all of our possessions for cash and bought plane tickets that would take us to JFK International Airport. Pops, Ammi, Flim, and I arrived in the States with three thousand dollars; eight suitcases of clothes, dishes, and valuables; and a steel trunk full of brass Buddhas and Santas—which Pops planned to use to start an import-export business.

When we landed there was no one in the five boroughs that we could call. Joining the bustling throngs, we stepped out into the smoggy air of New York City, wondering what to do. Out of desperation Pops approached a small man that he correctly identified as Pakistani, who was standing beside a hotel shuttle curbside. The two men engaged in a game of "Where are you from and who do you know?" In a few minutes Pops had learned that an acquaintance of his from med school in the Dominican Republic was living in Brooklyn—and conveniently his wife was out of town, which meant that his apartment potentially had space to host guests. We gave the old friend a call—an hour-long process that involved finding U.S. coins and mastering a foreign pay phone—and were rewarded: he came to our hotel to pick us up in a blue Chevy, hosted us for a few days, and helped us find an apartment in an Orthodox Jewish neighborhood where bearded men in big black hats and women in long skirts stoically walked to the synagogue on Saturdays.

Flim and I attended public school. Before sending us off, Pops made it very clear that we could eat only *halal*, which meant no pork or meat of any kind that wasn't prepared in the Islamic way. In addition to many yarmulke-wearing Jewish children at school, there were thugged-out black kids wearing jeans backwards like Kris Kross, and fake-thug Italians with Vanilla Ice haircuts. The school also served numerous Chinese, Taiwanese, and Korean children, as well as Lithuanians, Russians, and Ukrainians. Finally, there was also a large contingent of Albanians, with whom I started hanging out because they were Muslim—but whom I abandoned after I learned that they ate pork, which was *haram*, forbidden.

It wasn't long before Ammi found a local Bangladeshi woman who held Islamic classes at her apartment every summer. Many other immigrant kids—Arabs, Indians, and Pakistanis—also attended. Girls in *hijab* and boys with baby beards trudged over to the building, jointly took an elevator to the apartment, jointly walked up the hallway, and then split up in two different rooms because Islam said it was immodest for boys and girls to do things jointly.

Prayers were conducted in the boiler room in the basement of our building, with quite a few other Muslim families in attendance. We even had an *imam*—an old man who lived down the hall from us and led prayers as if he were in the grandest of mosques. The paint in the basement was peeling, and on cold days the wind howled menacingly through cracked windows. On humid days the entire place smelled of feet. However, as much as I disliked our makeshift *masjid,* when I went down the elevator, my hands and feet dripping with water from the ablution, if old Jewish and Irish and Italian ladies sent derisive glances in my direction, I softened my face and appeared as serene as I could, pretending that I was on my way toward Paradise so that I could show the non-Muslims how lovely and empowered my religion made me feel. Such little lies were necessary to be a good Muslim in America, because here Islam was all about perception in the eyes of the non-Muslim majority (and that perception always had to be positive).

When Pops was unable to find a job and our funds ran down to a single subway token—this was several months into our stay—he took out some of the brass statues, polished them up, and went to Times Square, where he sold a few of so we could buy groceries.

It took a few years and many jobs before Pops gained admission to a medical residency in the United States. The journey took us to all four corners of America: Brooklyn to Nevada, back to Brooklyn, to Arizona, to Washington state, and eventually, by the time I was in high school, to Alabama. Whenever I left a city and complained about losing my friends, Ammi quoted the Quran and told me to "hold onto the rope of God."

She meant Islam.

2

By the time we settled in Alabama, in a town in the heart of the Bible Belt, Ammi considered herself a Salafi—an adherent of a conservative strain of Islam promoted by Arab missionaries situated at various mosques around the United States. In Salafi Islam believers had to emulate the Muslims of the seventh century as closely as possible. To learn more about Salafism, Ammi purchased volumes of *hadiths,* bought and devoured literature written by Abu Ameena Bilaal Phillips, and signed up for the magazine *al-Jumuah.*

Salafism also brought a revolution in her dress. When we had lived in Pakistan she had used to wear the *niqab*—not from choice, but necessity. When she first arrived in America and could actually choose what she wanted to wear she adopted Western dress and left her hair uncovered. However, after becoming a Salafi she began wearing the *hijab* and declared that "women who don't wear the scarf are not true Muslims."

Ammi also rejected the mysticism that Beyji had taught her. "All that Sufi stuff," she said, referring to spiritual exercises and the veneration for saints and holy people, "is an abomination and an innovation. Innovation leads to misguidance, and misguidance leads to the Fire."

Also, since Salafis believed that all graven images were a form of *shirk,* or disbelief, Ammi took down paintings from our walls and blackened the faces of the people appearing in calendars. Even our family portraits were done away with. "If you keep a picture of a person on your wall," she said, "on the Day of Judgment Allah will challenge you to bring it to life. When you aren't able to do it, He will throw you into hell." Just to be theologically safe, she extended the pictorial ban to all organic things—pictures of plants and fruits included. For some time she shut down the TV as well, since Allah could potentially ask her to animate the cartoons Flim and I loved to watch.

In the most dramatic affirmation of Salafism, which shunned song and dance as immoral, Ammi turned our garage shelves into a grave-yard of cassettes. She went into her drawers and boxes and spent hours finding her old Pakistani and Bollywood songs. All the artists that she loved to listen to—Muhammad Rafi, Lata, Abida Parveen, Iqbal Bano—were put in little shoeboxes and consigned to the darkest part of the house. The stereo was kept in use, but now the tapes were of religious sermons.

There were two people responsible for Ammi's Salafi turn.

Indirectly: Pops. Ammi saw him talking to the attractive young nurses at the hospital—he was a medical resident by this time—and tried to shame him for his flirtation by putting on the *hijab* and adopting the most blunt kind of religiosity she could find. Her Salafism was supposed to remind him that he was a Muslim upon whom extramarital relations were forbidden. It was also supposed to curb his spending, because Pops kept piling on credit card debt, leaving Ammi—who did the family's accounts—to deal with the outrageous interest rates, and she took full advantage of the gruesome imagery that Salafism used to frighten people away from usury.

Directly: it was Mrs. Rahman's doing, a woman Ammi became friends with during our stint in Washington state. Long before we knew her, Mrs. Rahman used to be very secular, but when her oldest daughter went and married a Hindu, Mrs. Rahman blamed her own lackluster secular values for her child's pluralist leanings. She turned to Salafism and started wearing the *abaya*—a long robe—as well as the *hijab*. She also made it her life's mission to warn other women with children that the best way to protect the integrity of the family was with Islam. She took Ammi and a few other younger mothers for regular "fitness walks" at the mall, during which the indoctrination took place. Within a few months of their acquaintance, Ammi had stopped wearing the tight leggings she wore to blend in when we first arrived in America and, like her mentor, adopted the *abaya* and the *hijab*. Mrs. Rahman, who also wanted to assure the marital integrity of all the attractive younger wives, encouraged them to cease wearing makeup or perfume, "because as long as the scent of a woman stays with a stranger, she is accumulating sin."

Ammi and Mrs. Rahman used to have two pet projects. One involved giving *hidaya,* or religious guidance, to an irreligious nouveau riche Punjabi couple with two young daughters. The co-conspirators set up barbecues and dinner parties involving the couple, hoping to turn them religious. When food didn't work, Mrs. Rahman took a more direct approach: she picked up one of the girls, smoothed her hair, pointed her toward her father, and reminded him that "on the Day of Judgment you will be held responsible for her honor." The family never did turn religious.

Their other project involved a pair of middle-aged hippies next door, American to the core, who had adopted two girls from Kashmir, ages three and five. Ammi and Mrs. Rahman had concluded that since Kashmir was a Muslim-majority area, the girls, had they not been adopted, would have grown up Muslim, and therefore it was their obligation, as pious Muslims in the West, to reintroduce the girls to their birth religion. Ammi offered to babysit the girls and tried to teach them how to put on the *hijab* and recite Islamic phrases. When our neighbors found out what was happening, they promptly moved away. Meanwhile, Ammi and Mrs. Rahman fumed and cursed the biological parents in Kashmir.

Ammi's belief that she knew what was best for other Muslims was shared by Pops. Most of *his* targets, however, were Arab Salafis at the mosque in Alabama.

One day Pops went to the mosque for one of their free dinners, taking Flim and me with him. It happened that a Salafi brother named Yusuf was giving a lecture about how lucky everyone was to be Muslim.

Before the meal, Yusuf asked Allah to bless the grocery store where the meat had been purchased. He then asked everyone to be certain to recite *bismillah* over their meat in order to render it *halal*. Pops immediately stood up to warn his fellow believers.

"My dear Muslims," he interrupted. "This man is misguiding you. Is he not aware that in Islam it is not enough simply to say the name of Allah over our meat? Rather, we have to say the name of Allah over our meat *in the act of cutting it,* which is something grocery meat doesn't offer. Also, grocery meat has not been cut in the Islamic way. They *shock* the animals to death here. Muslims have to *bleed* the animals to death. Cut the carotid artery and let all the blood drain out. I spit this meat. It is not *halal*."

Brother Yusuf, still holding the microphone, tried to defend himself, but his English began to fail him. "I am simply a-sharing what Allah—"

"You *lie* in the name of Allah!" Pops shouted.

"Please, doctor, enjoy your meal and we can discuss in the privates."

"I will not."

A wave of commentary ran through the mosque, part bewilderment and part anger. Yusuf looked for a way to check the consternation. His anxiety caused his accent to worsen. "Brothers! I have estudied zees issue very close. Why I mislead?"

"Will you stand in front of Allah on the Day of Judgment," Pops cross-examined, "and testify?"

"I—"

"You cannot!" Pops interrupted again. "You are a man and not a Prophet. You cannot do intercession. Not for me. Not for my children. Not for the rest of this congregation. You are a liar. O Muslims! This man is taking all of us to hell!"

With that he handed Flim and me our coats and told us we were going home.

That was the first of many heated encounters Pops would have with the Salafis. When the Arabs at the mosque insisted on following the Saudi calculation of the lunar calendar in order to celebrate Ramadan, Pops told them that he was "an American and not a Saudi" and intended to sight the moon with his own eyes. When mosque elections took place, which essentially involved one Salafi appointing another one to the presidency—Salafis considered voting un-Islamic—Pops went and made a big hoopla about democracy, transparency, and determining membership by establishing a dues-paying system, "which was how *true* Muslims were supposed to run an organization." Eventually, Pops defected from the mosque and joined the nascent Blackamerican mosque downtown. They were Salafis too, but because they were shunned by the Arabs that Pops disliked, he overlooked their theology.

Ultimately it became clear to Ammi and Pops that although their methods were a little different, they were both driven by a desire to help other Muslims gain Paradise, so they joined forces and created the QSC: Quran Study Circle.

The main purpose of the QSC was to get together local families that had children and read the Quran in English. Friday evening was chosen as the official night, which Flim and I objected to vehemently, because that was when the two-hour block of TGIF sitcoms—including our favorite show, *Boy Meets World*—came on ABC.

The introductory meeting was held in our living room. Ammi moved all the furniture out and spread white sheets topped with cushions around the periphery. In the middle there was a small tray of almonds and some cans of Sunkist orange soda. (Dark colas were disallowed, because one of the chemicals in them was not *halal*). Males and females, in a wide span of ages, sat on opposite sides from one another.

A problem presented itself as soon as the meeting began. "We have twenty people, but only eight copies of the Quran," Pops noted.

"Also," said Auntie Fiza, a doctor at the local hospital (and no relation) who had a number of sons my age, "all our translations are different."

This caused a small debate to break out, which was resolved when Ammi said that she would order a standardized translation the next morning and QSC would reconvene in two weeks.

Two weeks later twenty copies of the *Noble Quran* translation arrived from the Saudi Embassy, and the Quran Study Circle was recalled. Ammi and Pops were as excited as Flim and I were irritated.

As soon as the meeting began, however, the group's theological differences came out in the open.

"This Quran isn't right," Pops said, flipping through the Noble Quran translation.

"You can't say that about the Quran!" Auntie Fiza retorted.

Pops ignored her. "What are these brackets?" he demanded, pointing to the editorial comments inserted into the translation. "These brackets are *not* part of the Quran."

"Forget the brackets," Ammi said, pointing to the footnotes. "It's a good Quran. Look, there, at the bottom of the page! It even has *hadith*s to explain the verses!"

"I don't accept that either," Pops said. "*Hadith*s aren't for explaining the Quran."

"Then what are they for?" Auntie Fiza said.

"They're nice stories," Pops said. "Stories that we can use to guide our actions. But the Quran is above nice stories. It is the Word of God."

"I think that the Ahl-e-Hadith are right," Ammi said, referring to a denomination whose members considered *hadith*s to be equivalent to the Quran. "Using *hadith*s is fine. Even advisable."

"I won't accept this translation," Pops declared. "The best translation is the one by Abdullah Yusuf Ali—this one here that my son is using. Yusuf Ali was a scholar. More important, he followed a particular *madhab*," Pops said, referring to one of the four schools of Islamic law. "Being true to a *madhab* is the most important thing."

"But the Noble Quran is free!" Ammi said loudly. "Look, they even come in different colors. Red. Green. Blue. Gold."

"I will use Yusuf Ali," Pops said, his voice ringing with finality.

"If you use Yusuf Ali," Auntie Fiza said, "you'll always be on a different page than we are!"

"So be it. Better lost than Lost. May Allah guide the true Muslim."

Over the many months that the QSC lasted, Pops was never on the same page as the rest of us; he often peeked over my shoulder to see where we were. He did, however, manage to get revenge: there were many instances when the group reached a complex passage of the Quran and couldn't make sense of the *hadith*s cited in the Noble Quran's footnotes. At such a point Pops would stand up and say, "Now let me read to you what a great scholar of Islam, Abdullah Yusuf Ali, has to say on this topic." Then he would read the whole commentary, even if it was twenty pages long.

During the study circle I always kept quiet, except when it was my turn to read a few verses; I never asked questions or offered an opinion. I spent most of my time wishing I could go into the other room and turn on the TV to watch *Boy Meets World*'s Topanga—with her plump lips and thick hips. I desperately wanted to see her kiss somebody.

Flim shared my sentiment, though we generally kept quiet about it. On Friday nights, when the clock hit 8:00 p.m. he would poke me on the foot. "Right now *Boy Meets World* is on," he'd say resignedly.

"Be quiet," Pops would glare, squeezing his hand. "Don't you see that we're doing *Boy Meets Islam*?"


Through the QSC I became better acquainted with Saleem, the eldest son of a local family. He was my inverse, my antithesis, my doppelgänger. He had recently transferred to my high school but before that had spent ten years at a Catholic academy, an experience that had left him deeply scarred. "Ten years with the Nasara," he said, using the Quranic term for Christians. "I couldn't take it anymore. Couldn't take Mass. Couldn't take the nuns. Bunch of religious rednecks!"

Even though Saleem had gotten a 1560 out of 1600 on the SAT and a 35 out of 36 on the ACT, with a 4.0 GPA and guaranteed admission at Princeton—all honors that I didn't have—he said he wasn't cut out to study "all that secular garbage." He wanted to go to the Islamic University of Medina in Saudi Arabia, where he would study his hero, Ibn Taymiya, a thirteenth-century thinker prominent among Salafis; he wanted to learn Arabic and study the Saudi *hadith* specialist Shaykh al-Albani; he wanted to master Islamic economics like the California convert Jamal Zarabozo; he hoped one day to run a correspondence course about Islamic theology like the Jamaican convert Abu Ameenah Bilal Phillips; and he wanted to travel the world debating Christians and showing the doctrine of the trinity to be utter foolishness like the South African polemicist Ahmed Deedat. His willingness to give up Princeton for the sake of studying Islam made me wonder if my own desire to get into a top college—where I would study secular subjects— was unworthy and un-Islamic.

In fact, I was doubly antagonized by Saleem: first for his being better than me in secular things, and then for his rejection of them.

Whenever the QSC descended into discussion, Saleem participated eagerly, and he always brought the conversation back to Christianity. He'd learned a lot during his days with the nuns.

"Did you know," he offered one day, "that there were like three hundred different gospel versions set out on a table during the Council of Nicaea? Then everyone fell asleep, and when they woke up there were only four left. If *that* doesn't prove tampering with the Bible, I don't know what does. This is why mankind needed the Quran! Christianity needed a corrective: Islam!"

Pops appreciated Saleem's zealous participation and was irritated by my silence. He often glared at me while Saleem was engaged in his long diatribes. Initially Pops made subtle comments to me that were meant to encourage me to participate more actively in the group. When that failed, he told me that I needed to be "more confident and more vocal, like Saleem." I always wanted to explain to him—though I never did—that my reason for not participating had nothing to do with a lack of confidence; I simply didn't like it when people spoke for the sake of hearing their own voice, as I often thought Saleem did.

Then one day several men in the QSC encouraged Saleem to lead *isha,* the night prayer. It was a great honor when older men, those who were generally expected to lead the prayer themselves, deferred prayer leadership to a youth. This upset Pops very much. He was annoyed that it was in *our* house that Saleem was being appointed *imam.* "They should be picking *you,* because you're the eldest son in this house," he said. "But they don't, because you don't give them a reason to respect you." In other words, because Saleem was louder about Islam than I was, he was considered more of a man. Even by my own father.

* * *

As QSC grew in popularity, more people came, and when they did, they gave long introductory lectures about their Islamic worldview to prove that they too belonged.

One day Ammi announced that Brother Shuaib, who was a professor at the state university, would come for a session. This was considered a sign of the study circle's expanding influence, because the professor was a well-regarded member of the community.

When it was Brother Shuaib's turn to make an introductory spiel, he closed the Quran and set it on his knee. Then he launched into a diatribe against the fifth Caliph, Muawiya. After that he gave a tirade about Muawiya's son Yazid, who killed Hussain, the beloved grandson of the Prophet, on the plains of Kerbala. "Muawiya the usurper and despot and dynastic tyrant produced a truly vile child!" he concluded with a flourish.

At first no one said anything. Never before had there been such an impassioned introduction by a member. As people thought about his words, they realized that Brother Shuaib must be a Shia, a member of Islam's minority sect who, unlike the majority Sunnis, believed that leadership in Islam should have been based on biological connection to Muhammad. Shias considered Muawiya and Yazid particularly repellant for spilling the blood of the Prophet's direct descendants; Salafis, meanwhile, considered Shias to be heretics.

Suddenly Ammi raised her voice from the women's side. "This is not acceptable," she said firmly. "You cannot come in here and curse a Companion of the Prophet!"

A surprised look passed over the professor's face. He fidgeted a bit, wiggled his squarish toes in surprise, adjusted his legs, and then gulped at his hot *chai*. He had assumed that because the study circle occurred outside of the mosque—where the hard-line Salafis ruled—he would be free to proclaim his Shia opinions. Now, looking around at a room full of angry faces, he realized that he'd miscalculated, as these people were even more hardline. He quickly excused himself and hurried out the door.

As soon as the professor had left, everyone put aside their Qurans and began discussing the (il)legitimacy of the Shia position.

"A Shia isn't even a Muslim," one of the aunties thundered. "It's part of Islam to respect the Companions. Muhammad personally promised Paradise to ten of them. Therefore, we can't say anything bad about *any* of them!"

Numerous anti-Shia comments rang out. Prominent among these was the claim that a Jew had founded the Shia sect to divide Muslims. Someone else suggested that Hussain had brought the massacre at Kerbala upon himself because he should have known that fighting a tyrant was hopeless. The evils of colonialism were blamed upon the Shia as well: "Because of the Shia Safavids in Iran," began one of the younger uncles, who considered himself an expert in Islamic history, "the Sunni Ottomans in Turkey weren't able to unite with the Sunni Mughals dynasty in India, and this allowed the British to destroy Islam. Blame the Shia for the success of the British 'divide and conquer' strategy."

That night, as the study circle became chaotic and splintered, Flim and I were able to sneak downstairs to a broken but functional TV in the garage and catch our sitcoms.

"We should invite Shias more often," Flim noted.

# 3

One of the ways Ammi kept Flim and me in line was by threatening to send us back to Pakistan. If Flim watched too much TV or I failed to do my homework, Ammi sat us down while she made a fake international call to an obscure relative and loudly discussed what kind of child labor Flim would be best at, or how fat was the Punjabi girl with whom my marriage was being arranged.

Pops's preferred means of regulation was to keep me busy with the Tablighi Jamaat, the merry band of missionaries from Pakistan who sent sorties to the West to make certain that Muslims in America didn't give in to hedonism.

I disliked being sent to hang out with them, but I had no choice. What Pops said, I did.

My first American experience with the Jamaat was in the Pacific Northwest. A Tablighi delegation composed of bearded and turbaned Punjabi villagers, most of them middle-aged men who didn't speak any English, wearing rolled-up pants and Velcro-closed sneakers, came to visit our mosque. It was an ambulatory group: they had walked all the way from Kansas, seeing a considerable part of America along the way. They held the state of Washington in considerable esteem, because "we have heard there is a city here called Walla Walla"—which they thought stood for "*Wallah Wallah*."

They spent three nights and three long days at the local mosque. Over my staunch objections, Pops commanded me to keep them company. With a long face I showed up at the mosque the first day. The Tablighis were delighted to meet me.

"*Mashallah!* Our friend! Where are you from? Do you speak Punjabi? Tell us about America! Come, come. Sit here and talk to us!" Like a celebrity I was led through the mosque's basement, where they were sitting on their sleeping mats, flipping *tasbih* beads or reading from the Quran while the designated *chai* server for the night wandered through ladling a stiff brown brew into their Styrofoam cups. I was passed from youngest to oldest—a toothless elder who put his arm around me and gave me an hour-long presentation on the *bismillah* verse. My celebrity, it occurred to me after a while, was of criminality. In their eyes I was an immoral, westoxified, and fallen entity who required their spiritual ministration to "be better." They compared life in the West with an illness and made me feel diseased.

In the morning, after a breakfast of *paratha*s and fried eggs, I was plopped into a rental car with three of the Tablighis and a driver they had hired, and we headed out to make *gasht,* or mission, in the local community. Since they didn't know anything about local neighborhoods, nor did they know a single Muslim in the city, they asked me where they should begin their proselytizing.

We ended up at the house of a computer scientist named Dr. Hameed, who used to be a member of the Tablighi Jamaat. Because he observed strict *purdah,* the inside of his house was split in two—a men's and women's section—by a curtain. After we sat down, Dr. Hameed praised the elders of the Tablighi Jamaat for finding him a good wife who practiced Islam absolutely.

There was a feminine cough from other side of the curtain, followed by the slight clinking of a tea tray. Dr. Hameed stuck his head through the perforation, whispered to his wife, and then pulled out the tray. I tried to see the other side through the fluttering curtain, figuring that his wife must be very frightening or very beautiful to be so protected.

We ate biscuits and sipped tea companionably. The silence was broken only occasionally, when one of the delegates lobbed Dr. Hameed a softball question about how computers could be used in the service of Islam. The Tablighis wanted to get out of there; they had nothing to add to the Islam of a man who kept his wife behind a curtain: he was already perfect.

For our next stop I took the delegates to an apartment complex at the edge of the river. We punched our way through the security system's electronic address book in search of Muslim names. I knew that the complex was full of twenty-somethings from Muslim countries who lived together in large groups and didn't pay much attention to Islam. Prime hunting ground.

We would knock at an apartment door, catching the oblivious Muslim students off guard, and let ourselves in while invoking "Islamic hospitality." At one place, as we sat across from four students—all men—our appointed spokesman talked in broken English about the virtues of being humble, the necessity of following the example of the Prophet, the need for rejecting corruption, and the importance of turning away from the three Ws.

"Are you referring to the World Wide Web?" asked one of the students. "I assure you, we don't surf the Internet that much."

"What is this undernet that you are talking?" asked our confused spokesman.

"What are the three Ws that *you're* talking about?" countered the now-confused student.

"I'm talking about Women, West, and Wideos," replied the spokesman. "If you are doing any of these things . . ."

The four students, sitting compressed on a loveseat, with a huge stack of lusty Indian films behind them, looked to one another and then stood up to try to block the Tablighis' line of sight.

"No, no, no! We don't do any of those things! How can you even suggest that? You might as well accuse us of murder! We are modest Muslim men from Pakistan! We are just students. We are here to study."

The magnitude of the lie embarrassed the Tablighi brothers and they excused themselves. They felt as if they had failed in their mission. Calling it a day, they dropped me off at home. I was thankful for the party-loving college guys.

Once we moved to Alabama another Tablighi delegation came for a visit, and once again, despite my repeated objection, Pops dropped me off to spend time with them. I was to make myself useful the first day and then accompany them on their mission work, via their automobile, the next.

This group was led by a young South African brother named Adil, who spoke fluent English with an accent that I thought sounded sophisticated. He said he was very happy to be in the blessed state of "*Allah*bama" and his final destination was the holy city of "T-*allah*-assee."

I put my head in my hands at the prospect of the long drive, listening to Quranic recitation and discussing various passages from holy texts.

Adil had picked up a bunch of young Muslims—most of them my age—from around the country. I was shocked to find that, rather than being pressed into service by parents, as I had been, they'd actually volunteered to travel with him. They talked eagerly about the American version of the Tablighi convention, or *ijtema,* where they had purchased Medinan musk and well-crafted skullcaps, had collected tapes of Quranic exegesis produced by the wizened Israr Ahmed and his Tanzeem group, and had consulted with the elders about what qualities they should look for in future spouses. I didn't feel a part of the group and wanted to get out.

My dissatisfaction increased when I learned that one of the teenagers was the son of a doctor we knew in the Northwest. I recalled that Ammi had been keeping an eye on his sister as a potential wife for me and wondered whether he knew about it. I considered arranged marriages an embarrassing and backward practice and stayed far away from him, just in case he was conspiring with my parents.

That evening, as the missionaries played ping-pong, drank big pots of *chai,* ordered and devoured a pizza, and then listened to Adil give a sermon from his sleeping mat, I stayed in the mosque library, biding my time, praying for a miracle that would get me out. Nothing.

In the morning, as the group planned their missionary activity, Adil decided that he wanted to visit the Blackamerican mosque that Pops frequented.

The mosque was a small, newly constructed house on stilts across from a cemetery in a blighted neighborhood near the football stadium. Most houses in that neighborhood had been reconstructed by the Muslims who bought them, after pushing out the squatters and the crack dealers. The entire length of the journey there Adil and his cohorts talked about how wondrous were these Muslims for improving their surroundings and their society like this. I wanted to ask why, if the Blackamericans were so wonderful, the Tablighi Jamaat—an organization aimed at castigating inadequate Muslims—needed to pay them a visit.

The mosque smelled of clean sawdust. We prayed in the main room and then joined a class in one of the adjoining rooms. With the students, we took turns copying the Quranic verses that were written in calligraphic style on the board; then we listened to the instructor teach the four young students about the principle of *tawhid,* or the Oneness of God.

Then, suddenly, various members from the Jamaat took the kids aside, individually or in pairs, and began lecturing them about how to wash up in the bathroom and how to wash their feet during *wazu.* These were basic, elementary things that all Muslim children of school age knew. And the instruction was conducted, not in a subtle and conversational manner, but blatantly, with an air of supercilious authority, the targets held in place with a firm grip on their shoulders. The Tablighis I'd encountered had always treated me the same way. Now, though—when I could observe them from a third-person perspective—I realized how shameless was their coercion.

Even aside from the physical restraint, the lecturing upset me. I considered it a mark of arrogance to walk up to another Muslim, one whom you didn't know and whose circumstances you weren't familiar with, and sermonize to him. It seemed like an assertion of supremacy, a usurpation of the individual's autonomy. It was rude and mannerless.

I didn't want to make a scene in the classroom so I dashed out of the mosque to take a walk around the neighborhood and blow off my anger.

Crossing a few streets, I entered an adjoining neighborhood. It was one of those surreal places forgotten since the Civil War, where bleak houses rested ponderously on crumbling stilts, where aged men with shiny eyes and grizzled faces leaned against handrails, where spilled sewage and trash were ubiquitous—a place acknowledged by the government only when a highway bridge needed to be noosed around it. Walking around on that hot afternoon, I imagined the place a hundred years earlier. What would have been different then? Nighttime light would have come from cracked stars instead of fizzled-out halogen bulbs. That was about all. The rest was the same: dogs voiding bladders, men who were lonely, and the glare of a despotic sheriff.

The scene made me wonder if some people were simply destined to be servile. I asked myself if I was one of them.

# 4

Ammi cultivated a small following of troubled women for whom she served as therapist. When Pops was at work, the ladies came to our house for long conversations over *chai* and cookies.

One of the women who came was a middle-aged *hijabi* named Janice. She had an unusual problem.

A long time ago she had entered into a financial arrangement with an Egyptian man: he agreed to pay her a monthly sum, and she agreed to be his wife on paper so that he could get a coveted green card. Along the way she ended up converting to Islam, and they took their marriage seriously. Three children later, their marriage ran into trouble when husband and wife went in different theological directions—Janice became a fundamentalist and her husband stopped practicing. Now she wanted a divorce so that she could marry someone who wouldn't reduce her chances to get to Paradise. However, the way her husband had been raised in an Egyptian village, *women* didn't give divorces, men did—and no matter how much she agitated for divorce, he wasn't going to give it to her. His refusal wouldn't have been an issue if she could have gone to family court and filed a paper at her own initiative. Problem was, according to the scholars she followed in all other areas of life, a Muslim woman couldn't initiate a divorce, only a man could. Since her husband was unwilling, she was out of options.

"What should I do?" she asked Ammi. "I don't want to fall for a pious man and be tempted when I'm still married. That would be *zina*."

*Zina* was a multipurpose Arabic term from the Quran that had no equivalent in English. It was a powerful word. Within it the sinful act and the associated punishment were conjoined. Depending on the situation it could refer to two separate things: premarital fornication punished by flogging, and extramarital adultery punished by stoning.

Ammi told the troubled wife that it would be all right for her to go to court and initiate a divorce. Janice, however, was wary of switching her understanding of Islam "just because it is now convenient."

"Maybe the strength of your faith is a sign by Allah that you should remain in the marriage and work on your husband's faith," Ammi suggested one day.

"Yes," Janice said. "Maybe I'll be able to bring him back toward the righteous path."

Still undecided, Janice came to see Ammi every few days, hoping to find a viable Islamic reason to get a divorce, and each time she left thinking that she should stay in the marriage. It went on like this for weeks and ultimately Janice stayed married.

I followed the Janice matter closely until something far more interesting presented itself. Her name was Amina Alam. She was a demure Pakistani immigrant from one of the nearby communities. In her late thirties, she was married and had two children who had been sent off to college. She wore long flowing *abaya*s in dark colors and mismatching *hijab*s. Amina Alam was an adulteress—or so she thought.

"As you know, sister," she said, sitting on the floor and rocking back and forth in front of Ammi. "It is a sin punishable by stoning for a married woman to sleep with a man who is not her husband."

"I know," Ammi said. "*Zina*."

"I believe that I've been committing adultery for the last sixteen years. What's going to happen to me?"

"You should seek forgiveness," Ammi said. "You should go to your husband and confess, and ask for his forgiveness too."

"That's the problem!" Amina said in frustration. "My husband is the one I've been adulterous with."

"This is confusing," Ammi said. "Are you playing a joke on me? One shouldn't joke about such things."

"No, I swear," she said. "You see, I've been married for twenty years. Four years into my marriage my husband and I had a fight. *Many* fights, actually. In each fight he grabbed me by the arm and said to me, 'I divorce you!' He said those very words—'I divorce you!'—three times. When I was growing up I learned that in Islam a man has only to say, 'I divorce you!' three times, and in the eyes of Allah the woman *is* divorced. This means I was divorced sixteen years ago."

"You're just remembering all this now?" Ammi asked.

"Yes," Amina said, hanging her head. "Sixteen years I've been married to a man who is not my husband. What should I do?"

"Just remarry him," Ammi suggested.

"That won't solve it," Amina said. "He's still the man with whom I committed *zina*. I can't face him. I shouldn't even be in that house with him. Islam says that we shouldn't be alone in the same space as men we're not married to. What am I doing? If we lived in an Islamic state, I would have been stoned by now."

That thought stopped the discussion for several minutes. Finally, Amina said, "Do you think I should move to an Islamic state so that I can be stoned as I deserve to be?"

"Don't be stupid," Ammi rebuked. "You're an *American* now. There's no stoning here. Here we believe in stoning only in theory. I think we need to ask one of the local scholars," she concluded.

"No!" Amina replied decisively. "I can't face their judgment. Besides, I don't want word to get out."

Ammi sighed. Then she got up and rummaged in her files. "Listen to me very carefully," she said. "I have a solution. My children use this new Internet, and I'm learning all about it. On it there are scholars you can ask questions of by way of a letter. We can ask them without using your name. They're far, far away—in South Africa or India; I can't remember. They'll tell us what to do."

Amina, who was now crying, pulled herself together and agreed. I was summoned and instructed to find an online *fatwa* service from which we could solicit an Islamic opinion. We then composed an e-mail to a group of scholars in South Africa.

It took the online scholars only three days to reply. Their verdict: Amina had been divorced sixteen years ago, and if she didn't want to continue living like an adulteress, she needed to leave her husband immediately. They also implied that she was hell-bound, but there was a chance that with just enough penance Allah might show mercy. They didn't say anything about stoning.

Amina wasn't with us when I read the verdict to Ammi.

"That Amina isn't as stupid as she pretends," Ammi said.

"What do you mean?"

"I think that for twenty years she wanted to get out of the marriage but didn't have the courage to leave. Now, with this story about getting divorced sixteen years ago, she's got influential Islamic scholars telling her that she needs to leave; otherwise, she's an adulteress. Now no one can stop her."

Ammi was right. When Amina found out about the *fatwa,* she was visibly elated. She left her husband within a week and moved to another state, where she got a job in human resources.

Of all the people I came across in adolescence, I identified with Amina Alam the most. She just wanted to be free.

# 5

I was prohibited everything related to the opposite sex.

Ammi had a pair of mantras that impressed on me the immorality of interacting with females. The first was based on a *hadith*. "When a woman and a man are alone," she said often, "the devil is the third." It meant that every single moment spent in the company of a girl was tantamount to Satanism.

Her other refrain, "A man is like butter and a woman is like a hot stove, and fire always melts the butter," had uncertain origins and equally uncertain meaning. However, it evoked in my head images of the various tortures in hell—which had been clearly described by the *imam* at the mosque and involved getting broiled in a cauldron full of pus—and was therefore effective despite its apparent absurdity.

Every time I felt an iota of arousal I was struck by fear. Then, trying to preempt the punishment that Allah and the angels were undoubtedly preparing for me in the afterlife, I tried to figure out a way to make myself suffer in this life. My behavior made Islamic sense: an *imam* back in Pakistan had once said that the reason Islamic authorities punished so harshly in this life was so that we wouldn't have to be punished for the same sin in the afterlife. I figured that since I lived in America now, and there were no Islamic authorities to give me penance through flogging, I might as well do their work for them.

Thus, when I went to a sleepover and ended up getting turned on while watching a soft-porn film called *Threesome,* I went back home and prayed for Allah to give me AIDS, the disease by which I believed Allah killed all orgiastic people. (Later, however, I prayed to Allah to veto my earlier request of death-by-AIDS, because I was concerned that if people learned I had the virus they would think I was gay, which all Muslims considered reprehensible.)

My general reaction to developing feelings toward girls at school was denial and avoidance. When a pretty, usually shy girl named Becky wrote me a love letter during film-hour in science class—it was stamped with a big, glossy kiss that smelled of bubble gum—I told myself that she was only joking; then, making certain that she could see what I was doing, I threw it in the trash can. Another time, when I developed a proper crush on a girl named Rachelle—a crush that I couldn't shake no matter how hard I tried—I convinced a friend of mine to ask her out and made a long list of all the other guys that I could potentially set her up with. It was easier to run away from girls I liked if they happened to be attractive: I simply told myself that I was too ugly for them. I used non-religious justifications for avoiding girls when I had to explain my-self, because I was too embarrassed to admit to non-Muslims that it was Islam—archaic, anachronistic, exotic Islam—that controlled me. Ad-mitting *that* would lead me to be viewed as an outsider—and I wanted nothing more than to be American.

There was one place where I pushed back against the restrictions: TV and film. I wanted to see every attractive onscreen girl I could. I wanted to see every instance of lascivious behavior. I wanted to see every inch of naked flesh. My reasoning was simple: since I'd consented to abiding by the rules imposed on my body, I should at least be able to *see* the things I was missing.

Unfortunately, Ammi and Pops had imposed a strict regime of media censorship almost as soon as we moved to America, which, like all such regulations, was only applied selectively, leading to resentment on my part. Two weeks after we landed at JFK, Pops had introduced all of us to the New York Public Library system, and we went regularly to the Park Slope branch as a family. It was there I discovered that you could get a copy of any film you wanted. On an early visit I picked out a film called

*My Beautiful Laundrette,* based on a screenplay by British-Pakistani author Hanif Kureishi. It was about Omar, an idealistic young man of Pakistani origin, who was trying to get ahead in life by taking owner-ship of a laundrette in a working-class neighborhood in South London. As Ammi and I watched, there came a scene involving Tania, played by the vivacious Rita Wolf, in which she lifted up her sweater and flashed Omar and his uncles in the company of her oblivious father.

"What a *wahiyat* film!" Ammi said, condemning the nudity as she shut it off. "This isn't us!"

As the screen went dark, I didn't move. Tania's dark areolas were burned in my head. To see a Muslim girl—like that!—set every fiber of my burgeoning youth on fire. I wanted Tania. I couldn't stop thinking about her. Day after day I passed by the film sitting on the VCR and wished I could just pop it in and look at those tits. But the strength of Ammi's reaction had evoked enough deference that I abstained. The night before the film was to be returned, however, the desire to see Tania was too strong: while everyone else was sleeping I turned on the TV, muted it, and popped in the video. I expected the film to resume at the part with the breasts; I told myself that I'd watch just those few sec-onds and then go back to my room. But when the screen came in focus, the final credits were rolling. At first I thought that perhaps the tape had malfunctioned, but then I realized that Ammi must have watched the film when Flim and I were at school.

Her hypocrisy angered me. If the film was *wahiyat,* she shouldn't have watched it either. Now I resolved to watch too, not just the part with Tania's breasts, but every other scene involving intimacy. In fact, when I got to the part with Tania's breasts, I rewound the scene many times over.

Over the years numerous TV shows were banned at home— somehow each containing an actress that I liked. The reason given was always Islamic: "Watching kissing on TV creates a desire to kiss in real life, which creates a desire to date, which leads to fornication, which is *zina,* which the Prophet would have punished by flogging or stoning and which is going to lead you to hell."

It was a stifling syllogism and my imagination became my escape.

I had always been a writer, weaving stories about heroic ants and edible *jinn*s. By the time I was in high school I set my craft in the service of sex and began writing erotica.

One of my recurring characters was Nadia Sumienyova, a gymnast, astronaut, and nymphomaniac. Her entire existence was sensual. One time she found herself on a mystical spaceship populated by a race of men who had one collective phallus—it was six feet tall and looked like the primordial me—that she promised to lick one hour per day in exchange for gaining the power of immortality.

One day I let myself engage in a bit of auto-writing. When I went back to read what I'd written, I saw that I'd retold (and revised) the story of Yajuj and Majuj—the tribes that the Quran said were trapped behind King Zulqurnain's wall and spent an eternity trying to lick their way out, and whose emergence would signal the arrival of the Islamic apocalypse. In *my* story, however, I had reimagined Yajuj and Majuj as a tribe of beautiful, naked women. The wall, hardened steel, was a huge penis: *my* penis, of course. It was licked by the women until ejaculation and then fell away flaccid. Then Yajuj and Majuj, so aroused by licking my wondrous penis, sprang out upon the world in search of sex. They jumped on the men of the world and killed them all through incredible blow jobs. Then they made out with all the remaining women until the Day of Judgment.

This sexual apocalypse ameliorated my desire to talk about sex, but only briefly.

Thankfully, I found an ally in an unusual place: Saleem.

Saleem and I talked about girls in all sorts of raunchy ways. We usually had these talks at a basketball court near his house, away from anyone's earshot. The only problem with him was that he tended to Islamize every discussion, which meant that the focus was on getting married first and *then* having sex. Still, we did get to sex eventually, and that was good enough for me.

"I can't wait anymore," he said dribbling the ball. "I'm sixteen and a virgin! How is this possible? I hit puberty at eight. I need to fuck."

"Me too," I agreed, both disturbed and excited by his word choice.

"There's this kid in Birmingham. I met him at the Muslim Sports Day. He got married as soon as he got out of high school."

"Is his wife hot?" I asked, hoping he would describe her.

"Dude. He's getting it on three times a day!" he said, ignoring my request for a description.

"Lucky bastard."

"So who do *you* want to marry?" he asked. We were both aware that asking who you wanted to marry was code for asking who you wanted to bend over and nail.

"How about that Egyptian chick, Amal?" I said, remembering a young *hijabi* that Saleem had pointed out to me at a Starbucks once.

"Yum," Saleem said approvingly. "She's got thick thighs. The thickest thighs in the Islamic *ummah*. But you need to tap that fast."

"Why?"

"She's Egyptian, man. Egyptian girls get fat quick. You need to ask for her hand in marriage soon. I bet you her parents would hand her over to you."

"I can wait a little," I said, not entirely sold on the idea of getting married during high school.

"Yeah, I guess you *can* wait. After all, *all* our women get fat," Saleem concluded with all the authority of a sixteen-year-old virgin. "That's why we're allowed to get another couple of wives when we're older."

I looked at him and smiled. Talking about polygamy was code for discussing threesomes.

"I'm going to get a Brazilian and an Indian in addition to my Egyptian," I said greedily. "Cover three continents that way."

"I'm going to get a Bosnian and a Colombian," he replied.

I imagined the scene and smiled again.

"Do you know why it's really important to reestablish the Islamic caliphate?" he asked.

I shook my head.

"So I can be appointed governor of South America. Then I can have my pick of Latinas for wives."

"I guess I'll take Los Angeles," I said. "Good diversity there."

"What would be your title? The Sultan of California?"

"Doesn't matter. I'd be too busy getting ass," I replied, trying out the new vernacular.

As Saleem went on speculating about how my caliphate in California—or *khalifornia,* as guys he read about on the Internet called it—could be actualized, I imagined my ideal woman: a virgin, stripper, actress, homemaker with a PhD.

"Where can I find such a girl?" I inquired.

"Have you tried AOL?" Saleem replied. "You can find everything on the Web. That's where I read about Ibn Taymiya."

A t first it was difficult to convince my parents that they should let me move the computer to my room, but they relented when I told them that, like Saleem, I intended to go online to learn about Islam. Flim wasn't happy about their decision, but I assured him that he could use the computer in my room whenever he needed it.

Going on AOL for the first time without any supervision was incredibly exciting. When the digitized voice greeted me with "Hello! You've Got Mail!" I felt tingles.

The quintessential component of socializing on AOL was the personal profile, because that was how a person determined if you were worthy of having a conversation with. Because I was desperate for attention, I crammed every characteristic I could think of into my profile, in the hope of attracting the widest possible range of girls. And I changed the description as ideas occurred to me. There was no accountability involved in editing myself endlessly. I could transform myself at a moment's notice—add to myself the things I lacked; subtract my liabilities.

AOL was perfect. It offered a means of communicating with the opposite sex that was severed from physical reality. Flirtation and arousal didn't go past the textual level. Chatting with women was nothing more than a thought-crime—and sexuality at that level couldn't be *zina.*

It all started innocently enough. There was Jess, a sixteen-year-old from Pennsylvania. We talked about our favorite tennis players, but soon she was telling me what kind of guys she was into and how many bases she had covered. Then there was Annie from Colorado, who said she was the heiress of a mob fortune but couldn't stand the sexual restrictions of Sicilian Catholicism; she wanted a boyfriend who would run away and travel the world with her. And there was Claire from Baton Rouge, who was an aspiring erotic novelist. She was bisexual, she said, and liked describing the difference between boys and girls to me. "Boys taste like stale 7-Up and corn; girls taste like strawberries warmed up in a towel left in the sun."

The easiest time to go online was in the evenings, but the best time to talk to Jess and Annie and Claire was at night, because that's when the chat rooms heated up. However, going online late at night was all but impossible for me, because if Ammi or Pops heard the modem screeching they came in and pulled the phone line.

I had to devise a way to cover my tracks. Islam came in handy.

I took a pair of prayer rugs and wrapped them all around the PC. Then I took my fattest books—the Quran and a couple of Ammi's big volumes of *hadith*s—and stacked them behind the tower to muffle the screeching. For background noise I put on a loud recording of Quranic recitation by Ajmi. Then I clicked "Sign on Now" and went to the living room to mislead my parents about my plans for the nights. "I'm about to prayer the *isha* prayer," I would say. "Then before sleeping I'll read some Quran."

During this time, when the modem would be reaching its highest pitch, I went to the bathroom and started making *wazu,* turning up the faucets in order to block any noise seeping from my room into the hallway. Just to give AOL enough time to sign on, I did a *wazu* that was five minutes long.

Once I was assured that the modem had gotten quiet, I went out into the living room and prayed. After asking Allah to make me a good Muslim, I went and talked to girls in Teen Chat 123.

This scheme took place every few nights. Those fifteen minutes of stress as I set the stage with my parents were followed by nights full of cybersex.

The Quranic recitation had to stay on, of course, so that no one became suspicious.

* * *

AOL sex lost its shine within a few weeks. Why bother to speak with someone a million miles away, where arousal was contingent on the integrity of a phone line, when at any time the Internet could, and often did, crash? If fantasies were to be imagined and nothing more, then why include others of lesser creative acumen—especially when my daydreams were far more detailed? Why engage in conversations where you could just as easily have been any of the other millions of screen names out there? AOL dropped out of the picture for good when I realized that when it came to the opposite sex, I didn't want carnality; I wanted intimacy. That required having physical access to women. It required *real* women.

The girls at school weren't an option, unfortunately. Shortly after I started at my high school in Alabama, a girl named Mary had gotten my home number and called up to talk, only to have Ammi tell her, "It's against my son's religion to talk to you." Word of her comment had gotten around so most of the girls at school had ceased considering me in a romantic manner. In order to elicit any interest from members of the opposite sex, I would have to publicly negate my devotion to Islam—a step I couldn't take.

I thought back to Amal. *She* was someone I could pursue. First because she didn't go to my school, and second because she was Muslim, meaning that the burden of my sin wouldn't be borne by me alone. We'd *both* end up in hell, whereas with a non-Muslim girl I'd be the only one to burn.

I went to Saleem to ask his advice about how to meet her. "Suppose I want to get to know Amal?" I asked.

"Ask for her hand in marriage," he replied. "Then you can start fucking her."

I wasn't quite ready for that. "How about I just send her flowers?"

"Why would you do that?" he replied. "Save the flower money to get some handcuffs or something."

I dropped the subject because I didn't want to tell Saleem that I needed to have my emotions involved. Something like that would make him think that I was gay. Instead, I got myself hired part-time at the

Starbucks where I'd first seen her, hoping to run into her again. On the way home every day I drove past her school and her neighborhood. I never saw her, though. Not once.

Eventually I realized that if I planned it right I'd be able to see her during Sunday school at the mosque. There was a moment before the noontime prayer when the girls came out of their classroom into the parking lot to get some fresh air.

The next Sunday, just before prayer, I broke away from the brothers and slithered around the edge of the mosque into the shadows. After a few minutes the girls emerged. They streamed out in their blue and salmon and pink *hijab*s, dillydallying before ducking through a side door. I saw all of them—girls, real girls, the flesh and the fashion of the faith—and I smiled broadly. Their soft clothes rippled on their bodies. The frilly bottom of their white petticoats stuck out beyond the hem of their long skirts. They lifted their *hijab*s and held an edge in their mouth while pinning back their crescent bangs. I gazed at the curvature of their waists and breasts and hips. They were beautiful, unbesmirched by the world around them. Sinless in a world of sluts. Virgins waiting to be wived.

Then I saw Amal, one of the last to emerge and thus at the edge of the group.

She was taller than I remembered, and thinner. She was in a long brown robe that hid her figure and wore a matching tan *hijab*. I was glad to see that she wasn't wearing gloves, because I'd heard of an old wives' trick which said that you could tell the shape of a woman's body by looking at the shape of her middle finger—though not at this distance. I squinted, then tried to catch the sunlight in such a way as to be able to perceive a silhouette through her clothes. As I approached, I tested the air with my nostrils to see if I could pick up her perfume. Nothing but the smell of the nearby paper mills. I looked down to see if her second toe was bigger than the big toe, because that was said to indicate whether she was domineering or submissive. What I saw so surprised me that I forgot to compare toe lengths: she was wearing nail polish. The fact that a seemingly pious girl would do something that was forbidden by the Salafis gave me a slight hope that she might be willing to engage in some subterfuge with me. Then I remembered that the prohibition regarding nail polish didn't apply when a girl was in her periods.

Suddenly the girls noticed me and the whole flock sidled away.

Thwarted, I grew angry. The nearness of these girls that couldn't be touched, even approached, even *befriended,* upset me. Why did I spend my life in conformity with Islam? Wasn't it supposed to be so that I'd have more in common with other Muslims? Have a community? If so, why did my fidelity to this faith, to the edicts of Islam, my perpetual presence at every Friday sermon and Eid prayer and observance of Ramadan, not grant me nearness to the female members of the faith? Why, in a case of egregious torture, were the Muslims I was most curious about the ones that were kept furthest away? Allah: I didn't want to violate them—I simply wanted to eliminate the chasm of anonymity that existed between us. I wanted to know them. To greet them. To get a name and to give my name. Wasn't the need for names divinely encoded? Wasn't it the case in the Quran that the first thing Allah taught Adam was the "names of things." Yet among Muslims of mixed gender this need wasn't just unfulfilled; it was considered the handiwork of Iblis, the devil.

In that moment it became apparent to me that if I was going to be able to live life how I wanted, I had to get the hell out of Allahbama.

To do that I had to become someone else.

# 6

I jumped out of my beat-up Ford Ranger with its sawed-off muffler and faded Confederate flag stickers, entered our cottage-style house perched on one of Alabama's many creeks, and prepared myself for my revolt. For many months I had been going by another name outside of the house, and now I was going to tell my parents that I planned to make the change formal in the legal system. It was my way of becoming who I was.

Everyone was home. Ammi had just returned from her classes at the university, where she had recently enrolled to study psychology, and was unfastening the safety pin on her pink *hijab*. Pops was in his green scrubs, getting ready for the night shift at the hospital. Flim was in the corner of the living room playing "Age of Empires" over the Internet (the computer having long since been returned to the living room). In the backyard, our new golden retriever, Rocky ul Islam Balboa, was barking at the neighbor kids bouncing on their trampoline on the other side of our brown picket fence.

"Why would you ever want to change your name?" Ammi said after I made my announcement.

"It's a horrible name."

"Abir ul Islam is a horrible name?" she asked, incredulous.

"Yes. A *beer* ul Islam is! Seven years in America people have been making fun of it."

"Like how?"

"Bud. Budweiser. Bud Light. Coors. Coors Light. Zima. Corona. Michelob. Rolling Rock. I've been called every major alcoholic beverage there is. Even fictional ones. Did you know people call me Duff Beer, like from *The Simpsons*? I know the names of as many beers as there are names of Allah!"

Ammi slapped me on the shoulder. *"Astaghfirullah!* Don't you compare God to alcohol! Can't you just tell people that your name is Abir ul Islam, emphasis on *Islam,* and that in your religion alcohol is forbidden?"

"Yes, I'll do just that," I said snidely. "Then the rednecks at school will want to have interfaith dialogue when they call me names!"

"Don't call them rednecks," Pops chided. "This state is our home now; we're rednecks too. Although our necks are more brownish-red."

"Fine. Freaks. Happy?"

"Don't say freaks either," Ammi interjected. "It's a bad word."

"Jesus Christ, you people!" I said, exasperated.

"Don't say Jesus Christ!" Ammi and Pops exclaimed in alarmed unison. "We don't believe that Jesus is God."

"Can we get back to the subject, please?" I said, having had enough of this religious turn.

"Yes, we can. Look," Pops said, taking on his most reasonable tone, "isn't this the Bible Belt? People take religion seriously here. If you just explain it to them—"

"I shouldn't *have* to explain my name," I said. "Just forget it. You people are too set in your ways."

"I can't believe you don't want to represent Islam," Ammi said, looking hurt.

"Why does everything have to do with Islam?"

"Because we're Muslims!" she said. "Muslims in a non-Muslim country."

"Before we even landed in America," Pops said, pride resonating in his voice, "we resolved not to give up Islam. Don't you remember the story of the naked woman in Holland?"

Oh, I remembered. When we were flying to America, we'd had a layover in Amsterdam. In the terminal we came across a perfume shop where there was a six-foot cardboard cutout of a topless Nordic goddess. When we neared her, Pops put his hand on the top of my head and swiveled it to face her. Shorter then, I was eye to supple thigh. "Look at this naked woman," he said. "America is filled with this kind of un-Islamic thing. Look all you want now so you don't sin later." The story about the naked woman had become a family legend. It was often retold—sometimes with the woman alive, sometimes as two women, and sometimes as a couple having sex in public—all to remind us that we had known about America's un-Islamic inclinations before we even got here.

"And what about *halal* food?" Ammi said. "We've worked so hard to maintain *halal* all these years, like good Muslims. That wasn't easy."

I remembered that too. Back when we lived in Brooklyn, before my first day of school, Pops sat Flim and me down in front of Ammi and explained the byzantine world of *halal* meat. No pork, no bacon, no sausage, and no pepperoni; beef and chicken were also out in this country, because they weren't slaughtered in the Islamic manner; fish was permissible, but we were supposed to tell the cook that it shouldn't be prepared along with pork, beef, or chicken. And if we had eggs or pizza away from home, we were instructed to make sure that it wasn't flipped or cut with a utensil that had touched pork, beef, or chicken. Finally, we had to make sure that our food was cooked in vegetable oil and not in lard or oils made from animal extracts.

"Remember that time you and I went to the farm?" Pops recalled fondly. "It was when we lived in Washington state. We went to Deer Park and put those chickens upside down in the metal ports and then took their heads and . . . *Bismillahi allahu akbar*," he said, making a slicing motion with his hand. "We did all that hard work so that we could eat *halal* like true Muslims."

"And we always made sure you had an Islamic education," Ammi said. "When we couldn't even figure out the subway map in New York and Pops had to be at work in Staten Island, I used to take you for Friday prayer at the *masjid* at Coney Island Avenue. And then we enrolled you in the Islamic school for the summer!"

"That wasn't a school," I replied. "That was a fat woman's nasty apartment. And the only thing related to Islam that she did was to split the boys and girls into separate rooms and tell us to convert every non-Muslim to Islam."

"Well," Ammi said. "At least there was a *masjid* in the building."

"Not really," I said. "The *masjid* was the basement of our apartment building near the water heaters. All the paint was peeling and the carpet was gross. It smelled like fungus feet, remember? And sometimes when the *imam* did prayer the dryers in the laundry room buzzed and scared the hell out of everyone."

"Well, it's important to be reminded of hell from time to time," Ammi defended.

"Then what about when we lived in Arizona?" Pops said, mulling over our numerous moves across America. "We took you to that *qari* at the beautiful *masjid* in the Mojave Desert that the doctors built. Man, that was some *masjid* wasn't it? It even had a one-way mirror separating the men and women—very smart."

"Qari Fazal?" I scoffed. "He was an illiterate villager from Pakistan who secretly wanted to beat all the students—and he would have, except I kept reminding him that if he did he'd go to jail."

"Stop being so negative," Ammi said. "What does criticism achieve?"

"I just want to change my name!"

"You really want to change your God-given name?" Pops asked.

I nodded.

"So what do you want it to be?" Pops asked. "Have you thought of something?"

"I want to be Amir. Just Amir."

"Amir," Ammi said tentatively, looking at Pops. "Am-iiir."

There was a long period of silence. Outside even Rocky Balboa became quiet.

"Why do you like this name?" Pops asked finally.

"Well, because it's not *odd!* All types of people have this name. I've met Jews and blacks who have it. I know of some popular businessmen with the name. Americans recognize the name more. It would make life easier. I just want to *live.*"

I didn't want to tell them that the name made me feel more American.

"So this would be your nickname?" Pops asked.

"No. I want to change it legally," I said. "So it gets changed on the school transcripts and for roll call at school and in all my records."

Pops thought over it for a while and then patted my back. "You'll need a new Social Security card, I guess, and you'll have to go to Probate Court. I think you fill out a form there and explain your position to a judge. If he says fine, then I'm fine."

I was shocked by how easy it had been, all things considered. I pumped my fist and smiled in relief. Only then did I turn to see Ammi's reaction.

She had moved to the couch and was sitting with her arms folded, pouting.

"I'm not happy about this," she said ominously. "Your name was Abir ul Islam, and now you'll be just . . . Amir? Don't you care that I rubbed your chest against the walls of the Ka'ba? What about our *mannat,* our covenant with Allah?"

"Pops said I could do this."

"Your Pops is wrong this time. You got that name, Abir ul Islam, Perfume of Islam, because you were promised to Islam in Mecca. You were supposed to spread Islam as if it were a fragrance. I rubbed your chest on the Ka'ba," she repeated.

"Tall tales."

"No. Do you know that you didn't start walking until you got to Mecca? What about the fact that during *hajj,* in the middle of the night, you just got up and went into the desert? What eleven-month-old does *that?* You were drawn to the places where the Prophet Muhammad walked. Islam—it's in your blood. You are Abir ul Islam."

"Don't Islam-shislam me," I said. "It's just Amir."

# 7

Amir had a multi-year plan for independence. He was going to apply for college far away from home. He was going to become a player. By the age of twenty-seven he would move to Amsterdam, work for equality at the Human Rights court, and keep a harem.

I applied to schools in New York, Chicago, and California. I used the Internet to befriend girls in those regions, hoping one day to meet them in person. At the same time, I distanced myself from all the backward people in Alabama—all the people I'd been calling my friends.

Then one day I met Una—blue-eyed, blond-haired Una. When she entered my life, I felt as if my plan was finally going someplace.

I met her at an academic achievement banquet held out of town. Her eyes were lively, and there was something of the Wild West in her presence that suggested a rowdy spirit. Her pale face had small freckles equidistant from one another except on one side of her forehead, where they congregated like a constellation. She did all the things I associated with all-American girls: she rode horses, played the piano, was on the school's swim team (which meant she wore bikinis), and liked to read infamous freethinkers such as Marqui de Sade and Voltaire. We kissed the first night we met.

After the banquet, we kept in touch via phone and e-mail. I started opening up to her and explained my family's fundamentalism. I expected her to back away, both hands up, but she seemed to become even more interested in me. Knowing that she liked me made me want to tell her that I'd be willing to challenge my family's religious dictates for her.

That was when Una sent me sonnets.

The poems, set in medieval times, dripped with the encounter of East and West. They were about ramparts and towers. Minarets and domes. She was Vienna and I was Ottoman. She was Andalucia and I was Almoravid. She was Desdemona and I was the Moor. She was a blond princess batting her eyelashes into the sun and I was a dark rider eclipsing the moon.

At first the poems seemed to suggest that even if I was willing to shun Islam, others wouldn't see me as anything but a Muslim. I took the poems as a sign that I couldn't escape my servitude.

But then I realized that the poems were special. They were liberating. In them Islam was understood not as a series of rules and regulations, but as geography, as aesthetics, as decoration. The poems allowed me to identify myself as a Muslim without having to take on the baggage that my parents and Saleem and the QSC added to it. Una offered an understanding of Islam—Islam as imagery, symbolism, exoticism—that seemed perfectly in sync with being an American. The old Islam was for Abir and the new Islam was for Amir—and he wanted Una to be his girlfriend.

I told Una that we should coordinate our college applications so that we could end up near one another. We kept our acquaintance secret for many months, hoping that no one would suspect anything between us. Slowly our applications were sorted out: Una would go to Cornell in central New York state and I would attend a private university in Manhattan. I would spend weekdays doing city things like reading Henry James and visiting museums, and during the weekends I would hang out with my all-American goddess.

Amir was very much ready for the next stage of his life. His American life.

# BOOK III

## The Fundamentalist—Abu Bakr Ramaq

*In which the author, newly arrived at college in Manhattan, embraces the superiority of Islam over all things, culminating with a trip to Pakistan, where he intends to (1) find a pious Muslim wife who will protect him from secularism's sexual temptation and (2) investigate his relationship with an ancient Caliph of Islam*

# I

Una didn't go to Cornell in the end. She left me for Stanford—all the way on the other side of the country—and I arrived in New York all alone.

The city immediately crushed me. When it rained, no one stopped to appraise the weather—taxis just flipped on their lights and people magically sprouted hoods. When it became sunny and I went to the park, a homeless man turned down the fish filet I offered him. The only flowers were red ones spray I saw painted on the side of a train. Even the English was different: the letters H-o-u-s-t-o-n, for example, were pronounced "Howston" and not "Hewsten."

I walked around the city endlessly during my first days there because I wanted to find a way to embrace it. I stood before the skyscrapers, trying to analogize them to something familiar, but I had never encountered things so massive. No other place compared to Manhattan, so I retreated into my imagination. I invoked a faraway place out of Tolkien's Middle-earth. A glittering Elven city, maybe. An eternal metropolis ruled by Aragon, perhaps. The towers of those imaginary kingdoms competed with the skyscrapers in Manhattan; the arabesques of that illusory sultanate challenged the beauty of the friezes at the library on Forty-second Street; the busy canals of that metaphysical capital teemed with boats as Broadway did with buses. Unfortunately, comprehending Manhattan as if it were nothing more than the beguiling doppelgänger of a city from my fantasies simply made me feel more estranged. I could say that I was in Manhattan's bloodstream, but not that I was in any way essential to the city. The recognition of this partition—between subject and city—was both instantaneous and painful. It forced me to seek out anything that was familiar.

I went to the university's residential services office because I heard of a dorm where you could ask for the specific kind of roommate you wanted—and I requested a Muslim.

My new roommate, Moosa Farid, had been looking for a Muslim to live with because the person he was initially assigned to turned out to be a "Luti."

"Man, I walked in on that white boy sodomizing another one," he said. "The room smelled like wet towels. Gross stuff. It was like I was back in the Prophet Lut's time. We know how God punished *them*."

In just a few days in the city, small-town Moosa Farid had become an expert in homosexuality. He hadn't wanted for it to happen, of course. It had happened, he concluded, because the gays were after him. How else to explain the fact that when he was looking for a place to eat he got stuck with a bunch of queers in a gay pride parade in West Village? What else explained the fact that during class orientation, of all the tour guides possible, he had gotten the flaming gay one? Why else would he go into a cafe and see his ex-roommate sitting with his legs crossed, being all faggoty with his faggot-fuck buddy? All these homosexuals were surely sent as a sign to remind Moosa Farid how much of a Muslim he was; how unlike Manhattan he was. And the more Moosa talked about homosexuals, the more Muslim I felt too.

As soon as we settled into our room, he started grilling me about Islam. "Do you eat *halal*?" he asked, "or are you wack?"

"I eat *halal*."

"Real *halal*? As in slaughtered in the Islamic way? Or just so-called *halal*, when you say *bismillah* over the meat like wack Muslims?"

"Real *halal*," I said, suddenly wary of this "wack" category that inspired so much animus in my roommate.

"Are you a player?" he asked. "Are you going to have girls here?"

"No girls. That would be wack," I said, testing to see if I had picked up the lingo correctly.

"Good." He nodded approvingly. "Tell me: are you going to join the Muslim Students Association?"

"Of course I am. Are you? Or are *you* wack?"

He laughed at the competitiveness filling the air. "I already know where the next MSA meeting is. Do you?"

"No," I conceded, realizing that he had won.

"How often do you pray?" he asked.

"I pray all five times," I said aggressively, though it was completely untrue.

"Me too," he said, nodding. "Let me ask you: do you shake hands with women?"

At first I thought it was a trick question. Didn't all human beings shake hands with each other? Certainly I'd shaken hands with people all my life. Then I realized that Moosa wouldn't have posed the question unless the answer was no.

"Come on!" I said, taking on an incredulous expression. "I'm not wack!"

"Me neither," Moosa said. "Touching women you aren't married to is *haram*."

"I agree."

"Do you lower your gaze?" he asked, continuing the inquisition.

I had no idea what he meant. Was this a code phrase that good Muslims used to identify the wack ones?

"What do you mean?"

"You don't know?"

I shook my head.

"The Quran says that you shouldn't look at women you're not married to. If you happen to glance at one, it should be only one look. So when you catch yourself looking at an attractive woman more than once..."

"... you lower your gaze," I concluded, putting it together. "I get it now."

"Right. If you don't lower your gaze, you'll go to hell. I'm surprised that you didn't know that. Haven't you ever seen that T-shirt that some of the sisters wear? On the front of the shirt it says, 'I know I'm hot,' and on the back it says, 'So lower your gaze because hell is hotter.'"

I shook my head. "Never seen those. But that's creative."

"Yeah. I saw one last year. I was looking at a pair of breasts in a mosque, and the shirt really put everything in perspective. Like, what is looking at a hot girl with mangolike D-cups when the punishment for looking at them is an eternity in hellfire? *Fi nari jahannum.*"

"I'll keep my gaze to the ground."

"I'm just looking out for your afterlife, brother!"

Once we'd established that we disliked homosexuals, weren't wack, and indeed executed Islam perfectly, we struck out to try to socialize with people. I suggested that we meet up with a Pakistani girl named Kyla I'd been chatting with on AOL; she was also on campus as a freshman. I figured this would be safe since she was Pakistani, and all the Pakistanis I knew were good Muslims—in other words, not wack. We made an appointment to meet Kyla at the student center near the security guards.

As we got approached we could see her waiting.

"That a pretty short skirt she's got on," Moosa said, turning to me. "That's pretty immodest!"

I immediately regretted setting up the meeting. "Let's go back," I said in a concerned voice.

"Can't. I think she's seen us."

Sure enough, Kyla waved and came toward us. She was the height of wackness. Low-cut blouse. Lots of cleavage. She kissed cheeks when she greeted. She took my wrist and pulled me close for a hug that I couldn't prevent.

Moosa was more adept: he avoided her sin-trap by backing away and saluting from a distance. He never did come any closer.

Kyla said she was delighted to meet other Pakistanis. When I'd made the appointment with her I had been too, but now my enthusiasm was dead. I was worried that Moosa would impute her wackness onto me. She kept trying to talk to me, but I gave her monosyllabic answers. Anxiety about what Moosa thought about me skittered around in my head until Kyla got irritated from my terse responses and stomped off.

When Moosa and I were alone, I wanted to say something to let him know that I didn't approve of her lifestyle and wouldn't try to hang out with her again. However, to say that I would ignore her *because* she was immodest wouldn't quite work, because that would suggest that I'd noticed her (lack of) clothing, which would mean that I paid attention to immodest women—and only wack Muslims did things like that.

"She's ugly," I declared. It was just as effective.

I soon got an opportunity to redeem myself in Moosa's eyes. A Jamaican guy we knew came over to the dorm when he heard that Moosa had a DVD burner. He brought a bag full of discs with him.

"I'll make you a business deal," he offered, scattering his stuff on my bed. "I'll give you a dollar for each one you burn, and if you want to burn an extra copy for yourself, that's fine too. I have two hundred blanks on me."

"You just want me to burn them?" asked Moosa.

"Yup."

"What do you do with all these movies anyway?" I asked.

"I'm a distributor," he said. "I sell them."

The deal was struck immediately and the guy left.

"That's a sweet deal," I noted as Moosa popped the first DVD in and the computer started whirring. "I wonder if he has a copy of *The Rock* with Sean Connery."

"Let's see if he has *Executive Decision*," Moosa suggested. "It has a Muslim in the story line, although like always they make us look evil."

Suddenly the film came onscreen and Moosa let out a massive yelp. "Shit! It's porn!" he exclaimed, clinging to the wall as if he'd been shot.

"Are you serious?"

I leaned over the monitor: sure enough, there was a gorgeous black-haired girl giving a blow job. Up and down, up and down. Her hair was so black it was purple. Up and down. The actress was stunning. Part of me thought that if Moosa was so scandalized, he should leave the room so that I could enjoy the goods. Rather than expressing what I really thought, I pulled back from the screen and took on a serious air, twisting my face into a disgusted sneer.

"That's wack!" I said, reaching forward to flick off the screen.

"What are we going to do now?" Moosa asked.

This was my opportunity to demonstrate what a good Muslim I was.

"Give back the DVDs, dude."

Moosa was reluctant. "Maybe I could just burn this set and not do anymore. I could keep the screen off as they copy."

"Yes," I said in a moralistic tone. "But it's porn, and that's *haram*. It's like distributing alcohol."

"I know," Moosa replied. "But it's not gay porn at least."

"Good idea running loopholes with God."

"I was just kidding," Moosa said, cowed by my hard line. "I'll give these back."

We were now even, the two of us, after what had happened with Kyla.

Moosa Farid and I found a crew of brothers from the MSA to hang out with. We all took turns talking about how we'd never been religious before but were trying to become religious, now that we were "in the real world," and we urged one another to confess salacious stories from our past.

Moosa went first and talked about how he regretted hooking up with some girl when he was a sophomore in high school. I went next and talked about how I had kissed Una, and how I regretted feeling tempted to go to the prom with a beautiful cheerleader, and how sometimes in class I used to touch the girls' bare skin at the place where shirt and skirt separated. Our honesty spurred the others.

"I became wack in high school," a tall brother named Aslam admitted. "I sinned. I sinned a lot. *Bad* sin, too. Ate pork. Got a blow job. Fingered a girl. Dated a blond. She was hot too. We don't even need to talk about her, but I've got her picture if you don't believe me. Looking back, I can't believe that I was seventeen and sinful. Man, when Muhammad bin Qasim, the great general of Islam, was seventeen, he was conquering India. I need a headcheck, you know? Something is definitely wrong with me!"

When any of the brothers rattled off their list of sins, the rest of us shook our heads judgmentally. Each swivel of the neck condemned the brother who had just finished speaking. Each turn of the neck pulsed disapproval. Our sardonic smiles sizzled with chastisement. "Damn, you were wack," we said. "You'd lost your sense of righteousness," we stressed. "You'd left the *sirat ul mustaqim*." We were like children learning a new language, one organized around accusation and excoriation.

We behaved like this because we all knew the prophetic *hadith* about the adulterer:

Once an adulterer went to the Prophet and confessed his sin before him and the glorious Companions. Then he pleaded to be stoned to death. The Prophet heard him out and then turned away, saying, "Don't tell me any more." The man ran around and faced the Prophet and again confessed his adultery. Yet again the Prophet turned away from him and said, "Don't tell me." The man moved to face the Prophet yet again and confessed for a third time. The Prophet then told the adulterer to go home and repent to Allah and never commit adultery again.

The actual moral of the *hadith* was that if a sinful Muslim sincerely repented, then the earthly punishment for his sin—even if it was something as grievous as adultery, which was theoretically deserving of stoning—could be waived by the authority responsible for carrying out the law.

However, the lesson that *we* drew was that in order to really repent for our sins, we had to prosecute and convict ourselves in front of others, as the adulterer had in front of the Prophet and the Companions.

Besides, since we were all brothers in Islam, we had an obligation to assist one another in our psychological flagellation. That would help keep us from repeating our sins in the future.

In short: it was out of concern for our friends that we had to berate them publicly.

Briefer: humiliation was kindness.

*　*　*

We didn't go to bars; we didn't date; we didn't hit strip clubs; we didn't do weed; we didn't go to parties. We all upheld the Islamic rules that our parents had had such a difficult time enforcing against us when we were younger.

What we did do was watch movies.

Every Friday and Saturday night—and sometimes even Friday afternoons—we rushed to the one of the city's many movie theaters and watched whatever was showing. Since films were the only form of entertainment we had, we had reached an unstated agreement that we wouldn't make reference to the ratings. After all, if we couldn't watch R-rated films, there really wouldn't be much to do. We normally took turns paying for one another, but when we watched an R-rated film we bought our tickets individually, to compensate for knowingly sinning. This was based on the Quranic verse that says, "None shall bear the burden of another."

It was during one of these excursions to the movies that I realized we all had a shared cinematic pedigree composed of three films with story lines about Islam: *Executive Decision, Malcolm X,* and *The Message.*

*Executive Decision,* starring Kurt Russell and Steven Seagal, had come out in 1996, and we had all seen it because it depicted a Muslim hijacker. It was notorious among Muslims, not just because of its depiction of a Muslim villain, but because it showed the cold-blooded hijacker praying and invoking Allah during his rampage.

We hated the film. The one thing that none of us could accept was that a pious Muslim was depicted as doing evil. After all, *we* were pious Muslims, and *we* weren't evil.

"That guy was a bastard," Moosa said. "But they were showing him praying and prostrating as if he were a good Muslim! That's not right."

"They always show Muslims negatively," Aslam said. "I saw a book once about how Arab and Muslim characters have always been depicted negatively in Hollywood."

"Except in *Malcolm X,*" Moosa said. "That movie was tight!"

"Except in *Malcolm X,*" Aslam agreed.

"The best part in *X* was when Denzel Washington went to *hajj* and became an orthodox Muslim. They could have extended that part," Moosa said. "Really let the people know what Islam is about."

"Denzel rules," I said.

"Man," Aslam said. "I wish there were more good movies about Islam."

"Something like *The Message,* maybe," Moosa said.

*The Message* was a semifictional account of the life of the Prophet Muhammad, starring the late Anthony Quinn as the Prophet's uncle. It was well loved among Muslims because it told—positively—the story of Muhammad's rise to power and prominence without depicting his face or showing any of the Companions.

"I loved that the whole story was told from Muhammad's perspective so you never saw his face," Aslam said. "That was brilliant. He didn't even talk. Just shook his head."

"True, but Hollywood is anti-Islam today," Moosa concluded. "They'll never make films like that again."

Indeed, a few weeks later Hollywood hit us hard. A film called *The Siege* came out, and we threw a collective fit because Denzel Washington—Malcolm X himself!—was in a starring role and not one we were happy about.

"Denzel betrayed us!" Moosa said. "The film is all about suicide bombers in Brooklyn, and I read that they're shown purifying themselves before killing people, as if killing were the same as being pious!"

"Denzel's in it?" I asked, astonished.

"So is that redneck Bruce Willis," Aslam said. "Man, you know it was all his idea. But why would Denzel go along? Did he forget that he played Malcolm X?"

We had a long argument about whether or not we should go see the movie. On one hand, we didn't want to financially support something that we thought would make Islam look bad. On the other hand, we wouldn't know *how* it made Islam look bad unless we actually watched it.

We discussed our dilemma in the university's prayer hall. The louder we argued, the more we became interested in the film. It was finally decided that all the MSA brothers would go to the cinema together; we'd sit in the back and jeer so that other people couldn't enjoy the presumably tasteless film. Once the "thug brothers"—called that because they liked dressing in gangster clothing, though they were actually a group of rich kids from Strong Island—heard our plan, they eagerly joined us. We marched to the theater talking about all the comments we'd make.

"Anytime Bruce Willis talks we should just start doing the call to prayer," was the idea most often heard.

Upon arriving in the hall everyone stopped talking tough and started munching on popcorn. As we watched the movie, I realized that I felt more conflicted than assaulted. I didn't like how the suicide bombers were depicted as pious, God-fearing Muslims when everyone knew that if you blew people up you were a bad Muslim. But at the same time, the film—which showed New York going under martial law—served as a warning about military excess in the aftermath of terrorist attacks. There was ambiguity in the story that I had not expected.

At the end of the movie I learned that the same confusion extended to the rest of the group. We'd gone in expecting to become angry—no, *more* angry—and we'd left not knowing what to say. Opting for the easy way out, we ignored the big issues and focused on minutiae: we called Tony Shalhoub a sellout for playing an FBI agent and mocked the way the film messed up little stylistic details. "Did you see how the guy doing ablution washed his arms *before* washing his face?" I said. "Hollywood sucks! Always demonizing Islam!"

After a few days no one even mentioned *The Siege.*

The only time I heard about it again was when someone told me that the guy who'd produced the film had gotten in a car accident and a stop sign had impaled him through the skull.

Moosa called that getting "God-smacked."

# 2

Moosa Farid often told me that his entire family, as far back as he knew, were Islamic scholars, and before that they were all Muslim kings. Aslam told me that his family were Seyyids, meaning that he was a direct descendant of the Holy Prophet. I felt like a loser compared to them, so I called Ammi to find out whether I had any glorious Islamic lineage.

"Can you tell me about my ancestors?" I asked.

Ammi was washing dishes and the pots clattered down the phone line as she spoke. "Sure," she said. "My family descended from Mongols. They were Genghis Khan's children."

"So they weren't always Muslim?"

"No."

"That sucks," I said despondently. "Well, what about the fact that the Mongols converted to Islam?"

"Not my family," she said. "We converted to Islam after becoming Sikh. Before that we were Hindu."

"Hindu?" I exclaimed.

Ammi picked up the accusation in my voice and became defensive. "*Initially* Hindu, yes. But my family has served Islam well. I told you about Beyji and my great-grandfather. What about him? He built a mosque and converted *jinn*s to Islam."

"Yes," I said, with barely contained antagonism. "But they don't count." I was irritated by all these people descending from Sikhs and Hindus. "Listen. Can you just not tell people that you come from Hindu stock?"

I could tell by the lack of background noise that she'd quit doing dishes and was concentrating on our conversation. "Why?" she asked cautiously.

"It sounds bad."

"No thanks," she said. "I am Rajput Bhatti," she added, affirming her Hindu heritage with pride.

"*Astaghfirullah!*" I exclaimed (having stopped saying "Jesus Christ!" to express frustration). I seethed on the phone. I didn't want to be associated with Ammi's side of the family anymore, so I looked for ways to diminish them.

"Isn't it true that your family didn't support the creation of Pakistan?" I asked angrily. "How shameful! All those Muslims that died for Islam—and your family opposed them!" I knew it was a cheap shot since just as many Muslims had stayed in India as had gone to Pakistan, but I felt resentful and wanted to let her know.

"You're right," she admitted. "My father didn't want Punjab to be split up. He felt that during the Partition of 1947 all the Muslims of India should stay in one united country."

"Let's forget about *your* family," I said, trying a different tack. "Isn't it true that in Islam we follow the father's side of the biology?"

"True."

"So tell me about them."

"Hold on," she said. "You do realize that on the Day of Judgment everyone will be raised under their mother's name?"

"Yes, but we're talking about *this* life," I countered. "In this kind of stuff, this life is more important than the afterlife."

Ammi began with stories of Pops's family from the time of the Partition of India and Pakistan. She reminded me about the aunts that jumped into the well. The story of the buried treasure. The nights in the open grave. The way Dada Abu had lost Dadi Ma during the transfer and then found her in a refugee camp. This was much better,

I thought. People who had died for Islam; who had showed how much they loved the religion by giving up their most valuable possession. I wanted to belong to *this* group.

"So what about before the Partition? Where were Pops's ancestors from?"

Ammi excused herself for a moment and went to ask Pops. I could hear them consulting for several minutes. Finally she returned.

"You guys are Siddiquis," she said.

"What's that?" I asked.

"It's like a family name, but it's also a caste. It comes down from Hazrat Abu Bakr Siddiq."

My hands began shaking, and my pulse picked up.

"You mean *the* Abu Bakr Siddiq?" I asked. "The first convert to Islam?"

"Who else?"

I almost dropped the phone. Abu Bakr? He was one of the most celebrated personalities of Islam. He accompanied Muhammad on the migration to Medina, and the two men hid together in a cave when their enemies from the Quraysh tribe came looking for them. It was across the mouth of that cave that a spider commanded by Allah wove a web, to make it appear that no one was inside. Abu Bakr was the man who affirmed Muhammad's story about the ascension to heaven to the skeptics in Mecca (which earned him the nickname "the Truthteller"). Abu Bakr was also very generous with his money, purchasing many slaves from oppressive holders and setting them free. Before his death, Muhammad appointed Abu Bakr to lead the Muslims in prayer, and this position led to his becoming the first Caliph after Muhammad's death.

"I need you to be absolutely certain about this," I said. "Confirm again. This could be a game-changer. Being a descendant of the first Caliph would be the most important thing to ever happen to me."

Ammi went to Pops and came back with the same story. "Pops thinks that his Pakistani birth certificate identifies his last name as Siddiqui. He dropped that name while growing up."

"So it really is true!" I hopped around my dorm room as Moosa looked on in amazement.

"Hazrat Abu Bakr's children moved from Mecca to Medina and then to Baghdad," Ammi said, repeating what Pops had told her. "Then in the thirteenth century, when the Mongols were destroying the caliphate in Baghdad, they went to India. They settled down in Punjab."

I imagined dark-skinned Arabs with hook noses like mine, dressed in flowing white robes, packing hefty camels and horses on a majestic avenue in Baghdad during its melancholy decline. I pictured them leaving for Basra in the middle of the night, crossing into Persia, and then traversing the Khorasan region toward India, where they must have crossed the five rivers and settled on farmland in Punjab, off the foothills of Kashmir. My imagination still soaring, I could see them settled in their new area: they converted beautiful Hindu girls, married them, and had many children. Hundreds of years later came the Partition, during which their descendants lost everything and then, in the name of Islam, migrated to Pakistan. Now here *I* was, a member of that clan, child of the first Caliph, all the way in America. The vastness of the story filled me with romance.

"Do we have a family tree?" I asked, returning to the present.

"Pops hasn't seen it, but he thinks his older brother in Pakistan has one that goes all the way back."

Triumphantly I began envisioning future encounters with Moosa and the guys. I imagined how, surrounded by a group of brothers, I would casually drop reference to the fact that I was a Siddiqui, a descendant of the first Caliph, and everyone would say, "Really? From the line of the first Caliph?" and I'd say "Yeah, bro!"—all in a very humble way, of course, because when you were an important Muslim, the best bragging was to pretend to be humble.

When I hung up the phone I lay back in bed, jubilant. I was a Siddiqui, from the tribe of Taym, the Truthteller's tribe, from the loins of the man whose intuition was so great that he used to decipher the dreams of the Prophet, from the family of that magnanimous merchant who freed the black slave Bilal, and thus a precursor to the Malcolm Xs of the world. My pedigree was steeped in Islam. Now it made perfect sense why Pops had made a *mannat* for me and why Ammi had rubbed me against the walls of the Ka'ba. I recalled that in 1258, even as the

Mongols killed the last Abbasid Caliph, they wrapped his body in a carpet because spilling caliphal blood was forbidden even in the religion of savages. That was *my* blood.

All of a sudden my life had meaning. Responsibility coursed through me. Having the blood of a Caliph meant, very simply, that I had to make certain I was a perfect Muslim. More than that, I had to accept that Islam was the perfect way of life. To do otherwise would be to demean my ancestors.

In honor of my revered ancestor I dubbed myself Abu Bakr Ramaq. The name Ramaq, which meant "spark of light," represented the passion I felt for Islam.

# 3

There were tangible steps a man took to express his love for his religion.

I grew facial hair so that everyone would know up front that I cared about Islam. I began folding up my pants above my ankles so that everyone could see I practiced Islamic humility. I began inserting an *alhamdulillah* and *subhanallah* in almost every sentence. I spoke English with a slight Arab accent that I cultivated, believing that Arabs were the best of Muslims. I let everyone know that I was getting rid of my music collection and replacing it with tapes of Quranic recitation. I often quoted Ibn Taymiya's proverb, "A thousand days of despotism are better than a single day of anarchy," when some Muslim around me agitated for change.

Further, what would be my love for Islam, the religion of mercy, the final message of God, the testament of total truth, if I didn't guide the non-Muslims of the world toward its blessed shade? I felt an overwhelming need to invite people to Islam—to do *da'wa*.

My first target was a Pentecostal girl named Rita, a fellow student at the university. She was a South Indian, and because her parents had already converted once—from Hinduism to Christianity—I figured she would be predisposed toward switching religions. Another thing that made her a good target was that she was willing to spend many hours talking to me. This was because she secretly liked Moosa, who refused to talk to women because they tempted him; by talking to me, she was at least able to remain in his vicinity.

I was confident that by the end of the academic year she would be a Muslim and God would reward me by cleansing all my sins. It was important for me to be as innocent as possible, given my lineage.

I started the conversion effort by trying to persuade Rita that Islam was the natural evolutionary advance from Christianity. I explained that the doctrine of the Trinity was illogical, pointing out that the idea of a single, monotheistic deity made much more sense. I told her that God and Jesus were separate entities, with God being divine and Jesus being just a prophet—a man carrying God's message, similar to Muhammad. I pointed out that, in fact, according to the lost Gospel of Barnabas, Jesus had prophesied the arrival of a man named Ahmed—which was Muhammad's alternative name—who would bring salvation to the world.

Rita always listened to me, then—promising to "think things over"—called it a night. The next night, though, we'd be back at square one.

I couldn't understand why someone whose faith was so weak that she needed to "think things over" after hearing about an alternative path wasn't able to see how secure I was in my faith—and from my confidence infer that I was on the true path, a path she should join.

After a week of this, her reluctance to become Muslim infuriated me. Our friendship was saved when, the very next day, Rita told me that she wanted to learn about Muslim history, not theology. Considering this a sign of progress, I promised that I'd give her a comprehensive lesson. I put it off for a few days so that I could prep.

The next morning I set about putting together a list of various facts in history that cast Islam in a positive light. But that wouldn't be enough, I realized. To convert Rita I'd have to do more than simply make Islam look good; I'd have to make it responsible for every good thing in the world. I decided that the best way to demonstrate superiority to Rita, who was majoring in engineering, was to show her that long before Western civilization attained technical proficiency, the Islamic civilization had been at the vanguard of science. I was certain this would convince her that Islam was the best religion.

Hitting the books, I discovered that Muslims had a long-standing fascination with flying. (I figured this was because of the story of Muhammad's ascension to heaven on a horse.) Armen Firman, a ninth-century Spanish Muslim, had tried to fly from a tower in Cordoba with a wing-shaped cloak; and even though he failed, he survived the crash because air became trapped in his cloak and slowed his descent (which made him the inventor of the parachute—sort of). In similar fashion, his compatriot Abbas Ibn Firnas tried to fly from a mountain with a glider, and though he ended up breaking his back in the landing, he lived as well. Later, Hezarfen Ahmed Celebi, a seventeenth-century Turkish scientist, became the founder of modern aviation when, long before the Wright brothers, he used a winglike glider and flew a distance of about one mile in front of Ottoman Sultan Murat IV—from the gigantic Galata Tower on one side of the Bosporus Strait to Uskudar on the other. He landed successfully as well.

Then there were the scientists and thinkers: al-Khwarizmi, the eighth-century inventor of algebra and quadratic equations; al-Haytham, the tenth-century optician who devised a version of the scientific method; Ibn Sina, the eleventh-century physician; Ibn Tufayl, the twelfth-century philosopher who anticipated the moral questions later evaluated by Defoe and Rousseau; Ibn Rushd, the twelfth-century jurist who gave Aristotle to Europe; Ibn Khaldun, the fifteenth-century Algerian who was the father of sociology; Iqbal, the early-twentieth-century thinker who said that the theory of relativity was wrong because it overlooked the spiritual power in the universe.

If the above information failed to sway Rita, I planned to pull out my trump card. Various *da'wa* references had taught me that a Frenchman named Maurice Bucaille had written a book called *The Bible, The Quran, and Science,* which had conclusively demonstrated that most of the advances of modern science had been mentioned in various verses of the Quran. I got hold of the book and it was indeed a gold mine of facts. Bucaille showed that everything from molecular biology, to astrophysics, to hydrology was discussed within Quranic verses. The book strengthened my faith, which convinced me that it would wow Rita too.

The final element of preparation involved peer pressure. I wanted to demonstrate to Rita that some of the most important people not just in history—my first list—but in *Western* history, had actually secretly been Muslim.

There was, of course, Napoleon, the greatest Western military hero. He was a Muslim: he adopted the name Ali for himself and told the Egyptians that he was the *mahdi,* or messiah. He was also reported to have said, "I hope the time is not far off when I shall be able to unite all the wise and educated men of all the countries and establish a uniform regime based on the principles of the Quran which alone are true and which alone can lead men to happiness." Then there was Goethe, the greatest German prose stylist. He was a Muslim, as his words in *West-Eastern Divan* revealed: "Whether the Quran is of eternity? I don't question that! That it is the book of books I believe out of the Muslim's duty." Emerson, the greatest American essayist, must also have been a Muslim, because he quoted Muhammed at the beginning of one of his essays: "I was as a gem concealed; Me, my burning ray revealed." Edgar Allan Poe, the great American short-story writer, must have also been a Muslim: he wrote a poem directly inspired by the Islamic angel Israfil. It opened: "In heaven a spirit doth dwell / 'whose heart strings are a lute' / None sing so wildly well / As the angel Israfel." The quoted part was directly from the Quran, and given that the Quran was a miraculous book that had converted all the pagans who heard it, Poe must have converted to Islam upon hearing it too. Finally, there was Nietzsche, the greatest of modern Western philosophers. He wasn't a Muslim, but he was certainly open to Islam; he said many positive things about it, showing a receptiveness to Islam that was a precursor to conversion.

I was very proud of my conversion dossier, but I didn't get a chance to use it on Rita. She transferred to Rutgers.

# 4

Abu Bakr Siddiq, the first Caliph, became the second most important figure in Islam, because after the death of the Prophet Muhammad, he fought the false prophets Musaylima the Liar and Tulayha son of Khwaylid. Siddiq's *jihad* against those pretenders assured Islam's permanence.

Abu Bakr Ramaq, the successor, the great-grandson many times over, also had a pair of false prophets he had to fight. One of them was usurping the role of the messiah from within Islam, and the other was inviting believers to secularism.

Their names were Osama and Salman.

My first encounter with the ideas of Osama bin Laden was in the form of a news story from 1998 entitled "Muslim Fury: 'War of Future' Claims First Victims."[*] It discussed the views of bin Laden and his supporters in the aftermath of Clinton's Tomahawk missile strikes at various training camps in eastern Afghanistan. The strikes had been launched from two nuclear submarines in the Arabian Sea as retaliation for bin Laden's blowing up two American embassies in Africa. After

---

[*] Christopher Kremmer, "Muslim Fury: 'War of Future' Claims First Victims," *Sydney Morning Herald,* August 29, 1998.

a long survey of various opinions, the article concluded: "Meanwhile, Osama bin Laden—deprived of his Saudi citizenship but now elevated to the status of folk hero in the minds of many Muslims—appears secure in his Afghan fastness, promising to answer Mr. Clinton 'in deeds, not words' and keeping in touch with his international network by satellite fax and phone."

After reading this article I came upon an interview that bin Laden had given to an unnamed reporter. In it he defended those who had attacked the American embassies in Africa. He also referred to Muslims as a "nation" that didn't need to recognize the nation-state borders and urged Muslims, all of them, to fight on behalf of God against the United States.

I was astonished that bin Laden, without any formal religious training, would hold himself out as a scholar of Islam. I considered such arrogance treacherous to the faith. When I expressed my concern, however, Aslam took me aside.

"You have to take this man very seriously," Aslam said.

"Why? He just seems like a fighter," I replied.

"Are you not familiar with the signs of the Last Hour?" Aslam asked in astonishment.

"The arrival of the Day of Judgment?" I said. "Of course I am. My mother taught them to me when I was just a boy."

"You must not know them very well, because Osama bin Laden was predicted in the prophecies of the Holy Messenger."

I was irritated by Aslam's implication that he was more knowledgeable about Islam than I was, but I was also curious. "And what did the Prophet say?" I prompted.

"There's a prophecy he made which says that, at a time when Muslims were thoroughly defeated, around the time of the arrival of the one-eyed Antichrist named Dajjal, there would arise from the region of Khorasan a group of Muslims with black flags. First they would conquer toward the east and then head west and liberate Jerusalem. At that point the messiah, or *mahdi,* would be revealed. That *mahdi* would then destroy Dajjal, and the entire world would fall under the heel of Islam, a period of power that would last forty years. Then the Muslims would be comprehensively defeated yet again, and that would signal the end of the world, bringing about the Day of Judgment. Do you know when that time is?"

"That could refer to *any* time," I said.

"It refers to now," Aslam replied. "The group of Muslims with the black flags are the Taliban. They're from Afghanistan, which was called Khorasan. When they go east it means that they will fight against India for occupied Kashmir. Then they'll head westward and liberate Jerusalem from the Israelis."

I was skeptical. "What about the *mahdi*?"

"Bin Laden is the *mahdi*! That's why I told you to take him seriously."

"How can that be?"

"The *mahdi* was prophesied to be from Arabia, just like bin Laden, and he's supposed to be tall and thin, just like bin Laden, and he'll have a mark on his back, which bin Laden probably has. Most important, though, bin Laden is with the Taliban and they have black flags. By the time he's forty, I think bin Laden will reveal himself."

"Who is Dajjal then?" I asked.

"America."

"Dajjal is supposed to be a one-eyed man on a donkey," I countered.

"Yes," Aslam said, "but Dajjal is a metaphor. The one eye refers to the camera, or media, which is what America uses to take over the world. And the donkey, that's easy. America's president is Clinton, and he's a Democrat. Their symbol is the ass."

Bin Laden's promises of deliverance rang hollow to me. He seemed like nothing more than an opportunist. Another in a long line of pretender messiahs. The worst thing about him was that he turned Islam into a shooting star. Into fireworks. Into a gunshot. He touched believers by the light of the faith but then encouraged them to become a flame, which he fanned into a conflagration. Such an affirmation of Islam was utterly pointless. It soon fizzled out. As Shaykh Abdal Hakim Murad said in his online essay "The Poverty of Fanaticism," extremist Muslims often got burned out on Islam, and eventually did things the religion prohibited, such as getting non-Muslim girlfriends, thus proving that their faith was weak. To make his point, Shaykh Murad gave the example of an Egyptian extremist named Hamdi who, years after launching attacks at Coptic Christians, ended up with a Christian wife from Australia.

I believed in an Islam that was permanent, unchanging, and solid. Being Muslim wasn't just a state of mind, as bin Laden argued, but a state of existence. Islam was all-consuming. A total condition. A state of submission to the will of the Almighty. It wasn't a system or formula or prescription that one utilized for a little while, in order to gain revenge against one's enemies. Islam was way bigger than that; it was the primordial state of being. Bombing and killing, marauding and murdering, taking up arms against America and Israel—these were a waste of time. They were childish acts carried out by insecure Muslims, by precisely those Muslims who judged success in life according to *worldly* terms.

What mattered, as I saw Islam, was the afterlife. That was the most important part of living. Bin Laden, meanwhile, was not concerned with the afterlife.

The other false prophet, a siren of secularism, the author of a book called *The Satanic Verses*—modernity's anti-Quran—was Salman Rushdie. He was out to undermine every Muslim's faith, it seemed to me.

I had heard about *The Satanic Verses* in Pakistan when the book, newly published, had spurred riots and book burnings. Back then I had lived in a world where all books and writing utensils were considered sacred. Ammi had often told Flim and me that "if a book so much as falls to the floor, you better pick it up; otherwise the Day of Judgment will arrive." When I heard that people were burning a book, I become anxious. One day I even snuck out to the site of a public protest after it had been cleared and poked through the burning tires to see if something remained of the novel.

That was then. Before I learned that I was a Caliph in waiting. Now I had to protect the flock of believers. Sitting in the stacks of the university library, I read through the novel in order to figure out how to undermine it.

It was a secularist's manifesto. The wondrous Prophet Ibraham was depicted as heartless. A girl in charge of a group of eager pilgrims cruelly led them to an oceanic death. An *imam* who resembled the Ayatollah Khomeini was shown as wily and power-mongering, rather than pious and honest (as any true, God-fearing *ayatollah* would be). The whores of Mecca took on the names of the Prophet's wives. Finally came the real problem: the part about the Prophet Muhammad and the circumstances surrounding the revelations that became the Quran. This part suggested that first Satan and then Muhammad's Persian scribe Salman had both tampered with the Quran, changing words outright.

It was this part that made the book vile to Muslims, because it promoted doubt. Skepticism opened the door for believers to think there was a chance that revelation wasn't from God, that the Quran was written by men and thus wasn't otherworldly. Widespread skepticism would be the ultimate victory for secularism, which had previously subjected the Torah and the Bible to just the same attack. What the secularists wanted—Rushdie among them—was to establish the supremacy of reason over and above revelation, something that all religious people had an obligation to resist, because if reason became dominant, the world would fail.

I had learned these things from reading the text of a 1999 lecture titled "The Changing Face of Secularism and the Islamic Response," given by Zaid Shakir in Aylesbury, England. In that lecture he claimed that secularism was un-Islamic. Whereas God said in the Quran, "I have only created *jinn*s and mankind that they might worship Me," secularism demanded that we worship the earthly, the immanent, the tangible. Shakir explained that secularism forced the people of the hereafter to become the people of the here and now. Rather than looking at death as a gift, which brought an opportunity to be near God, secularism looked at death as a curse, the moment when one became divested of the world. Shakir explained that secularism was trying to destroy the last normative religion in the world. It wouldn't use swords or guns to separate the creation from the Creator; rather, it would use a sinister idea called freedom.

That was what Salman Rushdie was selling.

My revolt against secularism involved shelving Rushdie's book in the art history section of the library when I'd finished reading it. That way no Muslim of a weaker constitution would encounter it, since Muslims—who considered images *haram*—didn't usually study art history. Hiding the book was way better than burning it—which drew attention to it.

# 5

After rationality, the most potent weapon that secularism wielded was sex. It was a pious believer's constant temptation, assailing from every angle, weakening us. My particular temptation was called Kara.

One day, when I was at the student center with Moosa Farid, we both saw a curly-haired brunette wearing a tank top.

"Damn," I said suddenly, unable to control my tongue. "That girl has nice tits."

Moosa stared at her also. "Wow!" he said. "And she looks Muslim on top of that."

"I'd like to get on top of that," I said, leering.

"We need to stop staring," Moosa cautioned, suddenly remembering Islamic decorum.

"Right. She's hot, but hell is hotter." I turned away as I mouthed the slogan, but my eyes were drawn right back to her.

"Hell is way hotter," said Moosa, sharing my weakness.

"I think we need to change that slogan," I said. "Something like: sometimes hell is barely hotter."

"Just lower your gaze," he warned.

"I will when you do."

"I don't have to stop," he said. "I'm still on my first look. You, on the other hand, broke the first look."

"What do you think she is?"

"The embodiment of sin."

"Ethnically, I meant."

"Arab. Look at those thighs. Thick."

"I want her," I announced dreamily.

"I do too, but I'm not risking hell for her. An infinite number of virgins are waiting for me in the afterlife. I'm going back to the dorm."

"Just a few minutes," I said. "I'll admire her for just a few minutes. I promise to make extra *nawafil* to ask God's forgiveness."

Left in peace to take in the scenery, I noticed that she wasn't wearing a bra. Her breasts stayed pert and afloat and rippled when she laughed. As she looked my direction my heart lifted, but then just as suddenly I was filled with despair. Why bother trying to meet her? I couldn't be with her in any case. She probably wasn't a Muslim, which meant I couldn't marry her—not because Islam forbade it, but because Muslims around me would censure me. And even if she *was* a Muslim, she was clearly wack, which would lead people to impute her wackness onto me.

Still, when she left the student center, I followed after her. When she turned into a lecture hall, I stepped closer to read the sign on the door. It was a student forum on women and religion. Interesting, I thought, and went in and sat down next to her, my heart racing, my conscience guilty, my body tingling.

She saw me looking at her and smiled. "My name is Kara," she said, extending her hand.

I mumbled my name and stared at her hand—a lovely hand that Western manners would have me hold but that Islam forbade me to touch. It would take the fire of *jahannum* to erase the sin of shaking that hand. As for looking her in the eyes, I had to avoid that as well, because that would lead to a temptation one couldn't resist.

"I don't shake hands," I said, with eyes downcast. "I'm sorry."

"It's fine," she said, retracting but not offended. "I thought you might not. I grew up with Muslims. I'm Lebanese . . . but Christian."

"Like Khalil Gibran?"

"You know the poet?" she asked, thoroughly pleased.

"I read his book *The Prophet* last month." Then I recited a verse I remembered: "For even as love crowns you he shall crucify you. Even as he is for your growth so is he for your pruning.'" I didn't tell her that I'd read the book because I thought it was written by a Muslim and had been disappointed to find out that he was Christian.

"That's my favorite line!" she exclaimed.

"Mine too."

Then we became quiet as if we had each confessed a tremendous secret.

I was relieved when another student rose and introduced the forum. For an hour or more I sat thinking of Kara as ideas about women and religion were exchanged around me. I didn't contribute anything to the discussion, but she talked several times, each comment revealing both character and intelligence.

"I'm going to go over to the cafeteria for a burger," she said when the forum was over. "Want to come?"

"Sure," I said, overriding my own intentions. "I'll have some fries and a shake."

Worried that a Muslim might see me with an immodest girl, I led her toward the back of the cafeteria. Still, despite the paranoia, I was sure that I wanted to be in her company. She was beautiful and intelligent and I wanted to impress her. As we ate, we talked about Islam. Our eyes kept connecting throughout the meal, and her easy smile made my heart beat faster. After we finished eating, we walked around the city, sharing a cup of *chai* at a Starbucks and another one at a Suheir Hammad poetry reading at NYU. Hours later we came to a stop at the university gym, where we planned on parting ways.

We stood looking at one another for a long moment. Then, just as I was about to walk away, Kara grabbed onto the buttons of my coat.

"Amir?"

"Yes."

"I have to tell you something."

"Yes?"

' "When his wings enfold you, yield to him, though the sword hidden among his pinions may wound you.' "

I stood dumbstruck. I recognized the words as a verse from Gibran. It was from the same section—Love—as the one I had quoted. The verse plummeted into some unexplored part of me like a pebble thrown into a lake from a great height. All this time in New York I had felt so lonely. Now here was a Gibran-quoting beauty who understood Muslims and was interested in religion. I felt an overwhelming desire to touch her. I wanted to make her mine. I wanted to kiss her mouth and taste Levantine leaves.

Yet I couldn't bring myself to do it. As she moved closer, I pulled away. I invoked Islam and Muslims and marriage and responsibility and the tortures of hell. Then I turned and ran in the other direction, chanting the Verse of the Throne as loudly as I could.

I left a broken button behind.

A few days later I went to an MSA meeting in the prayer hall. The brothers—sincere, severe, serious—sat in a semicircle facing the window, with me at one end. The sisters—soft secretive silhouettes—made a semicircle on the opposite side. The brothers actively looked away from the sisters so that everyone could see how hard they were trying to avoid getting tempted and ending up in hell. The sisters adjusted their *hijab*s to cover as much of them as possible so that everyone could see how hard they were trying to make sure they didn't inadvertently send brothers to the fire.

Just as the meeting began, the door was flung open and in walked Kara. She didn't have on a *chador* or a scarf. In fact, she was wearing tight jeans and a tank top. Her breasts were prominent, the cleavage at least as deep as the Prophet's trench around Medina. She walked over and sat down on the floor next to me.

"Hey, you," she said, bumping shoulders and smiling.

I was filled with dread. I scrunched away as if she were diseased. Her presence and her close proximity were reprehensible. I knew that the MSA sisters would look at us and assign her immodesty to me. The brothers, meanwhile, would act like nothing had happened, which was worse.

For a few tense minutes I tried to remain composed. Then, unable to bear the weight of eyes that consciously averted themselves, I asked Kara to step outside with me.

"You coming here was a very bad idea," I said, once we'd escaped into the hallway.

"I'm sorry," she said. "I just had to see you."

"You need to go," I ordered, punching the down button on the elevator to expedite her departure.

When the summoned car arrived, she stepped inside and the steel doors closed between us, while I went back to the meeting, took my seat, and remained very quiet. I knew—as did everyone around me—that I didn't deserve to be included. Feeling ashamed, I left the meeting early and went back to my dorm.

Locked in my room, I stood beside the window and looked out at the rowdy couples on the street flirting on a Friday night. With a mixture of fear and disgust, I watched people going in and out of a pub across the way—some staggering out drunk. There was a group of scantily clad women going into a Thai restaurant, followed by a young man with his hand on the small of a girl's back. All of these immodest sights and sounds seemed to be purposefully joined in a conspiracy against my faith. I could see what I had always suspected: behind everyday life in America lay temptation, lay the demonic beckoning of freedom; it curled out of the sewers, splashed down from the skies, and infused itself into each human body. I was witnessing the slow but steady imperialism of secular life. It was insidious because it wrapped itself in sex. I was being chased by women now the way Moosa Farid had been chased by homosexuals when he first got to campus. It was horrible.

I sat on my bed and cursed Kara. She had been irresponsible, coming into the meeting like that. Stupid non-Muslim girl! She didn't understand what was at stake. Nothing less than the future of Islam! She didn't understand what a meticulously crafted and fragile shadow this Muslim man truly was. She didn't understand that Islam was in a war, not just for its own integrity, but on behalf of all monotheism. Why did she make me want her? It must be because she didn't respect me, the way all of Western culture didn't respect Muslims.

The more I thought, the drowsier I became. Willing to drown my depression in sleep, I closed my eyes. Instead of darkness, I saw Kara—and I wanted her. I could picture her in my bed. I could imagine myself in bed with her. Clutching my sheets, I moaned into my pillow. I wanted to pick up the phone and tell her that I was coming over.

Suddenly tears formed in my eyes—tears of guilt and penance. Soon I was weeping, and I couldn't stop myself. I did what I had only read about: I cried myself to sleep.

When I woke up the next morning, everything was inexplicably clear: Abu Bakr Ramaq needed a pious Muslim wife. Otherwise, he would commit fornication and no longer be worthy of serving the religion.

# 6

Her name was Bilqis. I met her—where else?—on AOL, in an Islam chat during a theological spat between various sects. She was bored by the vitriol and wanted to talk to someone who knew Islam at a higher level. Enter yours truly. I made a few jokes. Invoked a few famous scholars. Told her about the spiritual war between Islam and secularism. We started e-mailing. She sent me a picture. I sent her mine. I decided that she was good-looking enough to be a good wife for me.

Bilqis hadn't been my first choice, though, because she didn't wear *hijab*. In the biographical sketch that I had once painted in Moosa Farid's company, my dream wife had to wear *hijab*. That's why, before Bilqis, I had first courted a *hijabi* named Selena. Unfortunately, things hadn't worked out with her. We had spent a lovely day together, sharing conversation and those ubiquitous Starbucks drinks—which she let me pay for—and then she had dropped me at my dorm when her boyfriend showed up. I had been left staring at her from my window with Moosa Farid reminding me, "You got played by a ho-*jabi*."

Actually, Bilqis wasn't my second choice either, because she lived far away, and I knew this would make it difficult to see her. In fact, after Selena but before Bilqis, I had courted a lovely, dark-haired Pakistani (who was contemplating putting on the *hijab*) due solely to her proximity. The problem with her was that I discovered she wrote poetry, and I—being an occasional poet myself—knew that poets were mentally unstable. I didn't want a crazy person to become the eventual mother of my children. So she had been vetoed.

Thus Bilqis became, through the process of elimination, my soulmate. Insert here images of burgeoning flowers, rambunctious rainbows, *abaya*-wearing cupids shooting arrows tipped with red crescents, and an Islamic wedding procession (without music, of course).

Whenever I had enough money, I traveled to see her: we tended to meet for a couple of hours every few months at a train station midway, where we sat on benches opposite one another so that we wouldn't feel tempted to commit *zina*.

"When are you going to tell your parents about us?" I asked her one day. "You need to be my wedded wife to protect my Islam."

"I can't tell them. My father would ship me back to the village we're from."

"Why?" I asked, surprised that I wouldn't be seen as marriage material.

"We haven't done things properly," she explained.

"What does that mean?"

"It means that we shouldn't have found each other."

"How should we have met, then?"

"Through destiny."

"Wasn't it destiny that we were in the same chat room at the same time?" I asked, smiling.

"Destiny means that, rather than you and I choosing one another, our parents should have created the conditions for our meeting. Everything arranged."

"Well, that's not what happened," I retorted. "Is there a way to solve this?"

Bilqis nodded and laid out a multi-step backup plan that would satisfy her parents and allow us to achieve our goal of marital union. It was as follows:

(a) The first goal was for us to become like strangers to one another, because if her parents became aware that we'd been in close proximity with one another, they would assume that we had fornicated. This would lead them to ship her off to a village in the old country, or to punish her (and me) by marrying her to an old and ugly cousin in Germany.

(b) I had to inform my parents that I wanted to marry a girl and get their approval. This had to be achieved without my parents learning that I'd had preexisting contact with Bilqis. The onus was on me to achieve this feat.

(c) Once I'd received approval from my parents, they—out of the blue—had to call Bilqis's parents and have a conversation about something mundane, such as the weather. The aim of this call would be to signal to her parents that there was a family out there in the world who had heard about their daughter completely by chance and wanted to ask for her hand in marriage for their son.

(d) At this point, Bilqis and I had to wait and pray that simply on the basis of that conversation about the weather, her family would invite my family over to their house for tea. This step required intervention from Allah because:

  i. Only divine fiat would ensure that her family didn't think the proposal was for Bilqis's older unmarried sister or older unmarried cousin.

  ii. Only divine fiat would ensure that the hearsay inquiry her parents would launch—into my character, my religiosity, my job security, my looks, my parents' religiosity, my earning potential, my family's gross and net income, the divorce record in my extended family, the skin color of the children born in my extended family, and the ratio of boys to girls born in my family—would produce results that would satisfy her parents.

  iii. Only divine fiat would ensure that two families who didn't live anywhere near one another would see fit to ignore geography.

(e) Finally, a look at our respective heritages would have to reveal that Bilqis and I were ethnically compatible. Due to the ravages of colonialism, with its divide-and-conquer legacy, as well as general Muslim bigotry, most Muslim races were incompatible with one another. Whether or not we would indeed be declared ethnically compatible depended on such things as her father's mood and his prior history with other ethnicities.

I eagerly went through the checklist with Bilqis. "I think we've got it covered," I concluded.

"No," Bilqis said sadly, stuck on the final point. "I just remembered that my father hates Punjabis."

"But I'm Punjabi," I said, feeling as hurt as if I'd been struck.

"My father says they oppress everyone in Pakistan."

"What does he care? He's not even Pakistani!"

"Oh, he cares. He says that the only people who are allowed to oppress one another are pure races, and Punjabis aren't pure."

"But no one is racially pure anymore!"

"Maybe not, but he particularly dislikes Punjabis. He says they're cowards for not using the nuke on Islam's enemies."

"What are you talking about? We produced Zia ul Haq and Nawaz Sharif. They imposed Islam on everyone."

"Won't work."

"So that's it? We're screwed?"

She sighed. "We could have hidden and hoodwinked everything, but ethnicity. . ."

I could see our marriage slipping from my fingers. I could see myself calling Kara and having intercourse with her.

"There are powers greater than ethnicity," I said.

"Like what?"

"Love!" I declared. "I'll tell your father I love you!"

"There is no love," she said. "Love is just when you pick one person and don't pick anybody else afterwards."

"What if we eloped?"

"I would be disowned," she replied, shaking her head dismissively. "My family would refuse to acknowledge me in the community."

"We could emotionally blackmail them—have a child as soon as possible and show up at their door with our little bundle of joy."

"That would work only on my mother. My dad would refuse to greet the child."

We sat in silence, hoping for inspiration. "What now?" I asked finally.

"We go our separate ways and hope that our parents will run into one another someday."

"How can you be so callous?" I asked, offended by her suggestion. "Don't you know that you're my soulmate!"

"I'm *not* callous," she said. "I'm hurting."

"No. I can't accept this," I concluded. "There actually *is* something higher than love."

"What's that?"

"Islam! The Prophet said that Islam stands above and beyond ethnicity. I heard it from Moosa Farid. I think there's even a verse about it in the Quran. About how God made us into tribes and stuff only for the sake of diversity."

"So?"

I explained that I would go to Moosa and ask him to help me make a long list of scholars and citations affirming Islamic universalism. With his help, I would show that Islam was beyond race. I would raise myself to such levels of Islamic piety and leadership that Bilqis's father would be hard-pressed to reject me. I'd become friends with all the main scholars of American Islam—Mukhtar Maghraoui, Hamza Yusuf, and Zaid Shakir—if that's what it took. I'd take all three of them with me to talk to her father directly. "In short," I said. "I'll show him that xenophobia is un-Islamic."

Bilqis smiled. She knew the persuasive power of religion. "Fine. So we are going to do things the Islamic way?"

"That's right," I said, puffing out my chest.

"Then that means we have to start behaving Islamically."

"What do you mean?"

"Well, it means that we can't touch one another."

"I don't think you've noticed," I said, "but we already don't touch."

"I know. But that's because we're reluctant and shy. Now we have to not touch for the sake of Islam. Our intentions have to be Islamic."

"Can do."

"Wait," she added. "It's going to be hard to stick to this rule if we keep meeting."

"Fine. We'll keep in touch via phone and e-mail."

"Thing is, if we keep hearing each other's voice—"

"—right, we'll become tempted to melt, like butter melts on a fire."

"So let's just talk on AOL."

"All right. Just that."

"Finally we're doing things properly," my soulmate said, exhaling loudly as if for emphasis. "By not staying in touch we have a shot at getting married."

In order to find Islamic scholars that might vouch for me with Bilqis's father, I started attending lectures around New York. One day Moosa and I went to see a prominent African teacher who was giving a lecture near Harlem titled "The Conditions of *Jihad*." He was considered very pious, and I really wanted to get him on my side.

The lecture was given in an old cathedral that was full of college students and young professionals. The seats were split down the center, as you'd expect for this speaker: women on one side and men on the other. The talk itself wasn't what I expected, though. No geopolitical jargon. Nothing about America or Israel. Just the macrocosmic relationship between striving on behalf of your religion in this life and success in the hereafter. The *shaykh* said that all military *jihad* was forbidden unless it was a defensive war waged by a government, and added that the highest form of *jihad* was against the temptations of the flesh.

When the lecture ended various petitioners crowded around the podium to talk with the *shaykh*. I got in line as well, but ahead of me was a large group of women. It turned out that in addition to classical jurisprudence and the rules of war, the *shaykh* was also a bit of an expert on women's issues.

"You gotta wonder if the *shaykh* takes advantage of the fact that he's surrounded by all these women all the time," I said to Moosa as we waited.

"Are you kidding?" Moosa exclaimed. He had read about this particular *shaykh*, apparently. "His new wife is eighteen!"

"What do you mean *new*?"

"He likes to upgrade. This is his fourth. You blame him? Look at the options he's got."

I looked over at the group of sisters. Each one was more buxom and full-bottomed than the next.

Something didn't compute here. Divorce was frowned upon by Islam, yet no one seemed to care that this *shaykh* did it often.

"Isn't divorce a sin?" I asked.

"Well, it's only *makruh*," Moosa replied. "That means it's neutral. God won't like it if you do it, but he won't penalize you. The Prophet's grandson Hasan married and divorced seventy-one women in his life."

"That's hard to imagine!"

"The brother was popular. Fathers would offer their daughters. He couldn't decline. It's probably like that for this guy too."

I looked at the *shaykh* with new admiration. His piety had to be truly immense if he was able to get away with numerous divorces. And here I was having trouble with just one marriage! I prayed for the day to arrive when I could be as pious as he was so that I could do things that would otherwise be questioned.

As I stood in line, a sudden commotion broke out behind us. An excitable congregant was shouting that since America used satellites to send sexual images and pro-Israel propaganda into Muslim countries, this qualified as a declaration of war, and therefore it was incumbent on Muslim scholars like the *shaykh* to announce *jihad* against America. A couple of older congregants tried to shout down the bellicose man for being a fool, but the man called them apostates and continued his tirade. Eventually the matter had to be referred to the *shaykh*.

Which meant I had to leave without getting a reference.

Bilqis and I decided that we would give ourselves until senior year before we talked to our parents. By then I would have had a chance to spend a couple of summers at Middlebury College, where I hoped to become fluent in Arabic; and that, in turn, would raise my Islamic credentials. The three-year delay would give us enough time to garner support among New York's Islamic intelligentsia. I also thought it would give me enough time to convince Bilqis to wear *hijab*.

Then something happened that caused us to accelerate our plans. His name was Yahya.

He was an older Pathan man from Bilqis's community who'd had his sights set on Bilqis for years. He'd been planning to go to her father and get permission to marry her as soon as she reached marital age. However, when he heard rumors that Bilqis had found some guy in New York, he flipped his lid. He started sending me threatening instant messages.

"What's up, punk?"

"Who is this?" I responded.

"Your worst nightmare."

"Do you have a name?"

"You know me, bitch. My name is Yahya. You stole my wife-to-be. I'm about to get all *pakhtunkhwa* on you."

"I don't know what that means," I typed honestly.

"Maybe you should ask someone who knows."

I called Moosa at his work.

"*Pakhtunkhwa* is an honor code," he informed me. "It basically means that you're going to die. Who told you about it?"

"Some guy that's been after Bilqis."

"That sucks," Moosa said. "Well, can I get your Quran MP3s before you're killed?"

"This is serious," I said, frustrated by a new obstacle between me and Islamically sanctioned sex. "Mother fuck me!"

"I don't think Islam allows that," Moosa quipped. "Although Khomeini said that if you were walking along your roof and fell down and your penis entered your mother, it wouldn't be considered incest under Islam."

"Well, that's a relief," I said. "But what if before pulling out you thrust a couple of times, because during the fall you became disoriented and thought you had entered your wife?"

"Good question. I'll have to ask a scholar about this."

"Anyway. Back to the important problem at hand," I said.

"I think you should scare this chump away."

"Threaten him?"

"Yeah."

"With what? Punjabis aren't warriors."

"Tell him that you challenge him to a *bhangra* duel," he suggested.

"What if he says that dancing is un-Islamic. Then he's got another way to diss me."

"Point taken."

"God," I said—almost a prayer. "I really don't want to die yet. I'm still a virgin."

"Look at the upside," Moosa said cheerily. "In Islam a murdered man is a martyr. That means you'll get seventy-two girls in Paradise."

"But I don't have any sexual experience. I wouldn't be able to please them."

"All right, then why don't you tell this guy that his code of honor is *haram* because it's rooted in un-Islamic tribalism."

That seemed like an amazing idea. Declaring things un-Islamic was always the safest way of winning an argument.

"It's not a permanent fix," Moosa cautioned, "but it should put him on the defensive."

"This whole Bilqis thing is getting out of hand," I said. "You know that book by Kurban Said that we read?"

"*Ali and Nino*? The one about the Muslim guy and Christian girl in Azerbaijan?"

"Yeah. I should just kidnap Bilqis the way Ali did Nino."

"You don't have a horse, though. I think it's tradition to use a horse."

"We could rent a Mustang."

"This is going to be so cool," Moosa yelped. "Can I perform your service?"

"Definitely. But after my service, where will I go to get it on with my wife? Didn't the Prophet say in a *hadith* that you have to play with your virgin?"

"He did. How about you rent one of those sleeping cars in an Amtrak train? That way if you get followed you can evade her family."

"What if during wedding night she's on her period?"

"I keep telling you to read Imam Ghazali. He says that if your virgin is periodic you should put a silk cloth on her privates and rub her until she orgasms. It's an Islamic duty for a man to pleasure his wife."

"Our scholars really knew their sex, didn't they?"

"There's a reason we should follow their precedence!"

"Yeah, man," I said after some reflection. "I'm not going to abduct anyone. It's illegal. Besides, I've got midterms coming up."

"Me too."

After hanging up, I turned back to the computer and started chatting with Yahya the way Moosa had suggested. I brought up all sorts of Islamic references and chose three of my favorite Islamic sayings. They would demonstrate that I was a scholar, not a fighter:

- The ink of the scholar is holier than the blood of the martyr.
- Search for knowledge even if it takes you to China.
- God loves nothing more than a pious youth.

Invoking Islam had the intended effect. Yahya became nervous. "Do you study Islam or something?" he asked.

"Yes," I typed. "I'm becoming a scholar."

"Damn. I had no idea! My bad, bro! I thought you were just some player going after Bilqis. I see that I was very wrong. I'm sorry for misjudging your character."

"Not a problem," I responded, smiling to myself, and then I proceeded to type out some pointers about better etiquette.

That night, buzzing on the power of Islam, I decided that I wasn't going to wait three years before telling my parents. If Islam could defeat vengeful ex-boyfriends, it could definitely persuade my parents.

# 7

G uess what? I've found a wife."

Back in Alabama for spring break that freshman year, I told Ammi and Pops the news over dinner. We were having *qeema* with *roti* and a side dish of curried zucchini.

"Excuse me?" said Ammi.

"He thinks someone actually wants to marry him," Flim said, ever the younger brother.

"There's a girl named Bilqis that I met. I want to marry her."

Pops cleared his throat ominously. "How old is this lady?" he asked, unwilling to attach a name to her.

"Eighteen—and I'd prefer it if you'd use her name: Bilqis."

"I see. Is this lady older than you?"

"A little, yes."

"This isn't a good idea," he said.

"Why?"

"Where we come from, men are five years less mature than women."

I couldn't accept such a trivial rebuke. I looked toward Ammi for support, but she didn't say anything.

"How old are you again?" Pops asked me.

"Seventeen."

"The thing about marrying young," continued Pops, "is that it takes away your ambition. Better to *become* someone before you marry."

This was the moment: I knew I had to invoke Islam in order to acquire mastery of the situation. "You people are aware that in Islam marriage is considered half the faith, right? There's a *hadith* about that point. I can show it to you in the books."

"Islam is between you and God," Pops said. "Why are you involving us?"

I was surprised by this statement. Until now Islam had been between all of us.

"Because I need your help. You're my parents. It's your Islamic duty to help me out. Bilqis's parents require that you call them to make arrangements and do everything in the Islamic way."

"I don't agree with that approach," Pops said, pushing food around on his plate. "I think they should call us."

"They won't, though. Bilqis said her family doesn't like Punjabis."

Pops scoffed loudly. Then Ammi scoffed. They were both insulted.

"You say you want us to abide by Islam," Ammi said, "but *they* aren't being very decent, are they?"

"Don't want Punjabis? We don't want them!" Pops thundered.

I stood up. "But I want *her*!"

"Forget it. We have dignity."

"Do this for my Islam. If I don't marry, I'll end up fornicating!" I stomped to my bedroom, convinced that my parents weren't taking me seriously.

I could hear Ammi and Pops arguing loudly in the kitchen, blaming each other for my hasty—and clearly faulty—choice in a potential mate. When they started blaming Bilqis for trying to steal their son, I was so upset at hearing my beloved's name besmirched that I stormed back into the kitchen and upturned the dinner trays. I flipped one tray too hard and everything splattered on my chest. My dignity shot, I retreated back to my room.

For a couple of hours the house was almost silent. Occasionally Flim could be heard walking up and down the hall, but that was it.

Eventually Ammi and Pops must have reconciled, because they came to my room together and knocked quietly.

"This Bilqis must be very pretty," Pops said once they were in and seated on the narrow bed.

"She is."

"You know who else is pretty?" Ammi asked. "Mountain girls. From Kashmir. Your father has a friend who has a daughter. Such rosy cheeks."

"I don't want a Kashmiri girl. I want Bilqis."

"This Kashmiri girl I'm telling you about looks like that actress—the one with the rosy cheeks."

"I prefer Bilqis."

"Son, let me tell you a story about mountain girls," Pops said, taking over. "I had this uncle. Big guy. He died before you were born. He was scary. One time he threatened to beat up a guy and the guy defecated in his own clothes. Anyway, this uncle's first wife died, so he went to Peshawar and he paid a Pathan and bought a young wife. Do you remember the stone-faced widow that lived near Dada Abu?"

"Are you suggesting that we *buy* Bilqis?"

"No. I'm suggesting that we buy a mountain girl that looks better because the dollar-rupee exchange is pretty good these days!" Pops said with a wink.

I realized that I was being mocked. My love trivialized. My feelings stomped upon. I actually began crying. Then I pulled myself together and made one final appeal to Islam. "Why can't you do things properly? Just call her parents, please. Where is your Islam?"

"So you want to do things the Islamic way?" Pops asked.

"Nothing more."

"There's a verse in the Quran which says that if your parents punish you, accept it, without so much as saying 'Uff.'"

"I know it," I said.

"Good. Because your punishment for getting into this stupid relationship is that you're going to transfer out of your college in Manhattan for a college in the South."

"No!" I exclaimed, horrified.

"You'll do it this summer," he said firmly. "I don't want to hear the slightest rebellion from you. The Quran prohibits you from disobeying your parents—and remember, you claim to be very Islamic."

"How can you do this?" I pleaded. "Please. This is despotism!"

Pops didn't waver. "What did your Ibn Taymiya say? A thousand days of despotism are better than one day of anarchy? Don't be an anarchist. Listen to your despotic father. That is Islam, after all."

That night was torture. I felt stars crashing around my head, and the sliver of the moon sliced my arteries open. I opened a copy of the Quran and cried into it. Bilqis was to have been my wall between the secularity outside and the Islam within. She was supposed to be my protection. I felt vulnerable.

As I lay weeping, there was a soft knock and Ammi came inside. She took my hand and brushed my face. "Don't worry about marriage. We'll visit Pakistan for the summer and see if we can find you a nice wife there." Then she kissed me and left.

When I returned to Manhattan I was terribly upset at having to give up Bilqis, though I did as my father ordered and called her to break things off. A day or two later it occurred to me that if I went to an Islamic country to find a wife, as Ammi had suggested, the girl wouldn't need to be convinced to wear *hijab* as Bilqis had to be. In fact, I might even find someone who wore the full *niqab*.

The possibility of upgrading from Bilqis filled me with excitement. If I had a *niqabi* wife, my piety quotient would be off the charts—I could even take multiple wives without anyone batting an eye.

Another advantage in going to Pakistan was that I could take some time to investigate my lineage to the first Caliph.

Suddenly the world was conspiring on behalf of my Islam.

# 8

Pops had to work so it was just me, Ammi, and Flim on the trip. We argued a lot during the planning stage about which airline to take. The clearest sign that a Pakistani immigrant had made it in America was when he returned in a foreign air carrier, but since we hadn't, we ended up taking Pakistan International Airlines to Karachi.

As I looked around me on the plane, I saw that the greater part of the passengers were working-class—rugged and worn from driving cabs and filling tanks on turnpikes, serving as cooks in *desi* restaurants named Shalimar. They laughed and joked the whole way because they were going home. For them America was simply a work station. It could just as easily be Dubai, Australia, or England. They were going back with paychecks that were meager in America but in Pakistan ballooned from the exchange rate. They looked forward to giving their families a chance to buy nice things. Maybe an AC for an aged mother. Maybe wedding clothes for a niece.

Others in the plane were like us. The quiet and morose bunch. We were the ones that had gone to the United States in order to make money *and* make a home—and had found that getting a paycheck in America was far easier than feeling a part of the country. Now, neither fully American nor fully Pakistani, we called ourselves Muslims and hoped that religion was enough to identify us in a world full of nations.

I didn't like where I was sitting. There were three college-aged girls in front of me. They wore jeans and short T-shirts, and each time they reached for something, I could see a span of waist and bare back. Immodest sluts, I thought. Why couldn't they be more like the girl sitting to my right? She was a pretty girl wrapped fully in a black *chador*. I wondered why the brazen types couldn't see how much more grace the girl in the *chador* had. I almost nudged Ammi, seated to my left, and pointed at the modest girl as a potential wife.

My proximity to the slutty girls caused piety to bubble up protectively inside me. I went off to join the Islamic mile-high club and prayed in the corridor near the kitchenette.

When I returned to my seat, I pulled my book from my carry-on: *The Life of Muhammad,* by Martin Lings. I had read it many times before, but this time I was focused on trying to memorize the names of the forgotten companions—men like Najiyyah the camel driver and Abu Dujanah, who wore a red hat during battle.

After some memory work in that book, I also pulled out Muhammad Asad's memoir, *The Road to Mecca.* It told the story of how Leopold Weiss, an Austrian Jew, converted to Islam after living with Saudi Bedouins and King Abdul Aziz at the beginning of the century. As I ruminated on the book, I recalled that Asad had eventually left Arabia and moved to Pakistan, where he became its first ambassador to the United Nations. Asad believed that Islam was the greatest force mankind had ever experienced. He thought that if Muslims could live their life guided by the "spark of flame which burned in the Companions of the Prophet," they would always be successful.

Getting up again to stretch, I walked up and down the aisles and thought about the idea of Pakistan. There was something empowering about it. In a world where there were so few examples of Muslims making anything, the creation of a nation-state, yanked from the smoldering ruins of colonialism and two world wars, snatched from the British Empire and the Hindu majority of India, established in the name of Islam and then sanctified by a migration that was comparable to the Prophet

Muhammad's flight to Medina, seemed like a massive accomplishment. Pakistan was an act of sovereignty carried out so that Muslims could pursue the purpose of life: worshipping God. Suddenly I felt honored to be a Muslim and honored to be going to Pakistan.

As the plane approached Karachi's Jinnah Airport, I hurried toward to my seat to buckle up. As I zoomed past the bathroom, I met up with the gaggle of immodest girls that had been sitting in front of me, recognizing them by their giggles. I instinctively drew away from them—even the slightest touch against them would have to be burned off by hellfire—before noticing that they'd switched into modest *shalwar kameez*es with full *dupatta*s covering their chests.

I was pleased by their change. It was a testament to the positive influence that an Islamic state had upon misguided believers.

We stepped onto the tarmac and wilted in the heat. Karachi's brownish pollution was palpable against my face. It singed the nose hair when inhaled and left an unpleasant taste on the back of the tongue. Despite the smog, old men—home at last!—puffed out their chests and inhaled deeply as they tumbled down the steps.

Inside the terminal we were greeted by my paternal Uncle Saad. He was a high-ranking officer in the military, which meant that he had an army of pages, servants, butlers, bodyguards, and drivers. At the airport he was able to press every porter, customs agent, visa inspection officer, and street urchin into service.

"Give your passports to me," he said to Ammi. Then he turned to one of his servants: "Get these stamped! Hurry up, you slow sonofabitch!" He ordered another servant to intercept our luggage before it made its way to the baggage carts. As the servant ran off, one of the bodyguards made a backhand and pretended to slap him. Uncle Saad saw the soldier's gesture and lashed out. "You fool! You think you're big time? Go bring drinks. Pepsi. Don't bring uncapped bottles like you did last time."

Uncle Saad led us past long lines winding into the customs office and herded us toward a special corridor for families with "connections." As we passed the people we'd flown in with, now pushing against each other in congested lines, cursing and swearing, or sweet-talking the self-important officers, I felt a sense of superiority. I didn't have to go through all that headache because I was connected to the military.

As I thought about it, though, that privilege made me uneasy; it filled me with guilt. Privilege was un-Islamic. I had read that the great Caliphs Umar al-Khattab and Harun al-Rashid used to dress up as common people and go through the city streets to feel part of the crowd. Similarly, one of the Companions of the Prophet used to put his servant on his camel and walk him through the streets. I'd read that Abu Bakr Siddiq had been so humble that he slept on the floor. The privilege and the hierarchy that the military imposed in Karachi seemed to contradict these stories from Islamic history.

This wasn't the way that an Islamic country was supposed to work.


Uncle Saad lived with his family in one of the designated military suburbs. It was a colony unto itself, with its own mosque, school, water treatment facility, market, and *tandoor,* and even the donkey carts that brought the vegetables served only the military. Uncle Saad and his wife were both educated and looked to Pops as a role model, because he had been able to get to America and was having his children educated there. When they saw me taking my books out of my bag the first afternoon we were there, they harangued me with questions about my "estudies."

I was perplexed by the zeal with which they wanted to emulate academics in the West. I wanted to ask them if they knew that a secular education was corrosive and corrupting to Islam.

The house was approximately a hundred yards from the mosque, where the *azan* was sung five times a day to announce the time for prayer. Yet I noticed that no one in the colony went to make regular prayers. The mosque seemed to be little more than a decoration that no one had much interest in.

At the house the TV stayed on most of the day. Every channel was from either mainland India or Dubai. Many stations featured music videos with scantily clad girls or songs full of innuendo. The VJs were all Western in behavior and clothing, and everyone was trying to out-MTV one another.

One day Uncle Saad took us for a tour of the colony and then to his base, where he put special emphasis on showing us the Officers' Mess—a sparse, English-style dining hall with antique tables, solid chairs, and finely engraved china with insignias etched into the bottom. I saw a table of wine glasses in a corner and asked him what it was for.

"Lots of the people on base drink," he said.

"Is it just the high-ranking people who drink?" I asked, "or does everyone?"

He thought for a moment. "Mostly it's just the top officers."

The notion that the foot soldiers and lower-level officers didn't drink gave me a modicum of comfort—it was nice that they weren't getting westernized. I resolved to talk with some of the lower-level officers and ask them how they allowed themselves to serve Muslims who drank.

One evening a military van with two machine-gun-bearing Pathan soldiers in the backseat picked us up and took us all to the commercial area, to go to an open-air restaurant on top of a ten-story hotel that seemed to cater to upper-middle-class families. When the restaurant attendant realized that we were from America, he started throwing in English words, and everything became "simply the . . ." The *daal* was "simply the best." The *naan* was "simply the fluffiest." The *biryani* was "simply the tastiest." His colonialized mentality disgusted me. He should have demanded that we speak his language, not the other way around. Muslims had to be proud of who they were.

As he led us to our seat, I saw massive piles of red *tandoori* chicken, and *kharay masalay ka gosht,* and chicken *jalfrezi*. At least the food is native, I thought.

We were seated across from a musical ensemble featuring a middle-aged guy with oily hair who took requests from the diners. He belted out old-school *ghazal*s as well as songs made popular by Michael Jackson and Frank Sinatra. I felt angry with him for bringing these Western songs into Pakistani society. Music itself was *haram,* and good Muslims ought not listen to it at all. But if people were indeed going to listen to music, then they should listen to their own and not try to copy the West.

I felt increasingly uncomfortable. Why was this establishment ignoring Islam? Wasn't Islam why this nation had been created? Yet people's attitudes, their definition of fun, the mix-gendered seating, the complete absence of Islamic rituals—all this was striking. It occurred to me that these people were thoroughly secularized, and that saddened me.

By the time we finally returned home from dinner, the Islam inside me was gasping for air. It seemed as if everything Karachiites did led them away from religion. Why did they pay so much attention to cricket, for example? It was a mindless sport that wasted the mind and kept people from worshipping God. Why did some of the programming on TV feature a mixture of Urdu and English—and more important, why had Pakistanis made English an official language? This was an Islamic country, wasn't it? The only official language should've been Arabic, the language of the Quran.

That night I dug into my books and found the gleaming orange cover of *The History of Islamic Philosophy,* by Majid Fakhry. Just holding the book restored some of my security. Opening its pages, I read about Imam Ashari, who vanquished the Rationalists; and al-Ishraqi, the founder of Illuminationism, a non-rational Islamic theology; and al-Ghazali, who vanquished the Philosophers; and Ibn Taymiya, who showed that Muslims didn't need logic because it was a Greek invention. I glanced through all the authentic Arabic and Persian scholars over history, and finding the name of Iqbal, the spiritual founder of Pakistan, at the very end of that list, gave me a sense of comfort. It proved that Pakistan was part of the long, flowing river of Islam—indeed, its culmination.

I concluded that Pakistanis who weren't true to this history weren't being true to themselves.

* * *

The next night Uncle Saad took us to a big-time party at a superior's house. The event was like something out of *90210* or *Melrose Place*. There were gleaming cars outside the enormous house, and servants in pressed uniforms ran around addressing every need. The event itself was in the garden, where food was served under white tents. Outside the tents there were countless round tables, laid out banquet style with fine china, and courteous waiters. The garden was stunning in its lushness, its damp geometry, and its crisply trimmed edges. Roses of all colors, as well as long rows of *chambayli*s and numerous other flowers, were banked against the main house, which gave off a golden luminosity from the chandeliers inside.

The main event at the party was a game of bingo organized by a couple of professionals. They passed out bingo cards to anyone who was interested and then spun a huge wheel with great aplomb. Uncle Saad quickly picked up a card for himself and began playing.

I wandered away from the table and went toward a corner of the garden where some young people were milling about.

As I got near them I stopped in my tracks. The guys were all wearing Western clothes—dress shoes, pressed slacks, and crisp, collared shirts with ties. The girls were variously dressed in tight chiffon dresses, backless *shalwar kameeze*s, and knee-length skirts. I crinkled up my nose at their immodest attire.

As I turned away to head back in, I saw a face I recognized: it was the *chador*-clad girl from the airplane—the one I had found so beautiful in her modesty. Now she was wearing a pair of tight jeans and a skimpy tank top, cut off at the midriff to show off a diamond-encrusted navel ring. I could see one edge of her thong as she sashayed over toward the group of teenagers. She didn't seem to recognize me but gave me a nice smile anyway.

Feeling almost ill from the encounter—I felt she had betrayed all of Islam—I went to look for Ammi, who was off chatting with my aunt.

"Why don't we go to the desert?" I suggested. "We should go and see Dada Abu and Dadi Ma."

"I've been trying to persuade them to fly out here instead," she said. "It's a hellish trip to the desert."

"But there's nothing for us to do in Karachi," I said flatly.

"We're here to try to find you a good girl to marry. Uncle Saad told me he's informed some of his colleagues that we're looking. You're an American citizen, which should be a draw. You'll have plenty of luck here, I think. In fact, there are some girls over there," she said, pointing toward the group I'd just turned back from. "Go talk to them."

"Forget it," I said, feeling angry by the *chador*-girl turning into a secular whore. "Those are *not* the sort of girls I want."

"What are we talking about here?" Uncle Saad chimed in, joining his wife.

"He's talking about going to visit the desert," Ammi said.

"Why would you want to do that?" Uncle Saad asked. "Tell your grandparents to fly out here."

"I want to go to the desert," I said firmly, "because I can tell you now that I'm not going to like any of these city girls."

"You want to go to the desert?" Uncle Saad asked. "Then tell me— have you ever grown a beard?"

"I grew a scruffy one at college," I said. "Pops told me to shave it off before we flew here. Why?"

"If you want to go to the desert," he said, "you'll have to grow a long one."

"But why?"

"Those people over there: they aren't like they used to be. If you don't have a beard, they'll beat you up."

"I don't understand."

"They say that men should wear a beard," he explained, "because that's what Islam says."

I found nothing wrong with that. "Well, they're right," I said. "Islam does stipulate that men grow a beard. If you don't have a beard, you're not a good Muslim. There's a *hadith*—"

"If you aren't going to like a girl here," Ammi interrupted, with a bit of doubt creeping into her voice, "then maybe we *should* look elsewhere. Besides, your grandparents don't seem interested in flying out, and I'm feeling guilty about coming all the way to Pakistan and not seeing them. Maybe we should go up north."

I nodded eagerly. After hearing that in the desert the men were expected to grow a beard for religious reasons, it seemed like Sehra Kush was the type of place where people actually cared about Islam. I wanted to get there as soon as possible.

Within a week Ammi had purchased a *niqab* and the three of us were on a train.

I stroked my face and willed my youthful stubble to grow long like a true Muslim's.

# 9

Neither garlands nor fireworks announced our homecoming. We were welcomed to Dada Abu's house by a naked toddler named Usama who ran to the ledge above the courtyard and urinated on me as I entered. I should have considered it symbolic; instead I just purified myself with water.

Flim and I were quickly separated from Ammi as long-forgotten relatives streamed into the house and greeted us eagerly. Being able to speak Urdu, I was able to respond to them adequately, but they were disappointed by Flim's incomplete grasp of the language. He was so young when we left Pakistan that he remembered only fragments.

"What has America done to this boy!" an uncle complained, and I felt a pang of shame for being an American.

Ammi, meanwhile, wasn't feeling particularly sociable. Feeling dirty from the train ride, she wanted to freshen up, but the water had been shut off for three days. Except for a sun-warmed bucket of stale water, there was no clean water with which to wash up. She asked one of the cousins to go and purchase bottled water from the nearby pharmacy, only to find out on his return that the caps weren't sealed. She made a disparaging comment about the desert's backwardness, and I felt angry with her for insulting a place where people were not only religious but pious.

"You'd rather be in Karachi?" I asked.

"Yes," she answered curtly. "They have bottled water there."

"They're irreligious there. I'd rather have a clean soul than clean water."

"That's fine," Ammi replied. "Just know that you're about to get diarrhea."

"The Prophet lived in a desert just like this," I reminded her sternly. "Things worked out fine for him."

Ammi turned out to be right: I did get diarrhea. However, when I went to use the latrine in the ground, I didn't indict myself for drinking bad water. Instead, as I squatted down I remembered the way I used to squat in the rooster position at the *madrassa*. It occurred to me that I should have embraced my childhood beatings, because they prepared me to be more adept at using a latrine. I exhaled a *subhanallah*. It was amazing the way Islam was everywhere.

After making sure that I'd greeted everyone, I took a walk in my old alley. The entire block had changed. Dada Abu had bought the house that had once belonged to the Balochi people; he'd torn it down and remade it in solid cement, adding a blue metal gate. This was now the primary residence, where he lived with Dadi Ma and one of my uncles, along with the uncle's wife and six children. My other uncles lived in various houses scattered around the neighborhood. Uncle Saroor, who had taken two more wives after black magic Gina, lived directly across the street in a multi-story home, keeping each wife on a separate floor.

There were visible signs of material progress. The houses with the dung patties on the walls were gone. The alley was paved. The gutters were covered. The pungent *nali* smell was fainter. There were no cows or donkeys blocking the main square. The big empty lot that used to be full of trash and wandering cows taking plump dumps looked as if it had been bulldozed.

The desert had also discovered privacy. Everyone had erected huge walls around their roofs. This meant no more roof-hopping and no peeking into other people's lives. No one left their doors open during the daytime either; and no children ran from house to house, chasing chickens or stealing an egg or sitting down arbitrarily at someone else's breakfast table. There were virtually no people in the streets. Even when the *azan* occurred, I saw no increased signs of activity in the neighborhood.

It was Dada Abu who finally helped me understand the neighborhood's newfound obsession with secrecy.

"You shouldn't leave the house except with a grown male relative," he cautioned Flim and me. "And you," he said to Ammi, "shouldn't leave the house at all!"

"Why not?" I asked, disappointed.

"This place isn't safe," he said. "There are strangers here. Foreigners." He was referring to the countless new sectarian and militant groups that passed through town.

Then he stepped closer and inspected the length of my beard.

# 10

I hated staying at home with the women. What made it particularly irritating was that they didn't treat me like the other men: when I walked past them, they neither covered their face nor threw a *dupatta* over their head. I considered this nonchalance an affront to my masculinity, and I blamed my lack of a legitimate beard.

I wanted them to scurry before me and be fearful of unleashing my masculine hormones. Instead, they treated me like a child.

There was one woman who did exhibit a bit of self-conscious modesty—my cousin Nyla. Whenever I came near her, she tossed her *dupatta* over her head or turned a bit to the side so as not to make direct eye contact. This suggested to me that she was wary of the possibility of temptation arising between the two of us; naturally, I became attracted to her and started following her around.

I spied her from a distance one day when she was in the kitchen. She squatted on her *chowki* and thrust her small hands into sticky dough on a tray, her thin body rocking back and forth. The *chowki* squeaked and the steel tray skidded on the cement floor as she worked and rocked. Her cheap *chooriyan* clinked on her arms. They were her only adornments. As I watched, one of the *chooriyan* snapped. She pulled the broken pieces off her arm and placed them in her pocket so that the children wouldn't step on them.

Nyla was a domestic dervish. She was a master of the kitchen. When she was working, she was under constant assault by the toddlers, who seemed particularly fond of her. The miniature Mongols wandered back and forth and tried to stick their feet into the food or upturn the tray of cut radishes. She withstood their onslaught by offering them vegetable bribes and sweet-talk.

At night, when everyone had finished dinner, Nyla cleaned the dishes at the trickling faucet. When—more often than not—there was no running water, she had to pump the *nalka* from a seated position, which required a great deal of force. As she did the dishes, the rest of the family, women included, retired to their *charpai*s on the rooftop, leaving her downstairs in the dark, scrubbing the brass pots with a steel sponge. When she was finished with that chore, she still wasn't done: she walked through the house and straightened out all the scattered shoes and slippers. She paid special attention to those that were flipped over, since it was an insult against Allah for a shoe to be upside down. Seeing her respect for God, combined with her modesty toward me, I felt a great deal of admiration for her.

In the middle of her daily duties Nyla often retreated to her sparsely furnished upstairs bedroom. In it, there was a tiny *charpai* that was leaned up against the wall during the day to give her more space. There were a few boxes with crocheted covers. There was a sewing machine, usually draped with a new outfit she was putting together. There were a couple of copies of the Quran wrapped in thick cloth to prevent dust from gathering on them.

During the midday breaks to her room, Nyla didn't go to sleep or, as I initially imagined, write her frustrations into a diary. Instead, as I discovered one day when I peeked in, she wrapped an old white shawl around her body—and prayed on a mat. Her eyes were downcast as her thin lips murmured *surah Fatiha*. Her face was placid and serene, with a hint of water still visible on the upper lip.

The sparse beauty of her room, along with the quiet serenity of her prayer, filled me with a sense of dignity and decorum. This was a *real*

Muslim woman: pious and patient, dutiful and persevering. If anyone was going to benefit from my American citizenship, it should be her. I felt as if God had brought me to Pakistan to serve as a conduit for Nyla's ascension to America. I was like the winged horse Buraq, who took the Prophet up to the heavens.

I went to Ammi and let her know my intentions.

"I want to marry Nyla."

"Our Nyla?"

"Yes. She's a Siddiqui, like me."

"But she's older than you," Ammi pointed out.

"I know. I don't mind, though. The Prophet's first wife was older than he was by fifteen years."

"Do you know this girl's story?"

"No," I admitted. "I've barely talked to her."

"She's the maid," Ammi said somewhat derisively.

"No she's not. She's my cousin."

"I mean that she dropped out of college to come live here with your grandparents. Now she's a glorified maid."

"Why did she do that?" I asked, genuinely curious.

It turned out that Dada Abu had given Nyla's father—one of my uncles—a loan, but he came down with lung disease and wasn't able to pay it back. Instead of financial repayment, he'd told Nyla to drop out of college and had given Dada Abu authority over her.

"This means he has authority over matters of her marriage," Ammi added.

"Fine. I'll talk to him myself."

"Won't matter," she said, waving her hand as if to brush the issue away. "You need to understand how these things work around here. A few years ago one of Dada Abu's more distant relatives passed away and left a bunch of children in your grandfather's care. He became responsible for raising them and getting them married. Nyla is already promised to one of them."

"Which one?"

Ammi named a distant cousin I'd met many times.

"Him? He's illiterate!"

"He's not illiterate," Ammi countered. "He's mentally slow. But he's gone to school every day of his life. Probably still does just because he likes it."

"So this college-educated girl is going to marry someone 'slow'?"

"That's her *kismet*," Ammi said.

"You have to do something to stop that," I argued. "You keep saying that you're a feminist. How can you support a marriage like that?"

"I'm an Islamic feminist," she corrected. "But I can't do anything anyway. This isn't my family; it's your father's. Just understand that there's a path that women follow. Girls get married. They get worked to the bone. They produce a baby every year—though God knows what the use of *that* is. Who's raising the children? No one. Raising themselves. They're like weeds. That girl Nyla won't last. She's too skinny."

I was stunned into silence. None of this made any sense to me. This was an Islamic country, and Islam was supposed to be about justice. Perhaps Nyla didn't have to end up with me, but it was downright unjust for her to end up with the neighborhood idiot.

"Pakistan was founded as a haven for Islam," I protested, my voice raised.

I'd hoped for confirmation from Ammi, but none was forthcoming. She had stopped listening.

I suddenly felt as if my wings had been chopped off.

# II

Unwilling to stay housebound, given the torment I felt in proximity to Nyla, I disregarded Dada Abu's edict and headed out to visit the men of the family at the *bazar*. My beard had started to come in, though it was far from robust, and I put on a pale yellow *topi*. Wearing dusty sandals and an old *shalwar kameez*, I could pass as a native. If I didn't say anything in my English-accented Urdu, no one would distinguish me from anyone else on the street.

When I got to the mouth of the *mohalla* and went past the mosque, I heard a yell behind me. "Hey, *bhai*. Wait, *bhai*!"

I turned and saw a guy about my age with a beard but no mustache running toward me, his hand holding on to his *topi*. He had a desperate look on his face. I thought I recognized him as someone from my extended family, but when he came closer I realized I didn't know him.

"You came from America, right?" he said. "You just got here a few days ago?"

I nodded, apprehensive because he seemed to know so much about me. He picked up on my unease and flashed a big smile.

"You don't remember me, do you? I know you haven't seen me in forever. I'm surprised you forgot me, though. Tell me: who did you use to play with when you were little—before you left and became an American?"

I jogged my memory, trying to place his face. Suddenly I remembered the cut of the jaw, the shape of the lips, the excitable eyes, and the broad-shouldered build. It was Ittefaq, one of my buddies from the *madrassa* years! He was older, weather-beaten, more muscular, bearded, and taller, but it was definitely Ittefaq. I said his name out loud and he happily shook my hand. Then we gave each other an awkward hug.

"I heard that someone came to town from America and wondered if it was you. I've been hanging outside your *mohalla* ever since, hoping to meet up with you."

The revelation that he had been watching for me struck me as kind of strange, given that we hadn't told anyone we were coming and that I hadn't ventured out of the house at all. I told myself that I was being too Western in my suspicion. After all, I knew that Pakistanis liked to stare at one another, which was something people never did in the States. Perhaps Ittefaq's willingness to wait for me was just another traditional Muslim custom that westoxification had caused me to forget.

"The *bazar* is still that way, right?" I asked, pointing.

"The *bazar*? Yes. You're going to the *bazar* right now?"

"I'm going to Dada Abu's shop. That's where all the men are."

"The *men* leave early in the morning," he said, as if to imply that I was less than a man for waiting this long to go join them. His comment stung.

Wanting to establish my masculinity, I pounded him on the back—harder than I needed to—and then gestured with my head. "Walk with me," I invited.

As we walked I asked him about what he'd been up to all these years, but he ignored my questions and kept asking me about America. Where did I live? What did I do there? What was it like? Did I go to school? Was I forgetting much of the Urdu language? Did I practice Islam? He asked that last question in an accusatory way.

"Of *course* I practice Islam!" I said emphatically. The force in my voice seemed to catch him off guard—and this pleased me.

He grinned apologetically. "I was just asking. Just making sure you weren't a CIA agent!"

He said it in a joking way, but I didn't think it was funny. I glared and looked away. First he had implied that I was womanly, and now he was essentially calling me a traitor to Muslims.

However, along with my outrage, I also felt insecurity. Ittefaq and the people of Sehra Kush represented the traditional Islamic life that was impossible to attain in the secular West, which made them purer than me, and if they thought that I was lacking in some way—if I wasn't man enough, if I wasn't trustworthy enough—then the presumption went against me and in their favor. I told myself to show a little more humility going forward.

As we continued toward the *bazar,* Ittefaq dug into his pocket and produced a little card. With an eager smile he handed it over.

"Check this out," he said. "It's something else."

I took it and inspected it. It was a stamp-sized picture of a topless Bollywood actress. Her mouth was in a sensual pout, her breasts large and glossy.

I admired her for a moment and then handed the picture back to him. I tried to indicate by my expression that I wasn't interested whatsoever.

"No!" he insisted. "It's fine. You keep that one. I've got more—many more! Put it in your wallet." He opened his wallet to show me that he'd done the same.

Not wanting to make a big deal about it, I shrugged and tucked the picture into my wallet as suggested.

Together we walked into the bustling *bazar.* There were hundreds of fruit carts and vendors and guys selling roasted corn and sugarcane juicers with windmill machines and little boys squatting at the streetside faucets washing pots by hand. Letting memory lead me, I walked toward Dada Abu's shop.

Ittefaq put his hand on my shoulder. "I have to go see my uncle," he said, pointing in the other direction. "You come with me. Let's go to his shop. There's *chai* and food there."

I didn't want to start exploring the city without touching base with my relatives first, so I asked him for directions to his uncle's shop. "I'll come there after I go and sit with my grandfather."

He nodded reluctantly. "Make sure you come," he said. "We'll eat and drink."

After saying my farewells, I pressed through the crowd to Dada Abu's store. I found him sitting in the back of the shop. He smiled when I arrived and pulled me into his sitting room by my wrist. After getting me a cup of *chai,* he began asking me questions.

"Why didn't your father come with you to Pakistan?"

"He had to work," I explained. "He gets only a certain amount of time off."

"He's always worked hard," Dada Abu said nostalgically. "When he was a child, he was the only one of my sons who was serious about studying. He was an example for everyone, but not everyone followed his example."

"He still likes studying," I said, recalling the way Pops had pored over his residency books.

"He must make you and your brother study hard."

"Oh, he does!"

"That's good. Very good. You must know that I'm an illiterate man. I only know business. I can sell anything, but being a salesman is low-class. Your father did right. He went and became a doctor."

I nodded.

"What do you want to be?" asked Dada Abu, looking at me intently.

"I want to be an Islamic scholar," I said.

"No," he said, "for your *profession.* A man needs a profession. *Everyone* can study Islam."

I tried to explain to him that I would get an advanced degree in Islamic philosophy and become a professor. Dada Abu shook his head.

"Not a good idea," he said. "Mosques and *madrassa*s are good for worship, and it's good to be a Muslim scholar, but a man can't make money from Islam. That's not allowed by God. You can't use the religion for money. So I ask you, what will you do for money?"

"I'll study law," I said, hoping to reassure him.

"Yes!" He nodded eagerly. "Yes, that is an honorable profession. Allama Muhammad Iqbal and Muhammad Ali Jinnah—founders of Pakistan. They were both barristers. Gandhi was a lawyer also."

Satisfied with my answer, he leaned back and lit his *hooka*. Then he closed his eyes again, gripping the nozzle of the *hooka* with his left hand. He smoked the bitter tobacco, causing it to smolder. The water gurgled softly. I leaned against the far wall and relaxed. A soothing tedium buzzed in the air, and the noise in the *bazar* sounded far away, a distant din of clattering feet and murmuring voices. As I looked through the shop toward the *bazar* beyond, I could see the hot *loo*—the infamous wave of noontime desert heat—emanating from the pavement; it gave the atmosphere a shimmering quality.

I finished my cup of *chai* and headed up the street.

In an alley in the *bazar* a sugarcane juicer's cart had been upturned and the vendor was rummaging around trying to contain the mess. First he bundled the big green sugarcanes; then he took care of his jugs and finally his machine. Although he was swearing loudly, invoking all sorts of incestuous relations and fecal matter, he seemed to be talking to the ground. Certainly he wasn't swearing at the culprits who had overturned his cart and now stood all around him.

A group of six or seven bearded men, their pants hiked up above their ankles, and checkered scarves worn over white *topi*s, stood in a half-circle around the cart. In a restrained voice the leader of the group told the juicer to shut his mouth and stand up.

"I told you I've got nothing!" the juicer pleaded. "You think I'm making any profit here? These bastard shop owners don't pay me a thing!"

"You're avoiding your duty toward God and the Prophet," the leader replied.

"What's happening?" one passerby asked another.

"They're collecting 'donations' in the name of God," the man said sarcastically, as if this happened often.

I couldn't believe my ears. The idea of religious men—men garbed in the clothes that pious people wore—extorting money from a defenseless and impecunious sugarcane juicer struck me as impossible. *Good* Muslims didn't do things like that, and everyone could see from these men's beards and wardrobes and the way they hiked up their pants that they took Islam very seriously; you could even hear it in their Arabized inflection.

No. There had to be a reason unknown to all the onlookers that had prompted the *maulvis* to accost the juicer. Maybe the juicer was peddling some form of immorality, for example. Or maybe he was a cheat who defrauded the patrons. Maybe he used bad merchandise. It had to be something like that which brought this punishment upon him; it had to be something un-Islamic.

The juicer fumbled through his pockets. He lifted the cushion on which he customarily sat and looked underneath. He lifted a corner of the straw mat on which his sugarcanes were spread and peered beneath. He was checking all the places where he might have kept money.

"See? Nothing—I have nothing!" he said to the men surrounding him.

One of the *maulvis* struck the juicer for failing to pay, knocking him to the ground. Another man delivered a kick. I didn't want to question these men who talked in the language of Islam, so I turned away.

When I arrived at Ittefaq's uncle's shop, a pair of boys were unfurling huge rolls of cloth for a customer. The brightly colored fabrics lay crisscrossed in front of the potential buyer, who rubbed his fingers on each sheet and then inquired about the price. Every time he demurred, Ittefaq's uncle stepped in and explained the type of cotton he held in his hand and why it was the greatest in the world. When the patron still continued to dither, the uncle calmly asked one of the boys to bring tea for the guest. Such hospitality put additional pressure on the reluctant patron. Once the *chai* arrived, the sale was put on hold temporarily. Ittefaq took advantage of the pause to introduce me to his uncle and his cousins.

As soon as Ittefaq mentioned that I was from America, everyone, including the customer, swiveled around in their seats, making me the center of attention. The customer, a clean-shaven man in his early thirties wearing a T-shirt and jeans, pointed his finger at me.

"Why did your Clinton shoot all those missiles!" he demanded.

He was referring to President Clinton's use of Tomahawk missiles to strike militant camps in Afghanistan.

"Do you know that some of those missiles landed in Balochistan and killed children?" he continued, his tone suggesting that I was equally responsible. "Your Clinton is killing innocent Muslims!"

I looked to Ittefaq for support, but he was completely, perhaps purposefully, oblivious to me. Everyone else jumped in with pointed comments linking me with Clinton. I felt besieged. I tried to think of the reasons that Clinton had used to justify the missile strikes, but I couldn't remember a single thing. My mind went completely blank.

Somehow I needed to change the subject away from missiles toward something, anything, that might earn me some good graces in the eyes of the hostile gathering. "After the Soviet Union fell," I improvised, "America needed an enemy. It has targeted Islam."

I couldn't remember exactly where I'd heard this idea discussed, but I recalled reading that a professor named Samuel Huntington had said something similar. My comment silenced the group, so perhaps my strategy was working. Imagining that I could turn the hostility around so that these people would trust me, wouldn't think I was a CIA agent but would see that I was a good Muslim, I went further. "America wants to be the world's only power. Just as the British took over the world centuries ago, now America is doing the same."

I was surprised at how easily these thoughts came to me. Feeling encouraged and powerful, I kept going. I recalled a particular e-mail I'd once received that had listed all the times the United States had invaded a foreign nation or supported covert action or engendered a coup d'état, and I did my best to echo its contents to the group. I started with the Spanish-American War and cited examples all the way up to U.S. sanctions against the regime in Iraq. Recalling my political science classes, I marshaled the views of Francis Fukuyama, who had declared that the West represented the end of history, and Kissinger's realist school of foreign policy, which said that *all* countries were enemies to the United States. Speaking forcefully, I explained that America was on a mission to turn Islam into its enemy.

Having exhausted my argument, I took a deep breath and paused, waiting for the frowns to turn into smiles, waiting for someone to say that it was nice to see an American helping Islam.

Yet no such recognition came my way. The men kept on chastising Clinton and Madeleine Albright and American foreign policy and me, as if I'd been a member of the president's Cabinet. Using some of the facts I'd told them, they made me feel as if it was my fault that Muslim children in Palestine and Kashmir and Iraq were dying.

I decided that leaving the shop was the best thing to do. Sidling out while the attention was focused on another speaker, I headed out.

"Where are you going?" Ittefaq asked, running after me and grabbing me by the arm.

I yanked myself away. "I'm going to the mosque."

Worship was my refuge. If I could go to the mosque and put my head to the floor, at least God would see that I loved Islam, would see that I wasn't, as the men in the shop had implied, a part of a massive American conspiracy against it.

"I'll come with you," he offered.

"Suit yourself," I said curtly, upset with him because he didn't seem to understand why I'd snuck out of the shop.

We took a circuitous road that led around the two *gol daira*s back to Dada Abu's *mohalla*. Suddenly Ittefaq grabbed my arm and pulled me around a corner toward a row of single-story cement homes in a narrow alley.

"Where are you taking me?" I demanded.

"Just come with me," he said cheerfully. "I have to make a trade."

"Trade what?"

He smiled wickedly and patted the porno cards in his pocket.

Heaving a deep breath, I followed him out of necessity, uncertain how to get home from there.

We entered one of the houses without knocking. Ittefaq's familiarity with the place made me wonder if it was his home, but I seemed to recall that his family had lived on the other side of town. I followed him past the empty verandah and into a bedroom in the back.

When we entered, I saw three older guys in *shalwar kameez*es. They had big beards and wore large turbans and the sort of vests preferred by mountain men. I stood near the door and waited for Ittefaq to complete his deal. After a moment's conversation, however, Ittefaq sat down and made himself comfortable. The largest of the men turned to me and glared while his associate reached around me and closed the door.

"I want to ask you about America," the big man said, looking over at Ittefaq as if for his okay.

"What do you want to ask?"

"It is not possible to be a Muslim in America!" It was a declaration and not a question. He had clearly already made up his mind about the subject.

"I am a Muslim in America," I replied.

"You aren't allowed to practice Islam in America. They don't let you grow your beard. They make you shave it off."

"You can grow your beard in America! No one stops you."

"America is not a religious place."

"That's not true. There are many Islamic scholars in America," I assured him.

"Those aren't real scholars," he objected.

Now I was stumped. When dealing with Muslims in America, I had always found that appeals to scholars settled disputes. Now, having been told that even the Islamic scholars in America were illegitimate, I found myself in a difficult position.

Before I had a chance to say anything further, my interrogator pointed his finger at me and shouted, "You are a CIA agent! You are a traitor to Muslims everywhere!"

I didn't know how to respond to this sudden accusation and stammered.

Upon seeing my weakness, one of the other men jumped into the conversation: "If you give allegiance to America you can no longer be a Muslim. Giving allegiance to anyone but God is *shirk;* it is the highest form of idolatry. We all know the punishment of those that leave the religion."

I felt myself blanch. He meant death.

"Wait. No. That's not—" I wanted to fight the direction this conversation was taking. I wanted to resist being cast out of Islam and rendered an apostate.

Fortunately, the second man changed course himself. "America is a nation of weaklings," he said in disgust.

"I exercise and lift weights," I offered, only to realize that he was talking about another kind of weakness.

"Americans are too cowardly to face Muslims on the ground!" he said with great passion. "They shoot bombs from far away. If they faced Muslims on the ground, they would certainly be crushed!"

The third man, who hadn't spoken yet, raised his voice. "Americans think they lift a few weights and this is training? When *mujahideen* train in Afghanistan, that's real training. I know about this. They are given nothing to eat and made to climb up mountains, barefoot with no warm clothes, and with nothing but a hunting knife to keep them alive. That's the kind of exercise that makes you tough and wiry and strong. Your stomach becomes taut and you become indestructible!" He smashed his fist against his stomach.

When I didn't respond, he continued with his bombast. He discussed the *mujahideen* from around the world that were flocking to "Shaykh Osama"—who apparently sat on the floor with all his soldiers in the spirit of Islamic equality—and he talked about how one day Osama was going to liberate the Muslims of the world. He went on to tell me that while America could send a thousand missiles, it wouldn't make a dent against those who were determined to bring America to judgment. He was convinced the *mujahideen* were invincible.

I couldn't understand why these men felt compelled to make such a presentation to *me*. Suddenly I saw through Ittefaq's friendliness: he was in with all these people, and he'd set me up!

He must have told them that an American he knew was coming to town, and they'd all gotten together and planned how to insult me. I thought back to the porno trading cards and realized that I'd been duped. Ittefaq must have figured I'd trust him more if he showed me nude women—and in fact he'd turned out to be right! Using the pictures, he'd been able to lure me away from my family and take me places where I'd be alone and without protection. Now he and his friends had insulted and degraded me, and when I went away they'd laugh about how "that American" was so gullible that he fell for the naked girl trick.

It dawned on me then that I hadn't been brought here to answer questions about the state of Islam in the West. These people didn't care

about any of that. They only wanted to air their grievances against the
West and to tell me that they supported bin Laden.

In other words, I, Abu Bakr Ramaq, descendant of the first Caliph,
promised to God at the Ka'ba, in search of a pious Muslim wife, was a
stand-in for the entirety of the infidel West. To be more blunt: I was *not*
a part of the *ummah,* the universal brotherhood of Muslims. The realization of having been constructively excommunicated left me feeling
sick to my stomach.

Yet the anger I felt wasn't directed at Ittefaq and his associates. It was
directed at myself. I had been tested by an offer of pornography, and by
accepting it I had essentially conceded that I was impious. No wonder
they didn't respect me. No wonder they didn't consider me anything
other than an extension of America. No wonder they didn't let me be
part of Islam despite all the love for the religion in my soul. My sin was
my indictment.

I pulled out my wallet, threw the picture toward Ittefaq, and excused myself.

# 12

The next morning Ammi woke me up by shaking my shoulder and yelling, "Get up! Someone is trying to kill your grandfather! He already has a heart condition. Those animals!"

I ran downstairs and saw that Dada Abu hadn't gone to work, nor had the other men. They were all inside the house with the gate locked. Dada Abu looked worried—his skin had taken on a darker hue of concern and he was shaking at bit—though he was clearly trying not to show his fear.

"He was sitting on the porch this morning, up the street near his brother's house," Dadi Ma said. "Two young men on a motorcycle drove by and slowed down in front of him. They pointed their guns at him and pretended to shoot. After driving to the end of the block, they turned around and made another pass. That's what happened, right?" She looked at her husband for confirmation.

Dada Abu nodded.

Speculation began as to who the assailants might be. The first theory was that it was thieves, but everyone knew that common thieves didn't intimidate. Another theory was that it was someone with a personal grudge against Dada Abu, since he'd recently been involved in some litigation about a piece of land.

"They told me they will be back," he said. "That's the last thing they said.

When he revealed this fact, everyone began chattering and gesturing.

"In all these years, no one has shown such blatant disrespect to an elder," Uncle Tau said.

"My father is a wise *buzurg*," my younger uncle said. "These people have no shame."

"Respect is dead," Dadi Ma concluded. "This is not the country it used to be." Spreading her *jai namaz*, she began making prayers to ward off the devil. She extolled everyone to pray, saying it was the best defense against aggression.

Ammi, meanwhile, tried to persuade Dada Abu against going to work. She didn't want him going to the mosque at night, either.

"I've done those things my entire life," he responded. "I'm not going to stop now."

"But your life is in danger," Ammi said.

"A Muslim that is murdered is a martyr. I am assuredly a sinful and hell-bound man. This will give me a shot at Paradise."

I wanted to laugh at the joke but couldn't.

Nor could Ammi. In fact, she began crying.

Once Dada Abu and the men had left for work, the women began to entertain the vague hope that the drive-by was just an act of random belligerence. That hopeful theory evaporated when strange phone calls started coming in during the day.

"I picked it up," Dadi Ma said after one such call. "I just heard breathing on the other side. There was obviously someone there. It wasn't just a wrong number."

"I had the same experience," Aunt Tai said. "If you don't hang up, they'll just stay on the phone and breathe."

"Just let the phone ring," Ammi said. "We don't need to pick it up."

"It's no use. They'll just make it ring ten or twelve times and then call back."

I wondered if we needed reinforcements. "Should I go to the *bazar* and tell them what's happening?" I asked.

"No!" said Ammi, grabbing my arm. "It's not safe for you to go outside."

Around midday prayer there was a lull in the phone calls. Ammi used the opportunity to call Pops back in the States, concerned enough about the situation that she didn't mind waking him up. Afterwards we went outside and sat down with the women, who were still trying to figure out who might be behind the intimidation. I had rarely felt so weak and useless.

"Is someone around here involved in drugs?" Ammi asked.

The women shook their heads.

"Who knows what it could be," my grandmother said.

Just then the phone started ringing again. I told the women to stay put and went to get it. Before picking it up I stared at it for a few seconds, letting the bell drill into my head. If the drive-by and the phone calls were related, then by picking up the phone I'd be putting myself in the middle of it all. Finally I summoned the courage to pick up the receiver.

"Hello?"

There was a pregnant pause on the other end. I heard breathing but it was sporadic, as if the person was surprised by my voice. After a moment or two there was a reluctant reply.

"Hello."

It was a young man's voice, but a single word wasn't much to go on. I tried to open up a conversation.

"Who is this?" I asked. "Are you looking to talk to someone at this number?"

Immediately the caller hung up, and for the rest of the afternoon no one called back.

I remained inside after the call and tried to think with a clear head. Wasn't it the case that the drive-by and the strange phone calls had started after I'd had my run in with Ittefaq and his aggressive friends? That was definitely a young man's voice on the other end. Couldn't it be Ittefaq himself? He had lured me out before; maybe he was now at the center of another, more nefarious game. It seemed like a plausible theory, but it didn't exactly explain why they would intimidate Dada Abu in the morning. I wanted to go out and share my theory with the women, but I decided against it because I didn't want to cause them panic.

In the early afternoon Dada Abu and the men came home. When the women told them about the strange phone calls, they didn't seem overly concerned. Their attention was consumed by something they'd heard while at the *bazar*.

"Somebody is planning an attack tonight," Dada Abu said.

"Here? At the house?" Ammi asked.

Dada Abu nodded. "That's what I heard. I can't know for absolute certain, but we're going to have to take precautions."

"Why is this happening?" Ammi asked. "What does it have to do with us?"

Dada Abu didn't say anything. He left the house to consult with his brothers about getting some protection for the night and didn't return for quite some time.

A meeting of all the family men had been called for that evening, and they met in the sitting room. I joined them.

"I've asked my friend Majid's sons to come over for the night," Dada Abu said. "They have weapons."

"We'll post the three of them on the upper walls," Tau suggested.

"Do *we* have any weapons?" Dada Abu asked.

"Just this," my younger uncle said, putting forward a revolver. Then he cracked it open dejectedly. "But I think the bullets are wet, so there's no way to know if it fires."

Dada Abu took it and turned it this way and that. "Hopefully we won't have to use it," he concluded.

"I have a sword at my house," my polygamous uncle said jokingly.

"You better hold that instead of one of your wives tonight!"

Instructions were given to all the men: lock up your house early, and don't let anyone visit.

"You," Dada Abu finally said to me at the end of the meeting. "Take your brother and mother up to the second roof. Put your *charpai*s in the center, nowhere near a wall."

This was explicit confirmation that the assailants were after me, or someone in my immediate family. When I told Ammi about Dada Abu's instructions and the implication that we were the targets of the attack, she took it in stride.

"I know. I heard from one of the milkboys," she said. "It's one of the Islamic groups. They're coming after us because we're American."

I nodded and then hung my head. So Ittefaq had ill intentions after all. He and his friends really did hate me. They didn't care how much love for Islam I had in my heart. I was just an American to them. I was just someone to be abducted. I had come to the desert in search of good Muslims—the sort I hadn't found in New York or Karachi—and I had instead been greeted by Islamic thugs.

Night fell and we took our *charpais* up to the second roof. Dadi Ma and Nyla bravely came to join us.

Majid's sons showed up soon after. They carried huge assault rifles and wore holsters with heavy pistols; bandoliers of ammunition crisscrossed their bodies. Two of them took a position on the ledge hanging over the main wall of the house to prevent anyone from climbing over and jumping onto the veranda. A third son went up to the first roof and sat in a chair. He couldn't be seen from the outside but could pounce on anyone trying to climb up the back of the house. His position seemed the most important, since he could see up and down the street as well. He was given a flask of tea to keep himself awake. My younger uncle and Tau paced up and down the staircase running from the veranda up to the second roof, where we were located. Dada Abu sat downstairs holding the revolver that might not work.

As the sky darkened, I lay down with a knife under the pillow. I had walked around the house to see how exactly the defenses might be breached. The most likely plan by the assailants would involve coming over with seven or eight men. Two or three would directly engage Majid's sons at the front while a couple went to the back and tried to clamber up. A lot depended on how the assailants wanted to attack. If they wanted to do things secretly, it would be a bit difficult for them, but if they were willing to shoot they could simply blast the door open and overrun Dada Abu. Trying to remain calm, I stared at the stars.

They were bigger and brighter in the desert, and they made different patterns than they did in America.

It struck me as absurd that someone was willing to go through all this effort just to get to me—insignificant little me.

Then I fell asleep.

When I woke up it was still dark, and the house was quiet. I worried that the guards weren't doing their job. For a moment I imagined that everyone else had been quietly killed and I alone had been spared. I got up and ran upstairs to check: there was the guard, sleeping with the Thermos in his hand. After shaking him by the shoulder, I ran downstairs to see if anyone was on the veranda.

Everyone, I discovered, was accounted for and alive, and nothing untoward had happened thus far.

I was settling back on my *charpai* when Ammi started me by whispering a greeting. She had been awake the whole time, she said, taking care of a few things and reading from the Quran. She gave me a comforting smile and I relaxed and soon fell asleep again.

I opened my eyes when the *azan* rang out in the morning. That call to prayer signaled a cessation of anxiety. A ripple of muted jubilation passed through the house.

As I rubbed my eyes Ammi threw a bag in my lap.

"Get up," she said. "We're leaving."

"What?"

"We're leaving. Let's go."

"Now?"

"Yes."

"Where are we going?"

"Lahore. Karachi. Islamabad. I don't know. Just away from here."

"What do you mean?"

"We can't stay here one more day. I already called your father to let him know we're coming."

"How will we get though town without trouble?"

"With the commandoes," she announced.

"What commandoes?"

Then I heard the loud rumble of a Humvee in the alley.

The previous night Ammi had managed to get in touch with Uncle Saad in Karachi, and he had called out a contingent of security professionals to drive down from Pindi and escort us out of town.

When I went downstairs I saw that the entire family was awake. Children ran excitedly from the house to the Humvee and patted it with awe in their eyes. A pair of toddlers pulled at a stoic guard's legs and tried to undo his shoelaces. A pair of serious men walked up and down the alley to make sure everything was clear.

Ammi had already made her haphazard goodbyes and sat firmly in the backseat, yelling at Flim and me to hurry up. I hurried out to join her, sadness coursing through my body as I realized that I hadn't been able to accomplish any of the things that I'd come to the desert to do.

It would have been nice to get a wife, but the more important thing had been to find out my family history and get the genealogical tree that linked me back to Hazrat Abu Bakr Siddiq. I never even got an opportunity to sit down with Tau and have him go through his files. Nor did I get to go to the *madrassa* and impress all my former instructors with my newfound intellectual understanding of Islam. I had dearly wanted to corner Qari Jamil and impress him with the finer points of Islamic law.

I thought about my aged grand-uncles, the pillars of permanence from my childhood. Living just down the street, they had been spared all the commotion of last night. In fact, I'd hardly seen them since we got to Sehra Kush. Now we were leaving, and they would stay here with all the secrets of my family history—the stuff about the Partition, the difficult journey across Pakistan since then, the entirety of the 1990s, all of it still lodged in their big hearts. I felt overcome with a desire to go and say goodbye to them. It was the respectful thing to do, especially since they would probably pass away before I ever returned.

Ignoring Ammi's calls to hurry, I ran over to their room. When I entered the tiny space the three brothers shared, they were unwrapping their turbans and making preparation to lie back down after prayer. Their white beards seemed richer and cleaner in the morning light.

"Circumstances require that I leave," I said loudly, knowing that they were hard of hearing.

All of them turned to me.

"You just got here!" my oldest grand-uncle said sadly.

"We didn't even get to talk," said another.

"Trip is over," I said. "Maybe I'll come back one day."

Then I went back into the street and walked to the Humvee. On the way I said hasty goodbyes to various aunts and to the little kids, and I hugged Dadi Ma. Then, full of shame and apology, I approached Dada Abu and excused myself.

"You have to go," he said stoically, "so don't make explanations. Just go."

There was both accusation and resignation in his voice. On one hand, I could tell that he thought I was running away. That was the loving part of him, the part that wanted to sit and talk with a grandson whom he hadn't seen for a decade. On the other hand, he knew that my departure was the right thing. That was the protective part of him, the part that wanted to keep me safe. As we hugged chest to chest, I realized that he wasn't as sturdy or as powerful as he used to be. I could feel Time hovering over him in that moment, weakening him with its invisible fingers.

I got into the Humvee and the guards locked up. Looking out the window, I waved at the assembled relatives. I felt like I was leaving a part of me with Dada Abu and my grand-uncles. These were the people through whom I was supposed to weave myself into the tapestry of Islam.

As the Humvee whirred into the desert, hurtling past the sand dunes, over the cracked bridges, and past the caravans of Gypsies in blue and purple, I felt as if I needed to blame someone for destroying my opportunity to connect with my history. Again, though, rather than blaming Ittefaq and his angry Islamic cohorts, I blamed myself. It was because I was an inadequate Muslim that they had consigned me to being an American and made me feel that I had nothing to contribute to the *ummat-e-islami*.

This was all my fault.

Not theirs.

# 13

We cut our trip short by four weeks and went to Uncle Saad's house in Karachi to wait for the next available flight to America. We ended up with a few days to kill before the flight, and we spent them slumming around his living room, too discouraged to do any sightseeing. Ruing my lost chance to get hold of the special family tree that would have showed the link back to the first Caliph, I raised the issue of our heritage with Uncle Saad over lunch our first day back.

"You know I came here to try and find out more about my history," I began.

"I thought you came for a wife."

"That too, but I really wanted to connect with Islam."

"Were you able to?" he asked. "Did that happen in Sehra Kush?"

"No," I said dispiritedly.

"Why not?"

"Well, I never got hold of our family tree."

"You didn't ask your Uncle Tau?"

"I never got a chance."

"Well," he said thoughtfully, "what are you looking for? Maybe I know."

Ammi, who was at lunch with us, spoke up. "He's trying to find all the connections to the Siddiqui name."

"I have the names going back four generations only," I told him. "That's all Pops remembered."

I took out my notebook and set forth my research. Uncle Saad read through it carefully.

"So you want to go further back than this?" he asked.

"I have to," I said. "I'm trying to get all the way back to Abu Bakr Siddiq, the first Caliph."

Uncle Saad stopped eating and looked at me quizzically. "*The* Abu Bakr Siddiq?"

I nodded eagerly.

A big smile spread across his face—a sardonic one. Soon it became a snicker.

"Why are you laughing?" I asked.

"It's nothing," he said, stifling another snicker. "I wish you the best. I do."

"No. Tell me right this instant," I demanded. "Tell me why you're laughing." My ears were hot with embarrassment.

"You really want to know?"

"Yes," I said, though I was pretty sure I wasn't going to like what he had to say.

Uncle Saad glanced at Ammi, then turned back to me. "That Siddiqui thing isn't real," he said, no longer smiling. "It's a joke. No, it's not even a joke; it's a forgery. No, it's not a forgery, because that implies an intent to cause harm. I don't know *what* it is."

"Meaning what, exactly?" I asked, the castles of pride in my mind crumbling.

"It's all an accident," Uncle Saad said. "The reason that we're named Siddiqui is because a couple of centuries ago one of our ancestors, a man who converted from Hinduism to Islam—his name was Savekhi—opted to take on a name that sounded close to his original name when he became Muslim. That's really all there is to it. Savekhi became Siddiqui."

"Hindu?" I said, my throat choking up. "Convert?"

"Is this right?" Ammi asked, jumping back in. "My husband told me the thing about being Siddiquis. *He* thought it was true."

Uncle Saad nodded. "When your father was growing up, we were new to Pakistan and had nothing. Dada Abu probably let him believe we were connected to Abu Bakr Siddiq to make him feel good. It was a convenient lie, since the actual Abu Bakr was a migrant and so were we. Or maybe it wasn't Dada Abu who told those tales. Maybe these stories were passed around by the government."

"But Uncle Tau has a book," I objected. "Pops said it has the family tree."

Uncle Saad waved a dismissive hand. "You can buy a hundred books like that. There are a million forgers who will happily tell anyone on the street that they're related to the Holy Prophet. Then everyone runs around calling themselves Syed or whatever. Biggest fraud there is."

Abu Bakr Ramaq, purported heir of Islamic royalty, descendant of pure Arab blood, child of Islam's greatest leader, started to tremble. The revelation entered my bloodstream, inciting an insurrection of rage. That rage was quickly followed by the hollow void of defeat. Images of tall Arabs in fluttering white robes, riding fast camels across vast deserts before settling in the alluvial fields of Punjab, leaving behind the Mongol savages—those images all disappeared in an instant. The luminosity of my fantasies, which had given those images their exalted flavor, turned to darkness. The vivid colors ran into my blood and become a blurry, indistinct mess. Everything threatened to tumble out of my tear ducts, but I held back by sheer willpower, unwilling to give up my last vestiges of pride.

Now the ancestor I saw in my head was a muddy, *lungi*-wearing farmer who was short and round and bald. Carrying a puny scythe, he squatted in a rice field, working for a Muslim feudal lord among a group of sweaty Sikh and Hindu men, all of whom were illiterate and dark-skinned. Perhaps there was a dot on his head from some pagan ritual; perhaps when he went home he ate a bland dish of rice and vegetables without any meat; and perhaps when he walked he was such a coward that he wouldn't even dare kill an ant or a fly because he was afraid he might come back as that creature in his next life.

Savekhi. The name echoed in my head. The name of a Hindu. A non-Muslim. I was a descendant of a *nothing*.

With a deep sigh I hung my head. A few days later, somewhere above the Atlantic, Abu Bakr Ramaq was extinguished.

# BOOK IV

## The Postmodern—Amir ul Islam

*In which the author returns from his disappointing sojourn
in Pakistan and begins exploring anti-Islamic ideas at a new
university, where he nevertheless insists on remaining associated
with Muslims and ends up becoming president of the MSA*

# I

I had exalted the people of the Islamic Republic of Pakistan as the highest of believers. I had vested them with the authority to judge my *iman*, my belief; my *taqwa*, my piety. If only those righteous Muslims had cut open my chest and seen how the four chambers of my heart pumped blood suffused with Islam—yet they didn't. I was sneered at by the very ones who were supposed to embrace me. I was rejected by the ones who were supposed to be purer—in character, in culture, in chivalry—than Americans. The brilliance that I'd associated with Islam just a few months earlier had now turned black. After a period of mourning and melancholy, I craved vengeance. I sought to undermine all that the presumably purer Muslims held sacred.

I transferred to a Christian university in Atlanta for my junior year and started studying philosophy. There I petitioned Dr. Conrad, a bespectacled, dark-haired professor with a Transylvanian twinkle in his eye, who wrote various books on atheism, to give me individualized lessons in a philosophic system called *postmodernism*. All I knew about it was that it was feared and reviled by Muslims nearly as much as Rushdie's *Satanic Verses*.

I went to Dr. Conrad's office once or twice a week for these lessons. Sitting amidst heaps of manuscripts and ancient books, we pored over the writings of the major thinkers in the movement. These included Foucault, Derrida, and Lyotard, as well as related thinkers such as Adorno and Horkheimer, existentialists such as Nietzsche and Sartre, postcolonialists such as Said and Spivak, and feminists such as Irigaray and Butler. Our meetings took place late in the evening when the halls of the Philosophy Department were empty. We talked in whispers, because he didn't want his colleagues to know about our secret soirees. "Too many damn theologians pretending to be philosophers at this university," as he put it. It was the theologians of the world that I most wanted to undermine.

When each session finished, I would stalk home through the night like a wraith in the shadows. I felt wicked and powerful. I was Muslim become malfeasance.

Postmodernism had a singular aim: it threw off the strictures of authority. It taught you how to unshackle yourself from the discipline and punishment imposed upon you without your consent. It exposed the myriad ways in which religious forces enchained humans, often without their knowledge. It was the inverse of bondage.

"According to Lyotard," Dr. Conrad said. "There are no metanarratives. This is perhaps the guiding principle of postmodernism."

"Meaning . . . ?"

"Meaning that there is no grand theory. Meaning that religion is insufficient to explain the world."

Unlike Islam, which postulated that we owed certain duties to one another because we were all children of God, postmodernism said that all relationships were power struggles and that duties weren't inherent in our nature but were imposed by the most powerful. Thus we have a father exerting himself upon a son, and the son revolting. Men ruling women, and women recognizing their subjugation and fighting back. The wealthy manipulating the poor, and the poor rising up and vanquishing the rich. Priests imposing their laws, and freethinkers cutting those laws down like twigs. Everything was connected by conflict.

Soon I was introduced to Richard Rorty, depicted on the cover of his book as a dapper, gray-maned gentleman in a white suit. In his short book *Contingency, Irony, and Solidarity,* he declared that there was no such thing as truth "out there." He said that language didn't have a fixed meaning; that language was just a collection of "malleable metaphors." Language wasn't divine, therefore; it was man-made—made by the *strongest* of men. This argument would frighten any Muslim, because in Islam, God had become Text, or language.

"A Muslim wouldn't agree with that," I pointed out. "Muslims believe that the Quran is uncreated. This means that the words in the Quran are one and the same as God."

"I'm sure, though," Dr. Conrad said, "that there have been people—perhaps Muslims themselves—who don't believe that the Quran and Allah are synonymous with one another."

I nodded. "There were. They were called the Mutazilites. Though there aren't any more of those."

Dr. Conrad shrugged. "They'll make a comeback."

"What would you say about the *huruf al-muqatta'at*?" I asked.

"Translation?"

I rummaged in my backpack and pulled out a copy of the Quran. "There are certain strings of letters in the Quran," I said, flipping through to the beginning of the second chapter, where one such string—*alif lam mim*—could be seen. "They occur in various parts of the Quran. Muslims believe that no human being knows the meaning of these letters. If all language is man-made, as Rorty alleges, then we should be able to figure out what these mysterious letter combinations mean."

I thought I had Dr. Conrad on the ropes. He pushed his eyeglasses up on his nose and stared at the letters.

"Oh yes," he said suddenly. "I read an article about these. The author, who was a Muslim, said that these letters are actually hieroglyphics from an earlier language—one that was prevalent in Arabia before the advent of Arabic. He said that the three letters found at the beginning of the Chapter of the Cow—those that you're pointing at—actually make a picture, much the way that Chinese words are actually symbols."

"So what are the letters *alif lam mim* a picture of?"

"A cow, I believe."

"There's a picture of a cow at the beginning of the Quran's Chapter of the Cow?" I exclaimed.

"Seems like a reasonable, rational explanation, doesn't it?"

I nodded slowly. "So then, according to a postmodernist, the Quran is simply a number of things that Muhammad pieced together from whatever was floating around in the air?"

"A postmodernist would say that Muhammad was simply doing what any great novelist does. Or, in Rorty's words, he was a 'strong poet.' Like Homer or Shakespeare."

"Then Islam is nothing more than a compelling story that a lot of people came to believe in unison?"

Dr. Conrad nodded. "A postmodernist calls that a myth. In Islam's case it spread worldwide, mostly because the Arabs were an ascendant military force, but also because Islam, with its messenger Prophet and archangel and monotheistic God, offered stronger imagery than what was out there at the time."

I gathered my materials and took my assignments home. Reading through my books, I noticed that while postmodernists appreciated religion for making advances in ethics and morality, they argued that people no longer needed to rely on religion to know the right way to behave. Religion was considered nothing more than a "personal idio-syncrasy."

"What does that mean?" I asked Dr. Conrad the next time we met.

"It means that religion is analogous to a nervous tick or an obsessive-compulsive disorder," he said. "Religion isn't something which is shared universally by all people, because all people aren't the same re-ligion and even people of the same religion don't practice the same way. Therefore, religion can't be universal and thus can't universally guide humanity's behavior."

"So how do we know how to behave?" I asked. "What *is* shared universally?"

"We look to reason."

"But how do we know what reason is saying?" I asked.

"One way to do it is to look at what everyone else is doing."

# 2

When I looked around to see what was popular among my mostly twenty-year-old peers, the big winner was sex. Consider:

My roommate Jon, an atheist who believed the future of the world would involve androids, set up a multi-screen porn cineplex in our dorm and played gangbangs 24/7.

My other roommate, Aton, an agnostic white guy with a fetish for Asian girls, chased multiple women at once and kept notes on their performance.

I regularly watched a couple having sex on the balcony across from mine. They waved at me from time to time.

One of the Baptist friends I made had long discussions with me about her preference for anal over vaginal sex: "It allows me to remain a virgin till I'm married."

I soon became envious of all this sexual license, and since I was new at school I took advantage of my anonymity and started going to clubs in the Buckhead district. I was underage and didn't have a fake ID, so I pretended to be an Indian foreign exchange student—"Eyum enjeenyuring pee ech dee"—to get past the bouncers.

My accomplice was an anime-obsessed Japanese girl named Princess whom I'd met in one of my classes. For my first outing she took me to the Havana Club, where—as soon as I was squeezed into a throng of well-lotioned legs, in the dark, with no witnesses—she became the representation of all the girls I'd ever desired. She was the girl in the dorm across from mine who liked exhibitionist sex; she was Nadia Sumienyova from the erotica I wrote as an adolescent; she was the girl in the porn that Moosa Farid and I had reluctantly turned off during our abortive DVD-burning career.

Reaching around her little waist, I pulled her tight for a moment. Then, as she leaned back against my forearm, my other hand explored in her hair, lightly tugging, then pulling her head back to expose her lovely neck. Our hips settled against one another. Her legs spread for a second and then pressed themselves on either side of my thigh. I put my hand on her lower back and ground against her. She hiked her skimpy dress up a little higher and rubbed herself on my rough denim. I put my mouth on her neck and licked her tentatively. She was salty but vulnerable. Opening my mouth a bit, I put my teeth into her. She relaxed against me and let me feed.

Suddenly the barriers of shame and modesty collapsed. I was Yajuj-Majuj bursting upon the world seeking apocalypse—although ejaculation would suffice.

M uslim girls were my immediate "target," because there were certain in-built advantages I could exploit. First, my aura as a "pious brother" was still intact. That reputation allowed me to go to Islamic conferences and conventions and initiate conversations with girls without having them think that I was hitting on them. "I'm starting an Islamic newsletter and we should keep in touch" was all I usually had to say to get a number.

The second advantage was my looks. I was tall and thin and innocent-looking, lacking in any strikingly masculine physical features. This made me seem less aggressive and perhaps less carnal than other guys my age. When it came to committing sinful fornication, the sisters who wanted to believe they were good girls preferred weak-looking men, because they assumed that aggressive-looking men might demand intercourse, whereas guys like me would take whatever we could get. Since it was very important for sinning sisters not to end up losing their virginity in the dating game—that was a gift they wanted to reserve for their righteous and pious future husbands—my slightly effeminate appearance reassured them.

I began my exploration with a girl named Jullanar, who came from a very conservative family: curfew at sundown and no privacy at home and no cell phone and ceaseless attempts by her parents to marry her off to cousins in countries ending with "stan." Given that her body really belonged to her father, and he didn't want any part of him to create erections among other men—since that would mean that he was indirectly a homosexual—she had to buy jeans from the boys' department at Sears in order to hide her curves. One time her father forbade her to leave the house because she was wearing her purse diagonally, rather like a sling, accentuating her breasts as the strap passed between them. Another time she got a long lecture from her father because she wore a black choker necklace. He literally ripped it off her because—he said—it made her look like a slut. All that repression had turned Jullanar into a closet exhibitionist. She craved attention no matter where it came from.

"There's this boy, he's a *desi*," she said to me about an Indian guy at her college. "He stalks me. He follows me from morning when I get to school till night when I get home."

"What a freak."

"I know, right! It's so hot!" she said.

"Wait. You like that?" I asked.

"God, yes. I love knowing I'm turning guys on. It makes me feel like a casual slut!"

I spent days turning my tongue in Jullanar—or dreaming of it—and spent nights scouting women online just in case someone more interesting turned up:

I maintained contact with a girl in Tehran who was looking to find a Westerner to marry.

I corresponded with a woman in Saudi Arabia who was already married but was trying to escape her husband and was looking for a good brother overseas.

There was a white convert from a troubled family who couldn't reconcile her Islam with her increasing levels of bisexuality. From time to time she called me to complain about the single-sex dance parties that the sisters in her community threw, where beautiful married and unmarried girls took off their *hijab*s. "They get into the little black dresses they have under their *abaya*s and then dance on each other!" she said in a fit of frustration.

I chatted on the phone with a sister who liked to call me after she'd finished the early-morning *fajr* prayer and before she went to work. An only child, she had me pull sex stories from the Internet featuring brother-sister action and read them to her on the phone. "I can't get to them myself because I share a computer with my family," she explained sheepishly. She tended to hang up as soon as she climaxed, leaving me feeling used.

Then there was Anis. She was a pretty little *hijabi* I first got to know online. Although she had just entered college in a distant state when I first "met" her, she was on the cusp of getting married to a guy from New York. Our e-mail exchanges were mostly about how little she knew about sex and sexuality. I was, of course, more than eager to relieve her of her timidity.

"You don't have to be shy about being explicit with me," I wrote. "Muslims enjoy discussing sex."

"Really?"

"Sure. Didn't you know that Imam Ghazali, one of Islam's foremost scholars, wrote a work called *The Etiquette of Consummation*? It contains instructions about what a man should do to and for a woman. Did you know that it's your right as a Muslima to demand sex from your husband—and he can't say no?"

"I had no idea the scholars said such things," she wrote.

"Surely you've heard of Ibn Hazm, the great Spanish jurist."

"Of course," she replied.

"He also wrote a lot about sex," I informed her, my fingers flying across the keyboard. "His most famous book is called *The Ring of the Dove*. It's a tome about courtly love, but the metaphor in the title actually refers to the head of a penis. So you see: the West learned its sexual explicitness from Islam!"

"I didn't know that," she wrote. "Well, if it's the Islamic thing to do, I think I'm ready to talk about sex. You can ask me stuff and I'll answer. Ask me anything."

I went straight to the head of the matter. "Have you gone down on your fiancé?"

"No," she replied. "He went down on me, but I told him I wasn't ready to do it to him."

"When do you think you will be ready?" I typed.

"I told him that next time we see each other I want to do it. Thing is, to be quite honest I don't know how it works. As in technically."

That was my in. "I could give you instructions," I offered. "Especially since I want to ensure that your courtship is successful and you end up in a proper Islamic marriage."

"That would be great!"

"There's just one condition," I stipulated.

"Anything."

"When you go down on him, you have to imagine that you're doing it to me."

"I was already planning on it," she wrote, adding the wink emoticon.

"Excellent!"

"Now *I* have a condition," she countered.

"Anything," I replied, taken aback by how unrestrained this *hijabi* was.

"When I imagine you, can I imagine that you're going to marry me? See, I have this issue: I can sin only with a guy that I can imagine I'll marry one day. So if I'm imagining sinning with you, I have to be able to imagine being married to you as well."

"That's fine with me."

Anis and I communicated regularly from that day forward. To my surprise, within a couple of weeks she told me that she and the guy she'd been going to marry had called things off, and now she wanted to give *me* the honor of being the first guy she went down on. That was an offer I couldn't refuse. In fact, I got in my trusty Ford Ranger—my parents had kept the truck for me while I was in New York—and drove overnight to go see her.

"I couldn't get us a hotel room," she said, getting into the car as if we'd already been introduced. "They wouldn't take cash!"

"We'll find a quiet parking lot," I replied, turning onto the main street of the rural town.

I stole glances at her while I drove. She was more beautiful than her online picture suggested. She was dainty and light-skinned, and her eyes were immensely sad. She wore Dior heels, a maroon *hijab,* a long black skirt, and a tight white blouse through which I could see the contours of her lacy black bra. I liked the way she wore her *hijab;* she wrapped it in whirls rather than safety-pinning the flaps the ugly way the Syrians and Malaysians did. At a traffic light I reached out and touched the texture of the scarf.

"Do you like it?" she asked. "I got it when I went to Mecca."

"Very nice."

"I'd like to give you a gift." She reached into her purse and pulled out a little cloth bag.

"What is it?"

She unfurled the cloth and I saw that it concealed a miniature Quran.

"I want you to have it. Look, it's even embroidered in gold and has silver calligraphy."

I didn't want to take it. It just didn't seem right that she should give me something so special when we'd just met. But I suspected that giving me the Quran cast a veil of sacredness over the obscenity we were about to engage in. Perhaps it made her feel better about her impending sin.

I smiled. "I like it," I said. "Put it in the glove compartment and I'll take a closer look later."

We drove around until we got to a park with a lake. Leaving the car, we took a walk around the water, stopping now and then to touch each other, and sitting on a bench to kiss. When we returned to our places in the car, I tilted her body back and reached over to unbutton her blouse.

She undid her *hijab,* letting a splash of auburn hair fall across my face. I squeezed her tresses between my fingers, wrapped the strands around my palms, and inhaled her Vidal Sassoon.

The rest of the day we made prostrations upon each other's skin. In case someone was passing by, I drew the *hijab* over our bodies.

"A man and a woman are like a covering for one another," she said, repeating a verse from the Quran.

# 3

Persuading girls to abandon the strictures of Islam, while it brought a wry smile to the corner of my mouth in the middle of a boring class, was not ultimately satisfying. I couldn't boast or gloat about it to anyone. I couldn't celebrate my success. The secrecy ruined it. What was the point of having power over another human being if it couldn't be publicized?

So I decided to break it off with Anis. We'd met only once more since our first delicious encounter and sometimes talked on the phone. Looking for an easy way out, I told her that I was going to leave school and run away with Yemenese Sufis in order to work on the state of my *nafs,* or carnal self. She thought I was just making excuses, but I insisted, saying, "I really need to work on my Islam, maybe do some spiritual *tazkiyah,* or purification; maybe evaluate my *aqida*s, my creeds." Those were Arabic terms, and I pronounced them like the pious did. Anis became quiet. She and I both knew it: she had been defeated by guttural inflection. She cried on the phone, declared her hope that I would never find love, and then hung up on me, leaving me to sort out how to redirect my energy.

The answer, as always, came in the form of Islam.

A leadership crisis had formed within the MSA. Apparently the few people being groomed as potential presidents were dithering and doubting their qualifications. Part of their reluctance was proper Islamic etiquette—following the example of the first caliph, Abu Bakr, a Muslim being offered a leadership position was supposed to turn it down a few times—but part of it seemed serious. The possible lack of a president seemed to have shaken the community, and the organization's elders were worried.

The whole situation reminded me of the upheaval in sixth-century Arabia. After the death of a man named Abdul Muttalib in the final quarter of the century, there was a leadership vacuum in the tribe of Quraysh—the primary guardians of the Holy Ka'ba. As lesser men haphazardly competed with one another, a figure by the name of Muhammad pushed himself forward as a leader. It occurred to me that perhaps Muhammad had been a postmodern before his time. He recognized the weakness of others and, like any strong poet, saw an opportunity to assert his authority.

I told myself that I had to be Muhammad to the MSA. In the spring of my junior year, I nominated myself for president and began campaigning.

My platform, which I prepared with no sense of irony, was one of social conservatism and restoring the moral center of the organization. The campaign speech was a skit featuring a sinful drunk brother who, by participating in one of my MSA meetings, reformed his ways and became a pious believer. The elections followed shortly, and I became the first-ever unanimously elected president.

I now had power over an entire flock of Muslims. What's more, I was the representative, the immediate authority, for one of the three Abrahamic faiths—the fastest-growing one. Though our campus organization numbered less than a hundred, I could speak on behalf of a billion people. When a former U.S. president or the Dalai Lama or Archbishop Desmond Tutu came by, I was sent a special invitation to do a meet-and-greet. I went to large Christian churches around Atlanta, where I gave talks and held Q&As about Islamic history.

I also became responsible for giving the Friday sermon, which made me the spiritual head of our little community. After Friday prayer I held court in the hallway as, one by one, supplicants and spiritual mendicants, brothers and sisters, came to me, shook my hand, bowed to me, and spoke their secrets in my ear: the brother asking how he should make his non-Muslim girlfriend turn toward Islam (with patience); the sister asking whether she should put on the *hijab* (yes); the brother who didn't know what to do about his parents' divorce (admonish them); the sister undergoing a nervous disorder (pray for a cure).

I was, finally, the *imam* my father had once wanted me to be. Islam had given me prestige. I placed great emphasis upon the fact that my full name was Amir ul Islam—Prince of Islam. It didn't matter that it was all a charade.

# 4

The responsibilities of leadership in the MSA were anything but princely.

Balancing budgets, begging the student government for money, vacuuming the prayer center, organizing dinners, setting up cheesy social events, attending interfaith meetings in the early morning, meeting with the heads of other MSAs in the area and pretending to care about their thoughts and concerns, and meeting with Rabbi Aaron, the Jewish campus chaplain, to try to establish a joint *halal*-kosher deli—these things, inglorious and tedious, occupied most of my time as president. The rest of my time was spent supporting my staffers, whether by making late-night runs to Kinko's to make colored copies or driving around the university and plastering up posters advertising MSA events.

I also learned that leadership came with a whole host of new restrictions. Consider:

Some congregants thought that my favorite shirt, which featured a man in a fedora and had the letters NPA—National Pimp Association—written underneath him, was now inappropriate.

When I commented that I would consider getting a small tattoo on my arm, some of the members told me that it would be in bad taste for the president to get inked, since some scholars considered the practice un-Islamic.

When I made plans to attend a birthday party at a club, I was given *naseeha,* or confidential religious counsel, by a brother who felt that this would reflect badly upon my office; and when I objected that I wasn't planning on drinking or dancing, and that in fact many of the MSA members themselves were going, I was told that most people would think I was there solely to monitor their morality and would therefore likely be viewed as the religious police.

In short, there was a downside to being "Muhammad to the MSA": I now bore the expectation of infallibility and heightened purity. A Muslim leader couldn't be just an average guy undergoing the same tribulations, committing the same mistakes, and liking the same things as everyone else. On the contrary, a Muslim leader had to be an ideal that other, less religious people looked toward as a way to motivate themselves to be more pious. A Muslim leader, rather than being himself, had to be what others thought a perfect Muslim should be. The trouble, of course, was that I was far removed from piety—postmodernism and my own nature had assured that—and therefore the only solutions were to genuinely achieve perfect piety or to fake it.

As a true postmodernist I opted for the latter and called it art. It was as Nietzsche had said: "giving style to one's character." I styled myself a slave of Islam.

My plan to depict myself as Islamically submissive had three elements: wardrobe, conventions, and public rituals.

First the wardrobe. Adopting the Islamic "look" was easy. It required mixing and matching the following clothes and accessories:

Chinstrap beard
Palestinian-style checkered *kafiya*s (2)
Multicolored West African *kufi,* a rounded, brimless cap (1)
Elegant white, crocheted *kufi* (1)
Green cargo pants and green dress shirts (2)—green being the color of Islam

Official MSA T-shirts (2) with Quranic verses from beloved
  chapters—*Surah Baqarah* and *Surah Nur*—imprinted on the
  back (maroon and blue respectively)
Long-sleeved pride shirt in white with "Muslim" written in gold
  lettering across the front
Pakistani *shalwar kameez*es (2), to be seen in, particularly in the
  student center
Gray Iraqi robe-style *thowb* (1), to be worn during Friday sermon
*Tasbih* beads (2 strings)—one string hanging teasingly out of a bag,
  the other hanging in the car
Islam ring for ring finger to symbolize "marriage" to the faith
  (sterling silver with star and crescent) (1)
Crescent necklace (sterling silver) (1)
Sterling silver wristband with Quranic verse etched inside (1)


The second component of my plan involved showing off my new
wardrobe at the Islamic conventions that were a big part of my job as
president. The best place to show off the fashions of the faith was the
annual convention of the Islamic Society of North America, or ISNA.

Every Labor Day the ISNA held a convention in Chicago. It was
the biggest gathering of Muslims in the Western hemisphere. Believers came from everywhere, filling Chicago's hotels. College MSAs
used funds they'd collected over the year to subsidize the trip for
at least some of their members. People went to listen to lectures by
superstar evangelists like Hamza Yusuf and Siraj Wahaj and to go to
the massive *bazar,* where everything from Medinan *miswak*s—teeth-
cleaning sticks—to Indonesian devotional music was available. There
were workshops and seminars and networking events for young professionals, where they discussed such things as how to tap the market
of rich Muslim doctors. For the bachelors and bachelorettes in their
mid-twenties—clearly past marital age—there were expensive match-
making banquets at which prospective spouses wore color-coded
name tags corresponding with their age. (Some of the parents, many
of whom accompanied even their middle-aged children, complained

that the colors ought to correspond to degrees or income, since those were the most important barometers of marital eligibility.) Often, prominent religious figures from abroad were invited to ISNA conventions. One time Shaykh Sudais, the lachrymose *imam* of the Holy Mosque in Mecca, flew in secretly during the middle of the night to lead the morning prayer. When he didn't cry during his recitation, everyone was disappointed and some brothers rioted.

The youth loved the annual ISNA event. We attended primarily to socialize with other Muslims of similar age and interests. Much of the hobnobbing took place late at night, in the various hotel lobbies. The best lobby was at the Hyatt. The youth ironically called it Club Hayat, which—translated loosely—means Club Modesty.

During the nighttime at Club Hayat youth broke up into a few identifiable groups. In each group boys and girls comingled and flirted, all under the guise of talking about medical school admissions, gender relations at their MSA, alternative (meaning lesser) career paths besides medicine, and the future of Islamic leadership.

Around eleven o'clock, Club Hayat emptied out a bit as the more adventurous youth snuck out to actual clubs in Chicago. Those not able to go—say, because they were dressed in full Islamic regalia, like yours truly—were filled with resentment and disparaged those "wack Muslims."

Around three in the morning, there was another clearing out of the Club. This time those who'd had the good fortune of finding a hookup headed outside to a car or upstairs to find an empty room. These pairs could be identified by their watchful peers: all of a sudden a sister would break away from her friends and walk toward the elevators by herself, followed, at an appreciable distance, by a brother pretending he was sleepy. They would get into different elevators, of course, that would—due to Islamic magic—stop at the same floor. (The elevators at the Hyatt were glass, so observers could catch all this.) Sometimes these encounters didn't work out so well, though, often because the girl and the guy had different expectations in mind. In that case, the guy would end up forcing himself on top of the girl, and she—feeling that she couldn't cry out for help since she was doing something sinful at what was supposed to be a place for learning Islam and being pious—would end up taking it.

All the remaining youth at the Club stuck around until the morning prayer. Then they prayed and snuck into their rooms with their sleeping (or wakeful) parents. The adults, who normally would have imposed nine o'clock evening curfews on their children, didn't interrogate or get angry if this late arrival was discovered, because this was an Islamic convention; everyone knew that at a large gathering of Muslims, all the participants were pious.

When I arrived at the ISNA convention decked out in my Islamic regalia I received a lot of attention from brothers and sisters. When I was riding with my fellow MSA-ers on the shuttle from the airport to the hotel, a group of youngish bushy-bearded brothers in long white *thowb*s, lecturing to one another about the benefits of living in a Muslim country and pledging to one another that they'd leave "this immoral America" as soon as they got their parents to pay off their student loans, glanced appreciatively in my direction.

My clothes had so much impact that a guy from another delegation—he'd introduced himself earlier as Razaq—saw me walking alone in the parking lot and came over to make a confession of his sins.

"I go to clubs," he said. "I don't drink, but I just can't stop going."

"Clubs are *haram,* of course," I reminded him.

"I know," he said. "I really try to do *halal* things, but it's hard. My parents aren't very religious. They're opposed to my sister wearing *hijab.*"

"Well, you don't wear a beard," I noted. "You should grow one to support her."

"She's a better person than I am."

I nodded. "But you have to want to be a better Muslim," I told him.

"How?"

"Being a good Muslim is about representing Islam," I said. "You must show Muslims and non-Muslims your love of the faith—usually with external symbols. Start with a beard."

Razaq shook my hand with great aplomb and thanked me for giving him guidance. "Bro, you'll be a great leader for Muslims one day!"

I already am, I thought.

Soon I initiated the final part of my three-pronged plan for achieving piety: public prayer. It came about as I thought back on the advice I'd given Razaq. I decided that if I could just do something big—something that would show all the Muslims in the MSA how much I loved Islam—perhaps that would create a moment of sublimation, a sudden eradication of all their doubts about me, and bring an immense infusion of gravitas to my tenure. In short, I needed a public display of submission. Something big and explosive. An act that would annihilate all doubts in one swift swoop. A flash of light that would burst across the landscape and let every onlooker know in emphatic terms: this Muslim represented Islam like no one else.

I petitioned the various deans and administrators at the university, seeking their approval to play the *azan,* the Islamic call to prayer, from the bell tower on an upcoming Friday. I went to a designated committee of three and had them listen to various recordings of the *azan.* Looking pleased with themselves for their intercultural tolerance, they agreed to play the recording by the *muezzin* of the Holy Mosque in Mecca.

As the appointed Friday drew closer, I became more and more excited. I made plans to lead the whole MSA out to the bell tower after the Friday sermon that afternoon. I sent out letters exhorting people from all across Atlanta to join us for a supplication after the *azan.* I even sent out gleeful messages to MSAs all across the East Coast, gloating rather prematurely about "our"—I meant "my," of course—success.

It was a cool fall afternoon. I delivered an impassioned sermon on the merits of being truthful and then we went outside as a community, men and women, old and young, student and staff, and we stood under the bell tower at two-fifteen. Shortly after the bells chimed the quarter-hour, the voice of the *muezzin* from Mecca rang out across the university.

"God is Great! God is Great!" rang the *azan.* "There is no god but God!"

Students sitting at the outdoor cafeteria looked up in confusion at this sound they'd never heard. They could see me, wearing a *thowb* and a *kafiya,* leading my community.

I looked around me at the fifty or so Muslims gathered in a circle. I had expected to see tears streaming down their faces, hands outstretched in prayer, faces wreathed in nostalgia and reverence as loud exclamations of *"Takbir!"* went up. I had expected to see warm smiles directed at me, both thankful and deferential. I had expected to feel as if we were one body, bound together by the beautiful voice of the *muezzin*. I had even hoped to see CNN cameras, representatives from other MSAs from up and down the East Coast, and perhaps representatives of national Muslim organizations who had come to read letters of commendation. The *azan* was supposed to be an act of transcendence so immense that afterwards not only would no one doubt my potency as a Muslim leader, but I, Amir ul Islam, would become a legend among America's Muslims. Maybe the news would reach Saudi Arabia and Pakistan, and in Arabic and Urdu Muslim journalists would write that a young leader in Atlanta, the president of his local MSA, had managed to hold one of the first-ever public calls to prayer in the West, and certainly the first one at an elite Christian university.

Yet as the tones of the *azan* rang out, it wasn't like that at all; it wasn't as I'd imagined and hoped. A couple of people got emotional, true; a couple of people smiled; a couple of people even thanked me. But no cameras. No organizations. No commendations. No international celebrations. In a swirl of breeze and fall leaves, everyone disappeared.

I was left standing alone under the bell tower.

# 5

Almost as soon as I had become president, I started feeling like I was losing the MSA. No one came to the Quran study sessions I held. No one was inspired by the sermons I gave. No one had sudden epiphanies about Islam in the middle of the night and called me to share them. I hadn't gained esteem in anyone's eyes; in fact, I was slipping.

I wanted to resign, but thoughts of my father's *mannat* came rushing back. The covenant was inescapable. It was the overriding imperative of my life. It encompassed everything, overriding all opposition. It couldn't be rejected; it couldn't be modified; it couldn't be foresworn. I was an implicit signatory to a contract that was inked in my blood, my history, and my future. I couldn't let the MSA fail. I couldn't let the community disintegrate. Even as a fake Muslim my allegiance to Islam had to be concrete.

The pressure I felt over both the MSA and the *mannat,* compounding the ordinary senior-year stress, kept building up. One afternoon I hurled my Islamic ring against the wall of my room, then rushed across campus and gave my necklace and bracelet away to girls in the student center. I tucked away the *thowb.* The phone rang repeatedly that day, but I ignored it. I wrapped a *kafiya* around my head and tried to sleep.

When the phone didn't stop ringing, I was eventually forced to pick it up.

"It's Sam," came the voice. He was a West Coast organizer who contacted me from time to time, asking me if I'd read his latest e-mail compilation about what was happening in the Middle East.

"Do you need something?" I demanded gruffly, not wanting to chat.

"Ariel Sharon!" he said loudly, referring to the leader of Israel's right-wing opposition. "He's causing trouble in Jerusalem. Trying to incite violence!"

"Who?" I had only vaguely paid attention to the name in the news.

"A butcher," said Sam. "An Israeli war criminal. Even the Israelis admit that he was responsible for the Sabra and Shatila massacres in Lebanon—attacks on Palestinian refugee camps in which as many as three thousand Muslims were killed. He walked into the al-Aqsa Mosque in Jerusalem in the middle of the Friday prayers just to show Israeli muscle in one of our most holy places!"

Sam was still talking, but I was no longer listening.

The conflation of the word "massacre" and "Muslim" had caused me to think about something other than myself. The Muslim world flickered in my imagination. I began thinking of the genocide in Bosnia, with its mass graves and organized killings; of Chechnya, where the violence against Muslims had caused me to confront Wolf Blitzer when he came to my university to show his daughter around; of Iraq, where half a million children died under President Bill Clinton's sanctions— deaths that his secretary of state, Madeleine Albright, called acceptable; of Kashmir, where the Indians occupied the land and forcibly resettled Muslims; and of the Muslim Uighur people in China, who were being brutalized by the People's Army.

Startled out of my funk, I realized that I had an obligation, as a future leader of Islam, to step up and say something, do something, organize something. God knew how many accolades could be earned in the process. I might even be able to make the MSA important again!

I quickly read up on the current Israeli aggression and wrote an article about it. I sent it to the campus newspaper, having signed it as

president of the Muslim Students Association. Announcing the affilia-
tion was the most important thing.

Sam was pleasantly surprised by the interest I showed and made me
one of his favorite points of contact. A few days later he called again,
this time bearing news about Rami Jamal al-Durra, a twelve-year-old
Palestinian boy who had been caught in cross-fire with his father and
been killed. Sam sent pictures of the terrible scene, with the bloodied
father clutching his boy in desperation. The powerful images evoked
sympathy. Split into a time-lapse strip, they were ready for distribution
to activists.

"Hold a vigil," Sam said. "Invite everyone. Raise awareness about
the killing of children."

I looked at the six pictures for a long time. If I couldn't bring the
MSA together after this helpless child had given up his life in the service of Islam, then indeed I was the lowliest Muslim to ever set foot on
earth. I had to make certain that I didn't let Rami down. The rest of us,
Rami's people, had to find a way to make his death meaningful.

That Friday I dedicated a sermon to the plight of all Palestinians.
Then, to specifically mourn Rami's death, I organized an event outside
the student center. Attendees read tragic poetry and held up candles in
the waning evening light. The event had the lachrymose atmosphere of
a wake. It was a funeral in absentia: at the end I read a eulogy called "I
am Rami." The aim of the eulogy was to evoke emotion, to elicit tears
and make people suffer—to suffer as I was suffering under the *mannat,*
suffering for the sake of Islam. With suffering we could become one
with one another, a seething and pulsating and crying mass of sufferers.
Only a crescendo of wails on behalf of suffering Muslims could ensure
my continued relevance.

After my article the paper called me to ask about the so-called second *intifada* and I told the reporter that I thought suicide bombings by
Palestinians couldn't be defended, but neither was Israeli aggression
justified. It made me feel honored to have my opinion sought.

As my voice spread around campus, pro-Israel students began writing scornful and angry responses via e-mail and in the university paper.
One of the letters to the editor referred to the Palestinians as "savages."

Sam found out about it even before I did and called me immediately.

"That's the language of dehumanization!" he thundered. "You can't let *them* get away with this!"

Using my authority as president of the MSA, I blasted a mass e-mail to all the prominent student activists, ethnic groups, and school officials, complaining about the offensive word. The e-mail spread all over campus, and there were many fierce and angry responses aimed toward me.

Suddenly something surprising happened: the members of the MSA, seeing their leader under attack, started coming out of nooks and crannies and extended their support. Not only that, but people who had never attended an event before—and in fact had never shown much interest in Islam—were suddenly not just aware of the MSA but looking upon it fondly. I had put "us" on the map.

"Are you the president of the MSA?" an attractive, dark-haired Latina asked me in the student center.

"Why?" I asked cautiously.

"Did you write that e-mail about the dehumanization of Palestinians?"

"Yes."

"That was good of you," she said, smiling. "Are you guys planning any events in the near future?"

"If you give me your e-mail address, I'll add you to my list," I replied, thinking that I could use that information to ask her out.

I soon discovered that it wasn't just at the local level that I was becoming well known. Sam had shared my words with other activists all across the country, and soon they began writing me messages of support and encouragement.

Their attention—the sort of attention I didn't receive for making the public *azan,* the sort of attention that had been denied to me among the believers in the Islamic Republic of Pakistan—confirmed to me that the path of resistance I had taken, this path of noise and agitation and ruckus—all of which was packaged in the word "justice"—was the path Amir ul Islam should've been on his entire life. I asked myself why I hadn't stood up for Palestine before. Wasn't it the case that many of the childhood heroes I had—Muhammad and the Caliph Umar and

Salahuddin—were remembered because they had some role to play in Palestine? If I wanted one day to be considered by historians as someone who deserved to be mentioned within the annals of Islamic history, I too had to stand for Palestine.

I decided to take the political activism one step further.

"My dear brothers and sisters," I said, standing up after the Friday prayer. "I realize that we're not in Ramadan, the month of fasting, but if you've been hearing the news from *Falasteen,* you know that our brothers and sisters are in dire straits. They have to face checkpoints and deal with Israeli settlers, and they're denied basic human rights like home ownership. To show our solidarity, our spiritual unity, with our brothers and sisters, we're going to observe a day of fasting. If you'd like to participate, please fill out the sheet being passed around. We'll meet at the café tomorrow morning at four a.m. to share a communal meal before the fast begins and to pass out white armbands that we'll wear for solidarity."

The congregants looked uncertain. They had never before heard of anyone utilizing fasting as a form of defiance—but when I got back the sheet I noticed that many of the MSA members who hadn't participated in activities before had signed up to join in the fast.

At the appointed hour, lots of people came to the café. Some had woken up specifically to get together and eat. Others had simply packed up their books in the middle of an all-nighter at the library and come to see what was up. Some came to support Palestine. Some came for the free food. Some came for the white armbands. Some came out of a sense of obligation or shame. Others came because of the novelty of it all. In the end, however, they came to stand around and listen to me speak.

I was the center of the spoke.

As tensions between pro-Palestine and pro-Israel students mounted over the passing weeks, various religious figures on campus became concerned. One of these was Rabbi Aaron.

After I was elected president of the MSA, he was one of the first people with whom I became acquainted. Since then, we ran into one another routinely at interfaith meetings. He had a position of well-established authority, and I wanted to emulate him. Often I would take walks with him and watch the way he invited reluctant Jewish students to *shabbos*. He had mastered the art of persuading impressionable youth. As I listened to the rabbi, I was spurred to learn more about Judaism, turning at his suggestion to the works of Martin Buber and Emmanuel Levinas.

Now Rabbi Aaron was troubled by my use of my position as a religious leader to advance a political agenda. He took me aside in the chapel where we met weekly and asked me about my beef with Israel.

I felt like I'd been caught red-handed. I couldn't admit to him that my pro-Palestine stance wasn't based on facts (except those that Sam fed to me) or even principle. I couldn't enunciate a reasonable, justifiable position, so I hid behind abstraction.

"There's a war, Rabbi. War is a state of nature. Hobbes says that in a state of nature peace can be achieved only if the more powerful put down their weapons first. Israel is the powerful party in its relationship with the Palestinians. Therefore, Israel must put down its arms. Then we will have peace. So to answer your question: I just want peace."

Rabbi Aaron opened his mouth and replied. I could see his lips moving, but I didn't let myself hear a thing. I was afraid that if I started talking things out with him, I'd start considering the alternative opinion—and that would make me less inclined to side with the Palestinians as zealously as I now felt I needed to. I had to remain closed to counterargument. I had to practice what Nietzsche, the grandfather of postmodernism, called the "will to stupidity."

As the rabbi spoke, I imagined putting my fingers in my ears and saying, "La la la la la la la la la la."

A few days later I heard about a pro-Palestine demonstration that was being organized by the local Arab and Muslim communities. It was scheduled after Friday prayer and was to be held in front of the CNN building in order to highlight media inattention to the plight of the Palestinians.

The rally was loud and full of young Arabs. They had with them all the items necessary for a good protest: Palestinian flags that they wore as capes; *kafiya*s in various colors and patterns; banners that could be carried by one or two people; and girls in *hijab* walking around forming human chains. When cars passed by, the protestors ran into the street. The atmosphere made me feel giddy. I belted out Arabic slogans, yelling them despite not knowing their exact meaning.

Various Arab guys heard me and asked me where I was from. When I replied that I was from Pakistan, they looked at each other in surprise and insisted that I had to be an Arab.

"You must be a Saudi!" one exclaimed.

"Why do you say that?"

"You've got so much passion for Palestine!"

The praise gave me such a sense of honor that I couldn't contain myself. There was nothing better, as a Muslim leader, than to be recognized as an Arab; after all, Muhammad, the preeminent Muslim leader, had been an Arab, and Islam had emerged from the land of the Arabs. Furthermore, I had been promised to Islam in the land of the Arabs. If Arabs were now recognizing me for being one of them, then surely I had to be on the right path.

I traded my bland black-and-white *kafiya* with a young boy who had one in the Palestinian colors of green, black, and red. I wrapped it around my head and ran around screaming, "No justice! No peace!" I wanted to be heard through the thick walls of power that CNN represented. I wanted union with the weak and the voiceless of the world.

I wanted Wolf Blitzer to do a story about me.

# 6

Until now the extent of Sam's own activism had been rather limited, because he lived in his mother's basement. However, he was always looking for a chance to play with the "big boys" at elite universities. He had a gold mine in me. Since I was, in many ways, *tabula rasa*, a clean slate, when it came to activism, but had access to a great deal of money through the MSA, he figured he could work through me. One of his great ambitions was to get the big three of pro-Palestinian activism—Noam Chomsky, Norman Finkelstein, and Edward Said—in one panel discussion.

"How amazing would that be?" he said. "Two Jews and a secular Christian laying out Israel's injustices."

I was just coming to learn each thinker's importance to the cause and nodded excitedly. "That would be special."

"Trouble is, they all cost a lot of money. I can't finance it, but I think your organization has the pull to get that sort of funding."

"I'll see what I can do," I replied. Over the next few days I contacted Chomsky, Finkelstein, and Said and inquired about their honoraria. The news wasn't good. "With the second *intifada* heating up," I explained to Sam, "they're all really busy and really expensive."

"How much did you offer? They'll come for the money."

"Chomsky's baseline is five thousand," I said, reluctant to disappoint Sam, who was playing such a role in my greater visibility. "I'm sorry, but I can't pay out that kind of money to just one guy. Maybe six thousand for all three."

"That's not going to work," Sam said. "Let me see if I can find other speakers."

After a few days Sam returned with information about a pair of lesser-known lecturers. One was a professor who would argue that Israel's settlements in the West Bank and Gaza were detrimental to the peace process. The other was a speaker coming from Europe.

"The professor is obviously solid," Sam said. "But the European is the more intriguing prospect. He's an observant Jew who formerly served in the Israeli military."

"So a pro-Palestinian Israeli European?"

"Pretty much."

"Is he cheap?" I asked, going straight to the bottom line.

"Very."

I told Sam I'd manage to get the funding through the MSA, and we came up with a schedule for both speakers.

"Send me their writings," I requested before hanging up.

Shortly before the European's talk, which was scheduled first, Sam sent me a sample of his writings. Despite being creative and evocative, they were aggressive and polemical. The writer was a veritable machine gun of rhetoric. He turned everything into Jew versus Gentile and claimed that the very idea of Jewishness was a conspiracy. Although he made seemingly sophisticated literary references to characters and authors such as Don Quixote and Thomas Hardy, he never moved far from his main point: putting the entire blame for Israeli actions upon Judaism.

Something about the articles didn't sit right with me. Reeking of bigotry, they argued that as long as Israelis were Jewish, peace wasn't possible. The obsession with trying to impose certain inherent tendencies upon Jews, all negative, reminded me of my tutor Qari Adil in Pakistan, who used to say that God had made apes and monkeys out of Jews.

I pictured the European writer in my head. Earlier I had imagined a dapper man with professorial glasses, but now he seemed more akin to a hungry rat. I went back to his writings, but they felt so blood-soaked that I couldn't even keep them on my computer. When I lay down on the bed to think, he chased me from the shadows. My stomach filled with acid and I felt like throwing up—I abstained only because I imagined he would run out of the shadows and lap the vomit up.

Suddenly my computer chimed the arrival of a new e-mail and I returned to my desk. Rabbi Aaron had learned of the event and was sending a concerned message to various community leaders and the university's chancellor—and me—requesting that the event be canceled. He thought that the speaker would create further antagonism between the communities.

Rabbi Aaron's concern confirmed to me that inviting the writer had been a mistake. Yet I didn't want to accept that I had erred. The world of Islam needed people to engage in *resistance,* I reminded myself. Besides, canceling the lecture would undermine my hard-earned status among Muslims.

I pushed my chair back and stretched, looking up toward the ceiling. At the highest level of my bookshelf, where I kept the Quran and other books I didn't read, my eye was caught by the turquoise-colored binding of a book written by the philosopher Emmanuel Levinas. He called to me, and I pulled down the book.

During World War II, Levinas's parents were murdered by the Nazis in Lithuania, and he himself had lived under German captivity. His wife and daughter had escaped imprisonment by hiding in a monastery. Levinas's encounter with the Nazis became one of the focal points of his worldview. He tried to devise a philosophy that would help him address the contradiction that what was presumed to be the world's greatest civilization was capable of producing murderous institutions like National Socialism.

Levinas concluded that the world had gone fundamentally wrong for three thousand years because thinkers didn't treat ethics as the most important branch of philosophy, opting instead to make metaphysics and science more important.

He based the importance of ethics upon the fact that even before a person could say, "I think; therefore I am" a person first had to prove that the "I" existed, which could happen only through what Levinas called an "ethical encounter" with another human being.

In other words, we recognized our self or "I-ness" only when we were singled out by another person's "gaze." Being recognized like this, in a face-to-face encounter—in an encounter that gave us our consciousness—was a privilege available only to humans. Levinas said that this entire encounter occurred in the realm of expressions. It was a force. We didn't know *when* it happened; it just did. It occurred even before we could think about denying it, and it rendered us responsible for each other. In other words, what most people called "love at first sight" occurred between every living being at all times, but most of us chose not to acknowledge it.

I recalled my encounter with Rabbi Aaron in the chapel the time that I chose not to hear his reply. We had been face-to-face, but I had behaved as if he were faceless. That feeling of being estranged from another human being was what people like the European speaker wanted. Such people wanted me to think of Rabbi Aaron as a Jew, and a representative of the state of Israel, and nothing more.

Levinas was a burst of light for me. He cut through the conflict-based understanding of humanity that postmodernism had imparted. He seemed to say that life was about more than the pursuit of power.

Unfortunately, the part of me that was Amir ul Islam—the *imam,* the head of the congregation, the one who had felt exalted by the affirmation of Arabs at the rally—didn't want to hear this new definition of life.

I tried to make him listen.

I got up and wrote an e-mail to Rabbi Aaron and other community leaders and told them that it was too late for me to stop the European from speaking. However, I said, in order to advance the spirit of harmony and reconciliation, and as a peace offering, I personally wouldn't go to the event and would pull the MSA's sponsorship from the speech.

Amir ul Islam rasped and clawed at my gesture.

Then he was gone.

# 7

Abstaining from attending the lecture didn't make me feel good, as I'd hoped it would. In fact, I felt as if I had let down my people. I felt like a traitor. A prophetic *hadith,* "My community cannot agree upon an error," echoed endlessly in my head. It said to me that any person who breaks away from the community is in the wrong.

Thus, when various members of the MSA asked me why I hadn't shown up at the event, I didn't tell them about Levinas. I lied and said that I'd been sick, or that I'd had pink eye, or that I'd felt the event would go more smoothly if I wasn't present. I didn't want to be different than my fellow Muslims or publicly register a complaint against the established consensus. Even though I felt as if Sam had foisted his ambition upon me under the guise of Islam, I couldn't bring myself to tell him to stop. I simply had to go along.

In that manner I passed the few months until graduation, and then I moved away to D.C. to be as far away from Islamic leadership as possible.

# 8

A few months later I was sitting in my office on the third floor of a
gray building a block from the White House. I had obtained a fellowship for aspiring lawyers at the U.S. Department of Justice, having
given up my goal of studying Islamic law. My new aim in life was to become an antitrust lawyer and defend small businesses against monopo-
lists and multinational corporations.

Melanie, one of my colleagues, sat across the desk from me with a
Starbucks cup in her hand. It was the beginning of the work week and
we were having our regular Monday discussion about big ideas. She
was my opposite in many ways, and we both enjoyed picking holes in
each other's arguments. We had previously talked about Christianity
and Judaism and feminism and existentialism.

Today's subject was Islam.

"I have a great deal of respect for Islam," said Melanie. "It's one of
the great religions in the world. It sets forth an additional monotheistic basis—besides Judaism and Christianity, I mean—upon which the
world can affirm human dignity. I think that's significant."

I objected. "I don't think human dignity is, or should be, based
upon religion. The basis of human dignity comes simply from the in-

herent autonomy and individuality of every person. Religions should supplement that but not be the exclusive source."

"I don't think humans are either individualistic or autonomous," Melanie countered. "I think all of us owe a lot to the communities we come from. You, for example, owe much of yourself to Is—"

I cut her off. "Owing the community?" I scoffed. "No. I don't owe a community anything. My interaction with a particular community has to do, solely and entirely, with the accident of having been born into it. From that moment on, a community may impart things to me, but that doesn't mean that I 'owe' anything to that group as an adult. You're trying to create obligations by making me feel guilty. I don't accept that."

"But we owe what's in our heads to the community we come from," Melanie said, beginning to sound heated. "In my case that's the Christian church and in yours it's Islam. Your thoughts aren't really your own. You're *nothing* without the community. It's through established practice, through engaging in the wider community, that a person's consciousness is created and sustained."

I started to feel a little heated myself. I felt as if Melanie was trying to set forth an argument that would push me back to Muslims when I was quite happy as I was. Since graduation I had tried very hard to make myself an individual apart. I had told my parents that they'd have to accept the fact that the *mannat* wouldn't be fulfilled. When I ran into an excited Muslim who'd heard about the public *azan* I'd done the previous fall, I told him I didn't want to talk about it. When I heard that the Secret Service had discriminated against a young Muslim leader during Karl Rove's announcement of new faith-based initiatives at the White House, I laughed in amusement. I dismissed multiple invitations to pro-Palestine rallies. I found other things to do at the time of Friday prayers and used my lunch break to visit the Smithsonian and look at nudes. I read all of Salman Rushdie's works. I wrote a play mocking the idea of the *mahdi* without worrying whether Muslims might consider it blasphemous. When I ran into a group of Muslims agitating for an Islamic state, I told them that their aims were foolish. I began befriending secular Iranians and Indians. I went to clubs. I went to Miami Beach for a getaway. I drank. I enjoyed smoking Nat Sherman cigarillos.

Now, thinking back on all that, I rebuked Melanie.

"I'd like to live as a man who doesn't owe anything to a particular community and doesn't have demands made upon him by that community. The poet Hafiz has a beautiful line that goes to this point: 'Not once has the Sun told the Earth: you owe me. Look at what beauty has come from that.'"

Melanie didn't say anything for a long time. Then she said—gently, sadly, prophetically—"The world doesn't contain such beauty, Amir."

She turned out to be right. The next day there was a mass execution in New York: two aerial scimitars lopped off heads in Manhattan.

P lease don't let them be Muslim!" I thought when the second airplane hit the Twin Towers.

I thought it again when a plane hit the Pentagon and we were evacuated from our offices, in case more death was to follow. I stumbled along with all the other pedestrians around D.C., looking to the sky to see if a fuselage was about to fall on us.

I spent the rest of the day watching TV at a friend's house in nearby Rosslyn, and we continued to discuss the likelihood of the attackers being Muslim. By evening I was back at my apartment in Bethesda, resigned to the fact that the attacks had been carried out in the name of Islam. That night I put on the *ghazals* of Ghalib as rendered by Jagjit Singh and I began writing.

I felt an unbridgeable distance from those militants across the globe that I'd long ago felt drawn to and then, more recently, had felt pity for. I had used to think that while their methods were disreputable, they were simply misguided people trying to rectify undeniable injustices around them. Now, having seen their vision of justice, and recognizing how far it was from actual justice, I felt only anger. What made their actions even more reprehensible was that they had carried out their murders in the name of Islam. In a singular moment they had destroyed all the hard work—of education and awareness—that Muslims the world over had done over the years. Just as Ittefaq's friends had excommunicated me solely because I was an American, bin Laden and his men had passed a death *fatwa* against the whole of the West, including the Muslims within. This showed that while the attackers waved the flag of Islam, they cared, really, for something else—something that had nothing at all to do with Islam. They were power-hungry postmodernists.

I lifted my pen for a moment and wished that someone who knew Islam well would stand up and denounce them. I wanted that denouncer to say to the fanatics that, in a world where violence is deified, there's no difference between worshipping God and worshipping Satan—and thus Muslims might as well prostrate themselves to Iblis.

I wished someone would stand up because I knew it wouldn't be me.

I set my writing aside and lay down on my bed, tucking my head beneath the cool side of the pillow. Soon after I closed my eyes, Ghalib's verses lulled me to sleep:

*My soul is full and it would be good to drain the blood.*
*The problem is limits: I have but two eyes only.*

# BOOK V

## The Reformer—Ali Eteraz

*In which the author, aghast at the militant and murderous
use to which Islam is being put, becomes an activist and
goes to the Middle East to start a reformation*

# I

It was midnight in Kuwait. The desert, dark and forbidding, stretched to the stars. The airport, looming large ahead of us, was an oasis of light. The plane touched down with a soft skid and a bounce.

I emerged onto the tarmac and inhaled the warm scent of Arab sand. In the blue luminescence I could hear the whisper of the ancient poets: Dhul Rumma and Antara, al-Mutanabbi and Labid—their *ghazal*s and their couplets, their odes and their quatrains. As I walked into the terminal, the faint sound of Quranic recitation coming from a young man's headphones served to remind me that, still, it was the verses brought by Muhammad that were supreme in this land where poetry was born, or, if not born, spent some of its formative eons. I suddenly felt tiny—as if the three decades I had been alive were not even a moment in a world that seemed eternal.

I entered the arrival lounge looking for my family friend Ziad. Amidst the robed locals and bulky American contractors, I found him easily. He was a tall, dark-skinned bald guy, with a strong mouth and straight nose. He wore blue jeans and a University of Vienna T-shirt. His shoulders were broad, and below his shirt sleeve I could see a calligraphic verse tattooed on his arm.

After we collected my luggage we got into an SUV—a Jeep—and sped out onto a highway that cut through the barren landscape, the road empty at this hour. The vehicle droned on the black asphalt. We went under a series of overpasses, and the moon blinked on and off.

Ziad asked me about the nature of my trip. He thought I was in the Middle East to find employment—that was, after all, what I'd told him when I asked him if I could crash with him.

"So what kind of job are you looking for?" he asked. "Do you want to go back into the legal field?"

"Let's not discuss this right now," I said, straightening up. Truth was I had no intention of looking for a job. "How about we talk about the beauty of the night? This is such a haunting drive."

"Is your résumé up to date? You did some contract work for a law firm recently, right?"

"Come on," I said. "Is this really necessary?"

"If you aren't here for a job," Ziad said, "what are you going to do for the next few months?"

I chewed on my nails. I pinched the bridge of my nose with my thumb and index finger. My contacts felt dry and scratchy. I could feel little particles of sand going into my throat and cutting into my larynx.

Then all my anxiety blew off and was replaced with bravado.

"You don't know who I am, do you?" I asked in a loud voice.

Ziad looked perplexed. "I don't follow."

"Who am I?" I asked, poking my chest emphatically. "What's my name?"

"Amir," Ziad said.

"No," I said. "No, no, no. You want to try that again?"

"Not really," Ziad replied.

"Ali Eteraz," I said. "That's my name."

"Ohhh, riiight. Ali Eteraz!" Ziad's voice became sarcastic. "You mean the anti-terrorist, anti-extremist, anti-Osama Islam blogger and activist who has written such essays as 'Open Letter to Reformist Muslims' and 'The Hoor's Last Sigh'?"

"Yes," I said, pounding my hand on the armrest. "*That* Ali Eteraz. The one who is going to foment an Islamic reformation in the Middle East."

Ziad blinked hard, bit his lip, fiddled with his cruise control, and sprayed water on the windshield. He didn't say another thing till we got to his apartment.

# 2

Ali Eteraz—which meant "Noble Protest"—was my newest manifestation, the latest phase in my attempt to satisfy my congenital covenant with Islam. Ali Eteraz was the force that shattered the abracadabra of silence that had cocooned me after the towers fell in New York, that had kept me cushioned from reality during the several intervening years of law school in Philadelphia. Ali Eteraz was the one who made me lift up my head and take stock of the world at a time when I was happy simply to play my video games, make my money, and try to start a family. It was Ali Eteraz who got me involved with Islamic reform—an underground movement involving Muslims around the world who challenged the theocrats and terrorists that had taken over the religion.

Signs of Ali's emergence preceded his birth. After 9/11, but before my conversion to reform, there were fleeting moments—upon hearing of a suicide bombing in Madrid, say, or a beheading in Iraq, or a blown-up girls' school in Pakistan—when my conscience would threaten to ignite. The combustion was never able to sustain itself, however.

That had changed in January of 2006 during the Danish cartoon fiasco. Upon the publication of a series of trivial and badly drawn cartoons in an irrelevant newspaper in Denmark, Muslims rioted in multiple locations, killing innocent non-Muslims and making an intimidating show of force. That such cosmic insecurity could be prompted by such comic absurdity was the final straw. "Enough!" said Ali Eteraz at that moment. "Islam doesn't belong to the idiots."

At the time I was a lawyer in Manhattan and lived in a penthouse on the Hudson. When I realized that there was a hunger in the world for someone to take a stand—a hunger that I myself had first felt almost half a decade earlier, when I yearned for a denouncer—I threw myself into my new persona. I put pen to paper and wrote outraged and incendiary essays denouncing the "snake lords" who manipulated Islam for military and political benefit, Muslims who supported the death penalty for apostates, Muslims who refused to accept that Islam promised equality of all people, Muslims who stifled speech in the name of religion—it was these Muslims who received the brunt of my criticism.

The issue of apostasy, deserting one's faith, was important, both to me and to the reformists. Too many Muslims who dissented against terrorism and theocracy were being declared apostates and attacked, maimed, or killed. I marshaled Islamic scriptures to demonstrate that apostates shouldn't be punished. I studied the works of scholars past and contemporary. I corresponded with students and thinkers around the world, and together we parsed individual Quranic verses, even single words, as well as countless *hadith*s, all in an effort to prove to our extremist co-religionists that there was no Islamic basis for the killing of apostates. It was tedious but necessary work.

The more I wrote, the more like-minded Muslims I met. Hailing from many countries, we became a small, decentralized network of activists. Some were well known, others anonymous. Some had prominent positions in universities, others wrote for newspapers, and still others were on the ground, right in the thick of the violence. Sometimes we kept in touch, and sometimes we pretended to ignore one another.

We wrote to *ayatollah*s in Iran who had passed death *fatwa*s upon journalists and implored them to reconsider. We wrote to Muslim governments, petitioning them to protect their female legislators. We raised funds to popularize and publicize a translation of the Quran that didn't promote supremacism. We created a letter-writing campaign against stoning. We fought legislation in Pakistan that would have punished women as adulterers even if they were raped. We gave talks related to the separation of mosque and state in Islam. We identified all the positive strains of reform in the Muslim world and passed that information on to media figures and writers in the West.

Our efforts were resisted by many die-hard Muslims. They called us apostates, seeing *us* as the radicals, and refused to speak to us.

We were also mocked by anti-Islam bigots. Because we dared to suggest that Islam didn't have to be authoritarian, they called us deceptive.

All these obstacles only caused me to become even more assertive.

Whenever I got discouraged, I told myself that in today's age, when the most vocal Muslims had apparently lost their moral compass, being a real servant of Islam required rebuke and dissent. It required being a renegade willing to protest, to wage a life-affirming counter-*jihad* against the nihilism of *jihadist*s, to toss away magazines of bullets and replace them with magazines containing bullet-points of knowledge. Only everyday Muslims like me—like Ali Eteraz—who were willing to stand up and resist the fanatics could prevent the Ka'ba's cloak from being ripped off and murals of blood drawn upon its denuded walls. Islam could be made beautiful only when there were no constraints on the creation of beauty.

Ignoring my work as a legal associate, I wrote more, researched harder, and spent more time on the Internet. Echoes of every bomb blast reverberated in my heart. The wails of those who were victimized by Muslim monsters haunted my soul. Islam was being destroyed, and I couldn't sit idly by. My life became one of resistance and tension. It had no room for mundane matters. Not for laughter. Not for love. Not even for calm and relaxation. I was part of something greater than history. There was a civil war within Islam and I had every intention of my side's winning.

I put everything into this war of ideas and I paid for it dearly.

I lost my job, my apartment, all my money, and my family. And apparently I was losing my war as well: the voices of violence were outshouting the voices of reason. Finally, in despair, after many nights consorting with Khayyam's beloved, I forswore the faith of my ancestors and told people I wanted to have nothing more to do with Islam. In my delinquency I bought a one-way ticket to Sin City, USA—viva Las

Vegas!—where I lived in a ghetto, wrote poems to dark goddesses, and intoxicated myself upon *ghazal*s. Roaches scurried through my chest hair at night, and in the morning I was wakened by boys throwing rocks against my window. It was an inglorious and miserable crash.

Once I was in Vegas, the only activity I engaged in was to park my car at the Stratosphere at the northern end of the Strip and then walk all the way to Mandalay Bay. On the way I would pass the domes of the Sahara, the gardens of the Alhambra, the sinking ship in front of Treasure Island, the burning water of the Mirage, the sad facade of the Aladdin, the dilapidated visage of the Sands, and the pyramids of the Luxor. I repeated the walk the next night, and the next. My eyes were sunken and my soul was morose.

My torpor would last approximately three months.

One night, when I was at the end of my walk at Mandalay Bay, I was suddenly fixated on two robotic camels munching on fake date palms in a plastic oasis at the end of a long escalator. Their appearance was so sudden and perplexing that I couldn't stop looking at them. I sat down on a bench facing them, the better to take them in. Then the camels spoke to me. "Go to the Middle East!" they said.

The camels, with their pronouncement, touched off an idea in my head. Suddenly I came up with a way to resurrect the reform, and myself.

That was when I had told Ziad I was heading over.

# 3

The next morning at breakfast, Ziad and I had omelettes with cilantro and tomatoes, along with Moroccan mint tea with the leaves still in. We took a kettle and our little green cups out onto the balcony overlooking the city.

To the right a palatial new building was under construction. I could see dark-skinned Indians and Sri Lankans going up and down ladders. The Arab foreman sat in his SUV talking on his cell phone.

To the left I could see the dome and minaret of a mosque. It struck me, now that it was bright out and I was refreshed from sleep, that I was in a Muslim country—and not just any Muslim country, but an Arab Muslim state. It was a stark reminder of the fact that the wheels of history had made their revolutions, and Islam, which began with Arabs but then got passed to Persians to Mamluks to Spaniards to Ottomans and Indians, had once again come back under the protection of the Arabs.

"Doesn't the call to prayer happen publicly anymore?" I asked, turning to Ziad.

"Five times a day," he replied. "Every single mosque in the city."

"How come I didn't hear anything this morning?"

"In the new houses the windows are soundproof."

"So what's the point of the public *azan*?"

"Gotta maintain the illusion of this being an important Islamic country."

"What if I—"

Ziad read my mind. "If you want to wake up for the morning prayer? You need to do what you do in the West."

"Set my alarm?"

He nodded. We sipped our tea in silence. I studied the architecture all around and I asked Ziad how he felt about the construction.

Sore subject. He complained at length about how long the nearby towers had been under construction and how the first and second waves of construction workers had given way to a recently arrived third—fresh—batch. "They never let them stay too long," he said bitterly.

As the sun rose higher and we started to become sweaty, Ziad finally prodded me to talk openly with him. I began by apologizing for my behavior in the car.

"I understand," he said.

"I was just trying to sound cool. I really don't believe that I'm deserving of even an iota of respect. The one thing that I'm good at—rhetoric, basically—doesn't merit much attention."

"You're a good organizer, it seems," Ziad said. "You can bring different types of people together."

"All I've done so far for Islamic reform is to act as a sort of cheerleader. I jump up and down with the colors of the movement emblazoned across my chest, and because I'm able to rabble-rouse and instigate, a few people start paying attention."

"If you're a cheerleader, I hope you shave your legs," Ziad said. "Because judging by your chest—"

"Very funny. All I'm saying is that I want to make a solid contribution. Something that's more tangible than words and Web sites and letter-writing campaigns. Something longer-lasting. Something that Muslims can touch and feel. And that's why I came to the Middle East."

"Why the need to be here?"

"It's the heart of Islam," I said. "The Arabs, as a whole, are considered Islam's elite."

"You know that most of the Muslims in the world—nearly 80 percent—are *not* Arab."

"I know that," I said. "But Arabs today are a symbol. They represent Islam in most people's eyes. And symbols are very important. Back when the Abbassid Caliphate was sacked in 1258 by the Mongols, the symbols associated with Islamic leadership—specifically, the mantle and sword of the Prophet—were moved to Cairo under the guardianship of the Mamluks, and thus it was they who became the presumptive leaders of Islam. Just because of the symbols. Today the caliphate is long gone—"

"Good riddance!"

"—but the symbol of Islam is now the Ka'ba, and as you're well aware, it's the Arabs who guard it. So if there's going to be anything that will sway Muslims in the rest of the world, it's going to have to be stamped by the Arabs—whether I as an American Muslim, or my friends in Pakistan, or Muslims in Indonesia like it or not."

"Didn't you write an essay arguing that Mecca and Medina should be made into independent protectorates like the Vatican? What was it called?"

"Mecca Is Not a Monopoly."

"Yes," he said, nodding. "I read it."

"In an ideal world, perhaps," I replied. "But to accomplish that now there would have to be far too much bloodshed. We need *less* of that. I'm not sure that I ascribe to that position anymore. The goal has to be to work *with* Arabs, not *against* them. This is the only hope for Islamic reform."

"So that's why you had to be here?" Ziad asked, looking thoughtful as he poured another round of tea into our cups. Then, handing me a full cup, he said, "I'm about to burst your bubble."

"Sure. Have at it."

"No one here is going to listen to you," he said with crushing finality.

"Why not?"

"You aren't a *shaykh* and you aren't a noble. On top of that, you're a Pakistani-born American. To many Arabs that makes you dirty *and* an imperialist. This is what you are in their eyes, even if your intentions are pure as the driven snow—and I don't doubt they are. This is all you can be to them. This is the rebuke you'll run into the moment you go into a *madrassa* or a mosque and try to get some support around here."

"I know what you're saying. Hell, I'm told I have no authority even among the Muslims in America—but I still persist."

I didn't mention that my persistence had already led to one monumental crash.

"I was only trying to give you a reality check," Ziad said. "I'm not a naysayer. I may not be a reformist, but I do want to help you."

I took another sip of tea. It made my insides hotter than my skin, and yet my body felt cool and light. Suddenly a great smile broke out across my face and grew into a grin. Then came outright laughter.

"What?" Ziad said, looking down at his pants. "My fly isn't open."

"If you walk past all the Arab- and Islam-themed casinos on the Strip in Las Vegas and then get on the walkway leading from the Luxor Hotel to Mandalay Bay, there are these two talking camels. One night we had a conversation—"

"Wait. I'm not following," Ziad said. "And I don't remember putting *hashish* in the tea."

"I'm not high," I replied. "Let's just say I didn't come all this way without a scheme tucked away in my dirty imperialist mind."

"Oh, a conspiracy. Now I wish you *were* high," Ziad said. "Let's take this inside. I don't want to be executed."

# 4

The aim of my plan was twofold: freedom of conscience and freedom of expression. If Muslims could believe what they wanted
without fear and say what they wanted without reprisal, I was confident
that the intelligent and humane among them would rise to the top and
excise the extremist cancer from Islam.

To accomplish my goals I had come up with a plot involving a
*shaykh,* a sculptor, and a princess.

## The Shaykh

A few months earlier I had heard that a scholar who had previously
risen to great heights among fundamentalists had taken an important
turn. In front of an audience of men and women who were clamoring
for the death penalty for any person who converted from Islam, this
*shaykh*—on satellite TV no less—had thundered, "This is not liberty!"

It was an important statement, because until now Islamic reformers
had been unable to demonstrate the principle of liberty through the
Quran and other Islamic texts. Whenever we made any citations or
references to liberty, our detractors quickly dragged us down in a battle

of citations, while freedom of conscience was further curtailed. This *shaykh,* however, had transcended the problem by turning liberty into an unimpeachable truth that didn't need to be proven. It just was. It was a monumental thing.

Since 2001 there had been many instances where the world had thought that an Islamic "Martin Luther moment"—something as dramatic as Luther's nailing of the ninety-five theses on a church door—had occurred. The instances that I'd heard about so far, like the woman who'd posted a women's rights manifesto on the door of a mosque in West Virginia, had all been staged and therefore were of only limited value. In my estimation, though, a genuine Martin Luther moment had occurred in the Middle East with the televised declaration of the *shaykh*—and yet no one seemed to be paying any attention.

My first goal, thus, was to get an audience with this *shaykh,* learn more about his positions, and then publicize his courage to the rest of the Muslim world. Once Muslims saw someone of the *shaykh's* stature— an Arab in a white robe who considered himself a fundamentalist— taking such a stand, it would (I dared hope) create a flood of other *shaykh*s echoing similar sentiments. I would then create an institute, a think tank, for the *shaykh* and his newfound followers. Their task would be to issue combative declarations against extremists, to challenge the reign of those who declared other Muslims apostates, and to write persuasive edicts linking Islamic texts with notions of equality, liberty, and community.

My institute would change Islam for the better.

## The Sculptor

The *shaykh* represented freedom of conscience, while an Arab artist I encountered—the sculptor in my threefold plan—represented freedom of expression.

When I was living in New York, someone sent me lithographs by an aged Arab sculptor. The artist had cast the human form into stone and clay and captured the magnificence and tragedy and tension of a body undergoing tumult and torture. He did this at a time when extremists declared images to be idolatrous, when the Taliban bombed the Bamiyan statues, when the Deobandis in India declared photography *haram,* when mere cartoons were considered threatening to Islam. This sculptor's courage—his insistence on affirming visual art in the face of all detractors—was inspiring. I decided that I would promote his work all over the world. His sculptures would be the hammer by which the idols of dogma and recalcitrance would be shattered.

Once the ban on images fell, all the other bans on expression would fall away as well. That was my hope.

## The Princess

Obviously, all of these ventures I had dreamed up would cost money. Or, as Ziad put it, "No shit, Sherlock."

The princess in my three-pronged approach would be the solution to that concern.

I had been following the immense amounts of money going in and out of the Arab countries. Financiers bloated upon oil wealth were buying real estate in Europe and America, including landmarks like the Chrysler Building in New York. They wanted to buy sports teams, purchase Grand Prix auto races, acquire huge numbers of the most expensive racehorses, and sponsor international tennis tournaments. They had purchased large stakes in the world's major banks, such as Citigroup; major oil companies, such as British Petroleum; major retailers, such as Barneys and Bloomingdale's. They had gotten involved in the American casino business: nine percent of the largest casino corporation in Las Vegas was owned by an Arab company. The largest condominium project in the world, a Las Vegas project called City Center, was also financed by Arab lenders. Arab banks had been able to muscle into the international banking scene by creating a subsector called Islamic finance, and it was the fastest-growing field of the securities industry.

"This means there's a lot of money here," I commented to Ziad.

"That doesn't mean wealthy Arabs are going to give any of their money to *you*," he pointed out reasonably. "They're obviously into business."

"I know," I said, stepping onto my soapbox. "But you have to figure that where you've got rich old guys in business, you've got rich younger wives into charity. In the Enlightenment all the great advances in arts and humanities were paid for by wealthy wives. Rousseau was patronized by a nobleman's wife. Voltaire had a queen. I bet the same thing will happen with Arabs and Islam: noblewomen will back universities; they'll finance theaters; they'll donate to museums and even fashion magazines. The super-wealthy equate culture with luxury, while activists like me equate culture with freedom. It's a win-win for both."

"How the hell are you going to get a princess to give you money?" Ziad asked.

"In Las Vegas the casinos are always looking for what they call 'whales.' These are well-known big spenders to whom the casinos make a presentation about their establishment, hoping to lure the spenders in. That's what I'm going to do. I'm going to meet the *shaykh* and the sculptor and come work with them to establish our think tank. Then we're just going to have to go from princess to princess until one agrees to fund us on a trial basis. If we can manage to perform well for a year, we'll have set up the world's first Islamic reformist institute. In the heart of the Arab world no less!"

"Interesting proposition," Ziad said, nodding. "But if you call a princess a whale, you'll get executed for sure."

# 5

When I wasn't with Ziad or plotting my schemes during those first few days in the Middle East, I was on the Internet.

Rogues and rebels; murderers and miscreants; polemicists and pundits; victims and women; whores and virgins. They had all flocked to it. The Internet was the place where the *jihadists* recruited and the counter-*jihadists* monitored. On the Internet patriarchs promoted ideas about the lesser station of women, and women militated for equality. Blogs and e-mail lists; forums and chat rooms; Facebook and instant messages; YouTube and MySpace. These were to Islam what the printing press had once been to Christianity. They blew the whole thing open. The Internet made it apparent that no one was in charge of Islam. It created a free-for-all. A Wild West of words and vitriol. Each Web site was its own OK Corral. Each pamphlet and video and essay was a gunfight. There were no sheriffs. There was no authority. There were no jails. There was no accountability.

I spent hours traversing its vast spaces. The aim was to find all the millions of pieces of news relating to Islam—coming from newspapers and blogs and governments—and then rearrange them in such a way that Islamic reform seemed to be the dominant force in the faith. When there was a terrorist attack, it was an opportunity not just to condemn the extremists (for their violence) and the orthotoxics (for their apathy) and the Wahhabis (for their political use of Islam), but also to popularize the names of key figures in the reformist movement, to plug their books, to market their pamphlets. All of this had to occur in the blink of an eye.

I called it "psy-ops for the future of Islam."

Ziad called it "psycho jihad."

# 6

By the end of the first week we'd fallen into a pattern: while Ziad was at work each day, I did the above-mentioned Internet surfing, wrote e-mails, put out calls to my contacts, and devoured newspapers. When he got home, we generally went out into the city.

We visited the major outdoor *souk* and haggled with aged sellers, went into the interiors of the large mosques, drove near the royal palaces, and ate Lebanese and Indian cuisine at fancy restaurants.

We marveled at the new building projects and counted the number of Porsches in any given parking lot.

As we drove up and down the streets, we saw migrant workers from South and Southeast Asia wearing thick overalls in various colors. They'd run out of the shade every few minutes with brooms in their hands, sweeping the sand from the asphalt under the sizzling sun. Ziad and I made a game out of trying to identify which country particular laborers were from.

"One hint I can give you to make your guessing easier," said Ziad, "is to *not* guess Muslim countries. They don't like having laborers from Muslim countries here."

"Why not?"

"They start agitating for rights."

As we were wandering through a mall one day, I saw some shelves of books in a corner shop that sold mostly cigarettes and candy. I went to take a closer look. Of the three rows of books, the topmost were mostly books of Islamic creeds, discussing such things as *tawhid* and the virtues of fasting. The second row was predominantly Arabic translations of Danielle Steel novels. The third row seemed to be devoted to alarmist books. The one on the end of that row had a picture of Dajjal, the Islamic Antichrist, on the cover, and the pages were full of end-of-the-world prophecies and predictions.

Moving on, we passed by a clothing store, where we saw two bearded men in robes taking a young man's cell phone from him. The boy seemed to be complaining, but the men didn't listen to him; they just yelled at him to scurry off.

"What was that about?" I asked.

"Long story."

"I want to know."

"That boy just got caught out by the vice police."

"I don't see any police," I said, looking around for uniforms.

"They're undercover. Those guys with the walkie-talkies that took the phone. They're just mall security taking their jobs too seriously."

"Jesus. Is he in trouble?"

"No. I think he just lost his phone."

"But why would they take his phone?" I asked.

"I guess the police have become technologically savvy."

"Meaning . . . ?"

"You know that you aren't allowed to talk to a girl in public, right?"

"Right," I said. "Sure."

"One way kids get around the ban is with technology," Ziad explained. "Boys and girls go to malls and hang out in their segregated corners, cell phones in hand. Then they all turn on the Bluetooth network and are able to identify one another using the screen names that show up. Basically, when you turn on Bluetooth it creates a map, and you can essentially see who's who just by moving your phone around. It's like finding treasure in a video game."

"That's amazing," I said, marveling at how fast technology evolved. "But what about the fact that the women are covered?"

"Easy," said Ziad. "Once you've identified a girl and she acknowledges you with her eyes or with a gesture, she'll send a picture over to your phone."

"This is incredible!"

"It's a new technology," Ziad said, "and it generally works pretty well, but I guess the police must have figured it out and started cracking down."

"So they took that boy's phone?"

"Yup."

"Let's follow him!" I said.

"Why?"

"That's a recruit! We'll tell him about our idea. How we're trying to usher in a culture of autonomy and freedom that opposes the vice police. We won't say we're reformists or anything. Just concerned Muslims."

"First of all," Ziad said. "I'm *not* a reformist."

"All right. *I'll* talk to him."

"Second of all, it's just a bad idea in general."

"Come on," I urged. "Let's just get him interested in the think tank. Don't you see? This is a sign. Right before us we see repressive Muslims in action! It's people like the vice police who give tacit and explicit support to all the authoritarian and extremist Muslims of the world. That boy is our ally!"

"I don't think that boy would want to work with you," Ziad said.

"Why not?"

"Because, look," said Ziad. "He's already gone and purchased a new phone."

Turning, I saw that the boy had gone up the escalator to another floor of the mall and, with his new phone extended, was walking around looking for girls on the network map. The mall police, oblivious, patrolled their route underneath.

It upset me that there had been a resolution and it hadn't involved me.

# 7

I found out that my designated sculptor was going to be overseas for a while, so I had to consign myself to waiting.

However, in the meantime I got a promising lead with respect to the *shaykh*. Rashad, one of the *shaykh's* young supporters in England, who wrote to me occasionally, was going to be visiting mainland Europe for a few days and was willing to talk with me there. He extended me an invitation to meet him in Vienna, and when I arrived he came to pick me up from my hotel in a limousine. He was about my age, in traditional Muslim clothing, and his head was covered. He gave instructions to his driver in Arabic.

Soon we were seated in Rashad's favorite Viennese restaurant. After making some small talk about the weather and our favorite philosophers (Nietzsche and Heidegger, respectively), we ordered our meal and began discussing reform.

"I read your seven-part series on Islamic reform in the *Guardian* newspaper," he said.

"What did you think?"

"It was different," he said warily.

"You didn't like it?"

"It was an information overload. Muslims aren't ready for all of that. Religions change slowly."

"That's why I want to meet with your teacher," I replied. "He has a better sense of the tenor of Islam than I do. He's in step with its rhythm."

When our food arrived, we ate in silence for a few minutes, appreciating tastes and smells.

Eventually Rashad broke the silence. "What do you want to talk about with him?"

"I just want to ask him some questions," I replied. "I want to have an honest discussion with him so that we can place issues of reform and moderation before other Muslims and show them that there's nothing reprehensible in being tolerant and egalitarian. I want to talk about how he went from being a youth who was involved in fundamentalist groups to someone who is quite critical of them. I want to know what battles he has with extremism. I want to know if the Islamists trouble him, and how he responds. What sort of narrative is he building that other Muslims in the world can adhere to? Where does he stand on the separation of mosque and state? Things like that."

"These sound like interesting subjects," Rashad replied, "and we do talk about them regularly. I'll speak with him and try to arrange a meeting. Perhaps someday soon you could just go over to his house and hang out with him and his family."

"That would be wonderful," I said excitedly, imagining a salonlike atmosphere in a large desert home. I could see myself discussing the finer points of Islamic history with an erudite teacher of moderation, tolerance, and liberty. I imagined the *shaykh* being something akin to Islam's John Locke and smiled at the thought of meeting him.

"I'm a little confused, though," Rashad said toward the end of dinner. "Why?"

"What are you trying to get out of meeting with the *shaykh*? It seems that you'll just become a glorified messenger for his ideas."

"When they started up the Pony Express to deliver the mail in frontier America," I replied, "the horse was as important as the mail."

"There seems little reward in it."

"It's a thankless job, but someone has to do it. Haven't you read about the heavenly rams? On the Day of Judgment they'll put people on their backs and zip them across the Bridge of Sirat, suspended over hell, and take them safely to the other side."

"You're aware that those are the same rams which had been sacrificed by Muslims at the Eid festivals in this life?"

Folding my napkin with exaggerated precision, I ignored him.

We both ordered dessert, enjoying Vienna's famed baked goods, and then parted ways. Before leaving, Rashad promised that I'd hear from him again about a potential meeting with his teacher.

As I thought back over the meeting in my hotel later on, I was pleased with the way it had gone. I hadn't come across as desperate or as a schemer—or at least I didn't think so. Thus the *shaykh* wouldn't be threatened when he met me, and if I could earn his trust then he might be willing to chair my institute.

Optimistic now, I started doodling potential names for the think tank.

# 8

Once I was back at Ziad's I felt good about the future.

Now while he was at work I started venturing out, often spending time at the malls. Eventually I got bored with that and headed farther afield, finding and delighting in hidden *souk*s. These were open-air markets, dusty and hot without air conditioners or fans, at which migrants from all around the world sold foods, wares, clothes, and used goods. Whereas the mostly Arab clientele in the malls wore *dishdasha*s and *abaya*s and *niqab*s, the market's clientele wore mostly denim, topped by collared shirts and blouses. Many of the women didn't cover, and there was no sign of any policing or monitoring. These *souk*s reminded me of the old Pakistani *bazar*s, seeming less formal and more jovial than any Kuwaiti mall I'd been in thus far.

The first day I discovered such a market, I walked around with a smile on my face. I sniffed cologne at one stall and then browsed through a magazine rack containing books from all over the world. I walked past a group of Filipinos, male and female, hanging about and carelessly chatting with one another. I heard clusters of Egyptians talking loudly with one another. A Lebanese man tried talking to me in English about how he was going to move to Canada. Toward the end of that day, as one of the Indian jewelers selling used watches closed up shop, his tiny companion, a dark-skinned Sinhala girl, walked past close enough for her hair to brush against his arm, and when they walked away, he momentarily reached forward with his hand and touched her fingers. I tried to pull out my phone camera to capture this moment of fleeting intimacy, this act of natural liberty, but by the time I got the lens in focus, the couple had gone.

After I got back to the apartment, Ziad and I went to a small café for dinner and I told him about my day while we waited for our food to arrive.

"It was lively," I reported. "It was loud. There was music playing. I didn't expect to see such . . ." I began, struggling for a word.

"Such what?"

"I don't know the word I'm looking for."

"You mean freedom," Ziad said, smiling. "You saw poor people in a Muslim country—"

"An *Arab* Muslim country," I interjected.

"—and you figured they'd be hard-core theocrats or fundamentalists."

I nodded. "Something like that."

"Quite the opposite," Ziad replied, nodding at the waiter as he brought our tea. "The people at the bottom of the rung—migrants and Bedouins—are pretty laid-back, both culturally and religiously. Same goes for the ultra-rich. It's the middle class—the mall-going, bureaucratic, Camry-driving portion of the population—which is uptight and stuck-up."

"I guess you're right," I said. "They do seem to be the most religious group. I've seen more women wearing the veil inside the malls than outside, for example."

"Being uptight doesn't only have to do with Islam, though," Ziad replied. "Women wear the veil today for all sorts of reasons that have little to do with religion. For most of the middle-class women it's so that no one confuses them for an immigrant."

"So bigotry instead of Islam?" I said sarcastically.

"Or classism. Or maybe even just fashion. Look, we can never understand why individuals do the things they do."

"Fashion? Come on!"

"Yes, fashion," Ziad repeated, pointing to a pair of *niqab*-wearing women in a far corner of the café. "Look at those girls. They're covered up, but they're in this café which is mostly men. That already indicates that they aren't constrained by Islam. If for some reason the café owner suddenly stopped permitting women inside, these girls would still find a way to be around guys."

"How?"

"You'd be surprised. Maybe they'd drive really slowly down the road, and guys would pull up next to them so that they could exchange phone numbers through the window. We'll drive up and down the main highway next Friday night. You'll see the pick-up scene there."

"I find that hard to believe."

"Just look at the shoes they're wearing," he said.

"Heels," I said, taking note. "Strappy ones. Nice sexy heels. So what?"

"I don't know many brand names, but those are guaranteed to be Dior or Chanel or Jimmy Choo. And if you go to the mall you'll find all these girls in the boutiques buying up a storm. Why would they buy stuff if there wasn't anyone to appreciate them?"

I nodded.

"And look at how they're watching the belly dancer on TV," Ziad added. "Clearly they have no problem with sexuality."

"But they cover their face," I noted. "That's repressive. We have to liberate women like them. Veiled women raise fundamentalists: the veil is the 'gateway drug' to extremism."

Ziad laughed. He sipped his tea and thought for a moment before responding.

"A veil is not a bomb," he said. "Besides, free them from what? The veil is a cultural symbol that has a long history. If you live in Kuwait for an extended period, you're going to run into a sandstorm. The sand particles are tiny, and they get into your eyes and nose and throat and clog everything up. I bet you that when one comes, you'll be covering your nose and mouth as well. That's probably how the people of this part of the world started wearing veils thousands of years ago. At the end of the day, though, if they want to wear the veil, that's their choice. Why not put up your feet and just admire the diversity of the world? I like to think of the world as a science fiction film. There are a whole bunch of creatures that look messed up to one another, but even if we don't like what someone looks like we should still talk to them."

"But there are people in this world—Muslims—who want to impose the veil on *everyone*. Those are the people Islamic reform is trying to stop."

"That's not *Islamic* reform, though," Ziad replied. "To 'impose' you gotta be in government. Any time a government imposes anything on you and you resist, that's just standing up to a government. Why do you bring Islam into it?"

"Because *they* say it's all about Islam."

"Just because *they* say it doesn't mean it's true. It's your job to see beyond that. Look, if the American government says that they need to incarcerate a segment of their population in the name of Pokémon, do you turn yourself into a Pokémon expert in order to try and prove that, no, Pokémon wouldn't do such a thing?"

Our waiter chose that moment to bring our food—felicitous timing, because I didn't have a response to Ziad's question.

He persisted. "You have to ask yourself what you're fighting for, Ali. Are you an enemy of Islamic fundamentalism simply because it pisses you off, or do you actually support liberty? If it's the latter, why do you have to talk about Islam all day? If it's the former, you have to ask yourself why you let your life be controlled by being pissed off. Or . . . never mind."

"Or what?"

"Or maybe you're just desperate to be relevant."

# 9

After my illuminating—but discouraging—talk with Ziad, I started working even harder on Islamic reform to compensate for the doubts I felt about its usefulness.

I started by setting up a legislation monitoring system for Muslim countries—a system that would track reformist laws in Iran, Pakistan, Turkey, and Egypt to start with but would eventually expand to all fifty-five Muslim-majority countries in the world.

The initial focus of the project was to be in the area of criminal law. The goal would be to identify all the various activists who favored repealing the anachronistic Sharia—or Islamic law—punishments, such as stoning, amputation, and lashing. I would then put those activists in touch with reformist scholars of Islam, who would help provide them with a religious basis for changing the law. In other words, the system would facilitate an alliance of reformist theory and action.

I printed out hundreds of documents in various languages, paged through history books by the score, and began translating articles by lawmakers and political leaders who supported progressive initiatives. I read the platforms of large political parties, compiled the names of major liberal clerics in every country, and trolled the Internet for reports by international human rights agencies.

The model for this project was the collaborative activism that had led, a couple years earlier, to the Women's Protection Bill in Pakistan. In 2006 a number of activists in Pakistan gained sufficient influence over legislators and leaders that they were able to get repealed certain Sharia-based punishments that had been imposed upon women by General Zia ul Haq decades earlier. The reform effort centered, particularly, around laws that imposed the punishment for adultery—stoning—upon a woman who was raped. The repeal effort had been nearly thirty years in the making but had stalled in the face of pressure from conservative clerics. Eventually, a number of reform-minded religious scholars allied themselves with the feminist cause, and that alliance gave the bill the new energy that got it passed.

My view was that since many of the reforms in the Muslim world—such as the Women's Protection Bill—required changing laws that had originated in some inappropriate interpretation of Islam, the most helpful thing for social activists would be to have a place where they could connect with religious scholars who could provide a religious imprimatur for achieving progressive aims. In other words, I wanted to make sure that Muslims' lives were improved, but I also wanted the credit for those improvements to go to Islam.

The project gave me a way to lose myself. I became consumed by press releases and news reports, by unjust laws and the search for religious justice. My agitation became a walking apparition that stalked the house.

Eventually my tension started to wear on Ziad. Whereas he had come home from work as early as possible when I first arrived, now he came home later and later. When we finally sat down to eat, he rarely talked, and if he did say something it was trivial. If I talked about my work, he seemed to bristle and become even more distant. We started cutting dinner short so that I could go off to my computer and he to the couch in front of TV, where night after night he fell asleep.

One night I decided to confront him. Perhaps the issue wasn't my work but something else entirely.

"Knock knock," I said, entering his bedroom.

Lying back with his head on the pillow, he wiggled his toes in acknowledgment. The curtains were pulled tight, and it was freezing in the room, the air conditioner on high. A pale aromatic candle burning in the bathroom sent its ghostly smoke into the bedroom. There was a big tower of novels on the bedside table, but none was open. An iPod sat next to him; though he wasn't wearing the headphones, I could hear faint music coming from the earpiece.

"This is your house," I said awkwardly. "I feel like I've taken over."

"You're my guest," he said. "It's not a problem."

"I can contribute more financially," I offered. "You drive me around but I rarely pay for gas."

"Our gas is subsidized," he replied. "Gas is cheaper than air in this country. Besides, you're the starving activist and I'm the established professional. There's nothing for you to contribute."

"This is weird," I said. "But I guess I'll just say it."

"What?"

"I know I sound like a wife here, but I feel like there's this distance between us."

I expected Ziad to change the subject. Instead, he confronted the matter directly.

"Of course there's a distance," he said, sitting up. "You're a reformist and I'm not. The things you're seeking to accomplish are different from the things I know. That doesn't mean I don't value what you do. It just means there will always be space between us."

"In other words, you're not particularly interested in what I'm doing," I said somberly.

"Right."

The realization made me a little sad. Not because I wanted him to think Islamic reform was the greatest thing in the world, but because for all the loftiness I associated with my work, that work was keeping me distant from the only person in the world who was helping me.

Remembering that communication is a two-way street, I set about trying to get to know what Ziad found interesting, given that all I'd done thus far was use him as an encyclopedia and a companion.

"Tell me," I said. "What's your orientation?"

He looked at me askance. "I see that you're still trying to get me executed."

I laughed. "Not like that. I meant Islamically. You read my work and enjoyed it. You oppose the theocrats and terrorists. You don't believe in requiring *hijab*s or beards. Yet you say you aren't a reformist. I haven't heard you say what you *are*, though: Shia or Ismaili or orthodox Sunni—whatever. It's a big mystery to me—you know, your theological orientation, stuff like that."

"It's too simplistic to be worth getting into."

"I'm interested," I said, pulling up a chair.

Ziad shook his head. "Don't worry about me. I keep rolling along. Why don't you update me, though? What's happening with the *shaykh* and the sculptor? And has Ali Ahab landed his rich Moby Dick?"

I waved my hand to dismiss his questions. I didn't want to talk about myself any more than Ziad did.

We sat companionably in the dark and silent room. The only noise was the faint pulse of music coming out of the headphones.

"What are you listening to there?" I asked.

"Your people's music."

"Really? I don't associate you with hip-hop."

"Your *other* people," Ziad said. "Punjabis."

"Let me hear."

Ziad handed me the iPod. "The Indian guy at the parking lot who washes my windshield told me about the CD that this song is from. Said his siblings loved the music and I reminded him of one of them. I don't understand it, but it's beautiful."

I put in one earpiece and began listening. I immediately recognized the heavy female voice. It was Abida Parveen, Pakistan's leading singer of folk and Sufi music. Most of her songs were from the tradition of Punjabi *kalam* poetry and mysticism that had been popular among Muslim saints, Hindu yogis, and Sikh gurus for hundreds of years, but was now ignored by most people, largely because ethnic literature no longer received patronage. The particular work that Abida Parveen was singing into my earpiece had been written by Baba Bulleh Shah, a famous Sufi saint born in Kasur, who had been the student of the spiritual master Shah Inayat. Bulleh Shah lived several hundred years ago in a period of great spiritual beauty in India. His life overlapped with that of the poet Waris Shah, who penned the greatest lyric poem in Punjabi, "Heer."

The prominent Sindhi Sufi Sachal Sarmast was also a contemporary of Bulleh Shah.

I knew the history of Punjab's mystics because I had long kept track of the work of these poets, using their lyrics to rebuke orthodox and extremist Muslims. It was something that was part of the "reformist arsenal" that we activists relied upon. The mystics' abandon, and their denigration of orthodoxy, was especially useful when reformists were sick and tired of dealing with religious recalcitrance and wanted to blow the conversation up with mockery and jest.

"This is great stuff," I said. "You don't understand it?"

"Nope."

"It's called *Ek nuqte vich gul muqdi e.* 'It is all in One contained.'" I plugged the iPod into Ziad's laptop so that we could both hear and turned up the volume. "The lyrics are mocking the dogmatically religious," I said, translating:

*Mindless prayer is for the weak*
*Foolishly fasting is how the breadless save bread*
*Only the ill-intentioned make loud religious proclamations*
*Only those make pilgrimages to Mecca that want to avoid daily*
*    chores*
*You can do ritual a billion times*
*But that is not the way to the Beloved*
*Until your heart is pure*
*Your prostrations are useless*
*Until you give up idolatry*
*You will be a stranger to the Beloved.*

I continued translating through the thirteen-minute song.

As the song wound down, I muted the volume and unplugged the iPod. "I really like Bulleh Shah," I said. "He was the most confrontational of the mystics. He had no time for the orthotoxics and the theocunts. If he were alive today, he'd definitely be a reformist." I turned toward Ziad, expecting him to have gotten as much kick out of the lyrics as I did.

Instead, I saw that he had gotten out of bed and paced to the corner of the room, where he was running his fingers over his dresser. I thought

I heard him sighing; sure enough, when I caught a glimpse of his face in the mirror there were tears running down his cheeks. He turned to me, his eyelashes wet and his lips quivering. He snatched the iPod from my hand, took a deep breath as if preparing to dive, and said simply, "Shut up with your reformist nonsense."

Feeling like I'd been slapped, I backed out of the shimmering blue room.

# 10

The fight over Bulleh Shah increased the tension between Ziad and me. We started avoiding one another. I stayed up late at night so I wouldn't have to see him in the morning, and he retired to his room almost as soon as he got home. If we walked past each other in the hall, we simply averted our eyes or walked in the other direction.

Things became so chilly that I called the airline to try to advance my ticket home.

It didn't go well. Apparently if I wanted to change my itinerary, I'd have to forfeit my return ticket and buy a new one.

"At full price?" I asked, horrified.

"Yes," said the attendant.

When I argued against the exorbitant pricing, the attendant told me to take it up with the airline's field office and hung up.

I had no way of finding the office on my own. I could get a cab, I supposed, but Ziad had given me severe warnings about the taxi service in the area. Some were not trustworthy.

My only option, then, was to ask Ziad to take me. However, this I couldn't bring myself to do; it would be unseemly and inexcusably rude, given the fragile state of our relationship.

My unwillingness to engage in further confrontation with Ziad over a ride to the airline, combined with the fact that I'd have to pay nearly a thousand dollars just to advance my ticket a few weeks, made me drop the idea of leaving early.

If I couldn't leave, I could at least renew my effort to improve things. I decided to buy a gift for Ziad and try to patch things up.

The DVD seller down the block convinced me to buy from him a new Pakistani film called *Khuda Kay Liye,* or *In the Name of God,* saying that it was the "total best film ever!" He even threw in the soundtrack CD for free. I thought it would make a good gift.

I'd heard of the film. When it was released in Pakistan, it had received numerous *fatwa*s from radical clerics and death threats from demagogues because it discussed difficult themes such as *jihad,* fundamentalism, forced marriage, and marital rape. Moviegoers had to pass through metal detectors in case they were planning on blowing up the theater, and they ran the risk of being killed by extremists merely for watching. Nevertheless, the film ended up being a hit inside the country and abroad.

I figured the film would intrigue Ziad enough to breach the stone wall between us. One evening while Ziad was eating dinner in front of the TV, I popped it in. When he tried to leave, I grabbed him by the arm. "Just be an adult and watch it with me," I urged.

*Khuda Kay Liye* is the story of two brothers, named Mansoor and Sarmad, from Lahore, Pakistan. They both work in the music industry. Mansoor, a modern Muslim, goes off to school in Chicago, where he falls in love with one of his classmates. After 9/11 he gets wrongly apprehended in the predictable security dragnet and put under custody by a shadowy American agency which engages in mental and physical torture that results in his being paralyzed.

Sarmad, meanwhile, begins following a fanatical *mullah.* He stops playing music and accuses his own family of being apostates and infidels. One day Sarmad's uncle from England arrives with his young daughter Maryam. The uncle is upset that she's planning on marrying a non-Muslim from London and convinces Sarmad to marry her. At first Sarmad is reluctant, but when he asks his *mullah* for advice he's given the go-ahead. Sarmad embraces the conspiracy and, after forcibly marrying Maryam, moves with her to a tribal area of Pakistan, where no one will find them. He eventually rapes her.

Once Maryam is able to escape to Lahore, she files a motion to annul the marriage. A dramatic trial ensues. Sarmad calls in his sinister *mullah* to have him testify that Sarmad was simply following Islam and therefore did nothing wrong. Maryam, meanwhile, desperate for help, goes in search of a reclusive reformist *shaykh* and begs him to testify on her behalf. The *shaykh,* played by the Indian actor Naseeruddin Shah, stands up in court, demonstrating with both eloquence and scripture that Sarmad's *mullah's* testimony was utterly fraudulent and bankrupt. Beyond simply affirming the rights of women, the *shaykh* decries the *mullah's* disregard for music, maligns him for the militancy he promotes, and attacks him for misleading impressionable Muslim youth. His testimony is so potent that it leads to a verdict in Maryam's favor—and leads Sarmad to dump his *mullah* and his extremist teachings. At the end of the film Sarmad is found using his musical skills to perform an *azan*. It was a perfect reformist resolution. Good Islam beating bad Islam.

By the time the twists and turns of the film were over and done with, the atmosphere in the room had changed. Ziad and I began talking in familiar ways again.

"Wow. That was intense," Ziad said, watching the final credits. "I feel like we should hug or something."

"Why don't you make some of that mint tea and we can *say* that we hugged."

"Only if you make a *hooka*," he countered.

It was late at night and cool outside, so I pulled two chairs onto the balcony and lit up the tobacco as I once did with my grandfather. Ziad brought out the steaming cups and we clinked them. Then we slurped noisily as we commented on the progress the laborers had made on the nearby building. We passed the *hooka* back and forth and made rings with the smoke. The O's rippled out of our mouths, hung in the air, and for a moment became necklaces for the stars.

I interrupted the reverie to talk about the film. "Didn't that movie really just cut to the heart of the civil war in Islam?" I said. "On one hand, you've got impressionable young men, who represent the strong, handing over the reins of their power to scheming *mullah*s. On the other hand, you've got smart women, who represent the weak, subjugated in the name of religion, looking for help from those who know the humane side of Islam."

"There seems to be something common to both sides," Ziad observed.

"Impossible. They're as different as night and day."

"No. They're alike. They both seem to believe that Islam is the solution. They're just arguing over whose Islam should be dominant."

"Authoritarian Islam and tolerant Islam aren't the same thing. The former is *not* Islam. They're two different things. Which side are you on?"

"What if I said neither?"

"There is no neither. You're either with us or against us."

"All things boil down to dominance to you, don't they?"

"Yes, they do," I admitted, raising my voice. "Dominance matters to the other side and it matters to us. The only difference is that when we win we won't kill everyone. I think that's an important distinction. Don't you?"

Ziad swished his tea around in his mouth and took big puffs on the *hooka*. "Why do you do this?" he asked, looking at me intently.

"What?"

"This Islamic reform stuff."

"I already told you. I'm trying to get a think tank going. I want to create a legislation monitoring program that allows us to track the modernization of Islamic law in various Muslim-majority countries. I want to challenge theocracy and terrorism from an Islamic perspective. I want to create a liberal *fatwa* factory. I want to promote the creation of images so that Islam has an artistic renaissance like that of the Europeans."

"I'm not asking you your *plans*. I want to know what your *motivation* is."

"My motivation is Islamic reform," I replied, speaking with exaggerated clarity.

"No. You aren't following. Why do you throw yourself into Islamic reform? Why do you care about that in particular?"

"I like helping people," I said. "Look, are you trying to evaluate me? Maybe deconstruct me? How about this: I help people because I'm not happy inside. I'm insanely lonely, and all this is a way for me to make myself feel better. Is that what you wanted to hear, Oprah? Should I shed some tears?"

"Now you're just mocking me," Ziad said. "Here's my issue. If you just want to help people, why not become a lifeguard? Why not work with the homeless in . . . I don't know . . . Philadelphia? Why are you chasing around *shaykh*s and princesses in the Middle East? Why are you putting up—"

"Islam!" I shouted, fed up with his obstinacy. "It has to do with Islam! I'm doing it for Islam! Isn't it obvious?"

I thought this would shut Ziad up, but it didn't. "Ali Eteraz, there are a lot of people in this world who know Islam better than you," he said. "Why not leave it all to them? Why not give your ideas and suggestions to them? Hell, why not go back to practicing law and raising the money yourself and becoming wealthy enough to buy your own think tank?"

I yanked the *hooka* nozzle back from him. "I want to get my hands dirty."

"Why?"

"Do you know the story of the Black Stone?" I asked.

"The one in Mecca? Yeah. It came down from Paradise, and the Prophet Ibrahim made it the cornerstone of the Ka'ba. You kiss it and it cleanses your sins."

"Yes. Did you know that it used to be white?"

"It did?"

"Yes. And now it's black."

"Your point?"

"It's black because billions of hands have touched it and made it dirty. Do you know what I want to do about it?"

"What?"

"I want to take a rag and clean it. Ever since I was little, that's been my dream."

Ziad laughed. "You're an odd one."

"Don't laugh: this is very serious."

"So you're on a quest, then?"

"Yes."

"I hate to repeat myself, but . . . why?"

"There are things that define a person's life. In my case it's a covenant that was made at the Ka'ba before I was born."

"A covenant?"

"Yes."

"Are you making this up? People don't do that kind of thing in today's world."

"Yes, they do. I'm living proof!"

"So what does your covenant involve?"

"Simple. In exchange for my being born a male, I would become a great servant of Islam. That's the deal my parents made. At birth I was given the name Abir ul Islam. It means Perfume of Islam. I was supposed to spread Islam like a fragrance. When I was still an infant, my parents rubbed my chest against the Holy Ka'ba. I took my first steps in the sacred city of Mecca. My draw to Mecca was so strong that when I was on *hajj* with my parents—I was less than a year old then—I crawled away from them and went off into the desert. Must have been following Muhammad's path, my parents assumed, once they got over worrying that I was lost. I grew up my entire childhood listening to this . . . this *legend* of what I was supposed to be."

"Some sort of Islamic hero," said Ziad.

"Yeah. For a while I even thought I was from a caliphal bloodline. Talk about the stuff of legend!"

"What happened with that?"

"Long story."

Ziad didn't say anything for several minutes. Mulling over what I'd said, he bit his lip the way he had in the car the first night I'd arrived. He fiddled with his cup and dipped his finger into the little remaining bit of tea. He licked his finger and made a sucking sound.

Finally he spoke again. "If you changed your gender," he asked, "would the covenant lapse?"

"First of all: I like my penis. Second of all: I don't appreciate you making light of this."

"I'm just trying to understand," Ziad said. "Really."

"I don't think you can," I replied.

"Fine," Ziad said, putting up his hands in surrender. "I'm going to sleep. Let's go off-roading in the morning. There's a place I'd like to show you. I'll wake you up early."

"I don't want to go," I said, sounding as petulant as I felt.

"I'm not hearing you," he singsonged.

When I got to my room I felt so annoyed that I figured I'd have trouble going to sleep. Lying in bed and thinking back on the confession I'd made to Ziad, I began to feel light and supple. I no longer felt angry. Relief overtook me. It was as if my mind was a walnut that had been cracked open by Ziad's incessant curiosity. I wasn't sure where I'd read it, but it was said that sometimes water actually spouted out naturally *from* stone. I felt now as if a hole had been opened in my ossified conscience. Soon I was drenched in myself.

I slept soundly and dreamlessly. I woke as refreshed as if I had just stepped out of a cool lake. In the morning I wasn't sure whether I felt so good because the night had spun silvery threads of joy into my heart, or because the forthcoming day held the promise of bounty.

# II

After mating with the desert, the city lay on her stomach snoring. There had been a sandstorm during the night, and a smooth, pristine-looking dusting covered everything. It wasn't yet dawn, and the moon was erotic gold.

When Ziad and I headed outside on our off-roading adventure, we found the black SUV coated in sand—a soft, fine-grained sand that felt like velvet. We used the edges of our hands to clean the windshield and the mirrors and then headed onto the highway.

There were no cars on the streets at that hour, though every now and again we passed a little mosque. The homes became larger the further we got out of the city until suddenly there were no more mosques or houses. We passed a few warehouses and some junkyards; then those disappeared as well.

The landscape resembled a good *ghazal*. Like that traditional form of love poetry, the desert was repetitious without being tedious. It had a melancholy tinge that was expressed with simple economy. It wasn't raw or forceful, yet it still felt imposing and impregnable. There was formality in its wickedness. It was ageless without being aged. Very rarely there was a singular man or a lone bird that inevitably disappeared in the sighing sand as the author of a *ghazal* disappears into his final couplet.

Ziad cut into a marked area and began to follow tire marks from earlier off-roaders. "The sandstorm would have wiped yesterday's tracks out," he said, "so someone must have stopped by recently." The knowledge that there were others in our proximity bothered me. I wanted to be alone with the world.

Ziad pressed the gas pedal down as we approached a looming bank. As he dropped into 4x4 mode, the Jeep roared, leaping into the air and then landing nose-first. He swung the steering wheel from side to side as we lurched down the backslope. The vehicle skidded calmly to the bottom, like a ship getting carried onto shore by a powerful wave.

After we took turns practicing downshifting and drifting, we parked the vehicle, took Ziad's bike out of the back, and hiked up a meager trail that led through clumps of rocks to a distant tabletop plateau. Ziad, with a camera around his neck, and carrying his bike over one shoulder, rushed ahead of me. He looked back from time to time, and I could see in his eyes a zealotry I'd never been before. His desperation to beat the sun to the plateau made him seem like an ancient Zoroastrian priest chasing after Ahura Mazda. I looked up at the sky and saw that the craggy moon was still visible, though in anticipation of the inevitable invasion by the sun it had fortified its light within its craters.

I couldn't understand Ziad's maddening pace. I wanted to shout out to him and say, "It's just the sun! It looks the same every day! It's just an ancient star that was destroyed billions of years ago!" Instead, I sighed and held my tongue. With one hand on each thigh, I pressed forward. By the time I got to the top, Ziad was contorting his body in myriad ways to capture the sun with his camera. I watched his acrobatic art for a little and then I started riding the bike around the rocks.

When I reached the far end of the tabletop, I stood with my back to the sun, looking across a vast desert. It struck me that just a few hours in that direction sat the city of Mecca, where the Ka'ba, the crown jewel of Allah, sat in the center of a thousand marble minarets, leaking the *aabe-zamzam* into the desert to nourish its pilgrims, with the Black Stone, its singular eye, giving God a way to gaze upon the profane world. If I just kept riding this bike, and it turned into a camel, and if I rode and rode, I would be at the place where my existence had started.

I spent the rest of the morning following Ziad around the plateau. It was hard to keep up with him. Sometimes he climbed on the bike and took a suicidal ride partway down at a steep angle, sometimes he stopped suddenly and lay down on his belly to focus his camera on a tiny insect—he took hundreds of pictures—and sometimes he had me stand between him and the sun and he captured my shadows. From time to time he would conceive in his head a scene that pleased him, and then he would hand me the camera and run to the spot—sometimes two or three hundred yards away—and strike a pose and tell me to take a picture. Then he'd come rushing back and look at the job I'd done, usually nodding in approval.

Even when we finally got back down from the plateau he didn't stop taking pictures. He took pictures of the SUV going up and down the sandy banks, me at the wheel. He stood in the center of a clearing and told me to drive doughnuts around him so he could take pictures of the blowing sand. The jaws of his camera snapped open and shut like the mouth of a voracious lion. Ziad ate everything around him.

Finally we got into the Jeep and, leaving the scant shade of the mountain, drove over to a raised clearing between two hills where the wind was more fierce. Ziad burrowed in the back of the Jeep and brought out a parachute kite, handing me the two-handed controls. Then he ran off and flung the kite into the air. With a powerful whoosh the kite caught an eastern gust and yanked on my arms. I felt as if I were trying to rope down a massive dragon with nothing but string. The gusts were so powerful that I was lifted in the air and even dragged forward a few yards now and then. To control the kite I had to dig my heels into the sand and get in a squat, my quads quivering from the force I exerted. Sometimes I didn't give the line enough slack or pulled too suddenly and the kite took a nose dive and slammed into the ground. Whenever this happened, Ziad whooped and ran over to untangle the string; then he flung the kite in the air again.

Once I figured out how to control the kite, I began enjoying myself. I sent the kite in threatening swoops over Ziad's head, which sent him ducking and rolling and running down the clearing in a panic. After a while he became fed up with taking evasive maneuvers and came over to take control of the kite. Now it was my turn to run around the clearing while the kite veered down and pecked at my head or slammed into me from my blind spot and sent me sprawling.

When in a *hallagulla* of laughter and sweat I fell down into the sand, I spread out my limbs and made sand angels. I left a line of sweat where the spine would be.

We flew the kite until the day became hot and the breeze died down. Finally we made our slow way back to the SUV and had a drink. Our faces were flushed, our skin covered in dust. Sand had gotten into our shoes and socks and under our clothes. The few hours we'd been out had made us darker, and we compared tan lines. We looked back up at the clearing and saw our tracks—footprints, and furrows where the kite had dragged us, and indentations where the kite had lacerated the sand.

After we cooled down, we got in the Jeep and made our way back toward the highway.

Suddenly Ziad pointed at a spot upon the hills. "What's that?" he asked, slowing down so that he could gaze into the distance.

I put the binoculars to my eyes and stared. Three forms slowly came into focus. One was an SUV high up on a sandy embankment at the side of a stony ridge.

"It's a Jeep like yours," I said. "I don't think it's moving."

"Do you think it's stuck?"

I adjusted my binoculars and confirmed. "I think so. I see two guys. They're just standing around near the Jeep. Maybe they're just hanging out."

"Unlikely. Let's go check it out."

When we got close to the ridge, we realized it wouldn't be safe for us to drive up where the other Jeep was. The sand was too deep and the incline too steep. We got out and approached the two men on foot.

They weren't men, as it turned out. They were a pair of Bedouin boys, no more than sixteen years old, who had brought their father's Jeep for an early morning adventure. Lacking 4x4 capability, the vehicle

had gotten stuck. They had spent the greater part of the morning spin-
ning their wheels, and the rear left wheel was now more than halfway
buried in the sand. We tried using a big plank that the boys had found
as a lever, but it snapped when we put our weight into it. Then Ziad
trudged down and back and brought a shovel from his car. The boys
took turns digging energetically. Each time they displaced some sand,
however, more sand shifted and replaced it. They tried to persuade us
to bring our Jeep and give them a push, but Ziad adamantly refused
because it would cause us to sink as well. In the end we drove the pair to
the highway, from which point they said they could navigate the rest of
the way back to their tribe. I was surprised by Ziad's unwillingness to
risk himself for the sake of others.

As we were driving back, the interior of the car full of sand, the taste
of the desert in my mouth, cuts from the kite's beak on my bare arms,
the smell of sweat and leather and exhilaration in my nose, I wondered
if perhaps the camels at Mandalay Bay hadn't told me to come to the
Middle East to carry out the silly scheme involving the *shaykh* and the
sculptor and the princess. Perhaps I'd felt compelled to come here to
befriend Ziad.

"How long have you lived in Muslim countries?" I asked suddenly.

"Two-thirds of my life."

"Yet you never became a reformist?"

"No."

"And you never became a fundamentalist?"

"Nope."

"And you never wanted to become an Islamic leader?"

"Nope."

I raised my eyebrows. "I find that astonishing."

Ziad slowed the car and glanced over at me. He brushed his hand
over his left eyebrow, dislodging little particles of dust onto his lap.

"Let me ask you something," he said.

"What?"

"How long have you lived in this world?"

"Pardon?"

"How long have you been alive?"

"My whole life, I guess."

"When was the last time you flew a kite on a mountain?"

"Never.

"When was the last time you got on the ground and took high-res pictures of insects?"

"Never."

"When was the last time you saved Bedouin boys in the desert?"

"Never."

"Well, buddy, I find *that* astonishing."

I said nothing. I felt like I was buried shoulder-deep in sand and someone was aiming stones at my essence. Yet rather than shattering me, the stones revealed themselves to be globules of light. They went down my mouth and gathered in my stomach. They became a pool of brilliance that coalesced and began to bubble. Then a mammoth geyser of laughter shot out from my navel and the beam of light was visible all the way to Damascus.

We laughed until we cried.

# 12

One day while Ziad was at work, I went walking through the neighborhoods looking for a barbershop. It didn't take very long to find one. It was set in a narrow alley behind a massive high-rise, with aged leather couches on the front porch where men smoked *hooka*s. Various types of people that I hadn't seen at the malls—Indian carpenters, Egyptian shopkeepers, and errand boys from unidentifiable countries—came in and out of the shop, smoking cigarettes and sipping mint tea from stained glass cups with thick bottoms. There was a TV in the corner, one that no one watched, on which a soccer match between two anonymous teams was playing. The glass doors of the shop were flung wide open and the desert's afternoon heat came in, encountered the shade, and moderated some of its anger.

The barber who took care of my cut and shave was a middle-aged man named Arif—assigned to me because he was the only one who spoke English. Looking at one another we both raised our eyebrows in recognition. Then I cautiously inquired whether he was Pakistani.

"Of course I am Pakistani!" he exclaimed, breaking into a smile. After shaking hands like old friends, we switched from English into Urdu and he told me about his family, the house he was getting built for them, and how he longed to go back and be reunited with his homeland. It seemed that homeless Pakistanis were everywhere in the world.

During the course of the shave, when my neck was exposed to the ivory-handled blade and a trickle of foam ran down onto my chest, he stopped and looked at me in the mirror.

"What are you doing tonight?"

"Nothing," I said.

"I'm going to a celebration. You should come."

I thought it over for a moment. For a second my stomach clenched as I thought of Ittefaq and the last time I'd been invited somewhere by a Pakistani. "What sort of people will be there?" I asked hesitantly.

"Just average people," he replied.

That wasn't much to go on. "What time does it start?"

"After midnight," he replied. As we exchanged glances in the mirror, I could see that he was confused about why I was being so reluctant. To a Pakistani, an invitation should be accepted out of consideration and kindness; it would be rude to refuse. When I stayed quiet, Arif shook his blade, wiped it, and then resumed scraping. Each time he wiped the little hairs onto the white napkin on the counter, he tried not to look at me.

Arif's silence and confusion weighed heavily on me, so I tried to make small talk. "What do you think about what's happening in Pakistan?"

He clicked his tongue and shook his head disapprovingly. "What is there to think? These people are giving a bad name to Islam."

"Which people?" I asked, suddenly alert.

"These people who blow people up. That's not Islam. Don't they understand that Islam is about moderation? They are giving every Muslim a bad name. In the West people think badly about us."

"Yes," I said, encouraging him. "These people are responsible for many deaths, including those of Muslims, and of heightening tensions between Westerners and the Muslim world."

"What can you do?" he said, sighing. "They're out of control."

I became quiet again. I wanted to tell Arif that if he joined me he world learn that the militants *could*, in fact, be controlled. I was envisioning him as the working-class hero of my movement to reform the religion, but I couldn't form the words. Instead, I told him that I'd join him at his celebration.

Around midnight Arif and I met at the barbershop to go together in his car and arrived at an empty field serving as a makeshift parking lot. We were far removed from the part of town where the glamorous shops and restaurants were located, though we could see the skyline in the distance.

Leaving the car, we walked toward a small, squarish structure at the end of the lot. Gathered outside it numerous people—all men— were shaking hands, embracing, and kissing cheeks. Arif patted me on the back with a pleased look on his face before introducing me to a number of people, most of them wearing traditional clothes. I quickly realized that all of them were Pakistanis. Urdu, Punjabi, and a little bit of Pashto flowed among the congregants. There was a lot of laughter, which puzzled me greatly, because I was expecting to be tricked, to be led into something somber and serious, something angry and political.

I could see that these men were all from working-class backgrounds. When I commented about that, Arif said, "Some of them come from the labor communities far outside the city—places where they sleep ten to a room." I nodded and looked around at the dusty feet in torn sandals, the clothes that smelled of dust and desert, the turbans of aged fabric. Yet all the faces seemed serene. Each time my hand was shaken by a smiling man, my brand-name shirt—the same shirt I'd worn for the interview with Rashad in Vienna—rubbed against a man who spent most of his life sweeping dust from the streets, or clambering up and down the ladders of a building in progress, or slaving inside a boiling shop. I wanted to fling my shirt off my skin: maybe it was the expensive monogram on my chest that was keeping me from the warmth and serenity that Arif and his dusty friends seemed to share.

"Let's go inside," Arif suggested, leading me into a throng of men taking off their shoes. We stepped into an open room that resembled a mosque but was decorated with banners, streamers, and numerous lights. Some of the banners had a picture of the Ka'ba upon them. Crisscrossing the room just above head level was a patterned decoration made from gauzy paper that rustled softly in the occasional breeze. Arif and I went and sat on the floor near the center of the room. From there I could see a group of old men seated in front, facing the crowd, their heads bowed and their lips murmuring.

Soon a younger man rose and walked forward to a podium, where he introduced a fresh-faced singer in a blue T-shirt and dirty jeans. "This guy's got an amazing voice," Arif whispered.

By now the room was full. People that weren't crushed together on the floor were standing along the edges. Others, Arif told me, had gone up to the roof to sit. As the crowd thickened and congealed, various people pressed into me from the back, the front, and the sides. Feeling a bit anxious, I tried to keep space for myself by extending my elbows and jutting out my knees, but to no avail. I noticed that Arif, rather than fighting the crowd, welcomed it: he leaned back against the man behind him, hugged another man in front of him, and gave smiles to the man to his right.

Finally the performer cleared his throat and began singing.

It was a *hamd,* a devotional song about God. This particular one was a mixture of many ethnic languages from Pakistan. As the young man sang, the crowd swayed, sang along, and raised their hands in jubilation. When the singer hit a particularly compelling verse, Arif or one of the other men near me would put his fist in the air and shout, *Haqq!*

The word meant truth.

Each shout sent a wave of euphoria through the crowd. It was apparent to me that all these hard-working men could understand *haqq*— not the word but the concept—but I couldn't. I began to feel like an outsider, someone who had been accidentally dropped into a group of people to whom he couldn't belong. My mind started wandering. What if a militant came and blew up the congregation? What if some hardline Wahhabi came by and arrested all of us?

Suddenly the young man at the podium began singing *Allah hoo Allah hoo,* the legendary *hamd.* Arif let out a *haqq* that was echoed by others. As the beautiful notes of the song coursed through me, all concerns were erased from my mind. I felt as if someone had cut open my head and was blowing into the tube that was my body. The feeling softened me somehow. It melted away my skin and sinew and made me a part of the men around me. These men who were raised from dust, lived in dust, and would eventually rest in dust. I felt one with them. I was *not* alone. We were many. We were all children of dust. I swayed in time to the music and when a sweaty man put his head on my back to rest for a moment, all I could do was smile.

The song accompanied us as we exited and even as we picked up our free tray of food from an attendant waiting outside. Even as we drove away, it kept pulsing in my veins.

When Arif dropped me off at the apartment in the wee hours, I wanted to tell Ziad all about the event, and about the sense of belonging I'd felt with the Pakistani laborers, but I found him asleep. I went out to the balcony and sat up awhile longer humming the tune to myself and smiling.

# 13

Over the next few days I didn't spend any time on Islamic reform. Ziad and I played tennis, argued through long games of Scrabble, and hung out with migrant Kenyans who taught us how to play Uno with regular playing cards. We went to look at calligraphy at a museum, drove out to a marina to attend a yacht party on the sea, and watched kids flirting at the mall. Then we went and bought a long hose at the hardware store and used it to wash the sticky desert sand from his car.

While I was spraying the vehicle, a man in a robe stopped in his Benz and, thinking me to be a laborer, gestured at me to wash his windshield. I agreed to do it as long as he let me fuck his mother. He cursed and drove off.

Ziad was impressed. "You came here as a beggar to the rich, and now you're giving them a piece of your mind."

After the car was washed we drove to the meat market and bought an assortment of different meats: chicken, New Zealand beef, baby lamb, and Ziad's favorite: camel. We decided to have a barbecue.

While the chicken was marinating and I was waiting for Ziad to finish making lemonade, I went to the computer and, for the first time in many days, checked my e-mail. I found a series of startling messages.

The first was from one of the *shaykh*'s acolytes, saying that he was ready to meet. She told me to send her the questions in advance so that she could point out—and I could toss—the ones the *shaykh* wouldn't answer.

The next was an e-mail from the sculptor. He advised me as to his availability and said that he looked forward to hearing from me.

The last one was the most surprising. Rashad had gotten hold of one of the *shaykh*'s silent benefactors—an older noblewoman with a reformist slant to her philanthropy—who might be receptive to ideas about expanding the *shaykh*'s regional and international reach. She was a professional philanthropist—the sort of person who looked forward to seeing a PowerPoint presentation. I excitedly printed out the e-mails.

As I was standing in front of the printer, I took a look out the window at Ziad, who was on the balcony grilling camel burgers. I could smell every spice he'd used in the seasoning. I also picked up the scent of basted chicken thighs crisping on the grill. I could hear the sound of clinking ice cubes when he took a drink of lemonade. I saw him wipe his mouth with his bare arm. The perfect picture of a life savored.

I wanted to go out and show him the e-mails. I wanted to tell him that my scheme had not been insane, that my plans had not only come through as I'd hoped, but had the potential of being so much more.

Yet a part of me felt reluctant. I remembered the gulf between us when I'd been caught up in my work. I didn't want a repeat of that. I was drawn to the voracious way of living that Ziad had shown me. If I threw myself back into my schemes, Ziad's way of living—living with abandon—would be lost. I'd be back into the fiber optic cables and press releases, back into the suffering that came with saving sufferers, back into the violence that was involved in vanquishing extremists.

I sat back down and put my head in my hands. What was happening? Was I really contemplating abandoning all my plans just because they would create some distance between me and someone who didn't agree with my aims? It was irrational! I didn't have a legal career anymore. I'd lost my family. I had no money. Islamic reform was my salvation—my way of becoming respectable and stable again, my way of having a place in society, my way of gaining status among the community of believers. Only the utterly insane would fail to act responsibly here.

And it was more than just material things. The think tank was to be the culmination of the covenant with Islam that had colored every manifestation of my being from childhood to adulthood. I had an inescapable duty to follow through on these plans. I owed it to myself; I owed it to Islam.

All of a sudden Ziad's voice through the window brought me out of my reflection.

"Hey, desk jockey! Are you coming back out?"

"You bet."

"The chicken is done. We're just waiting on the camel."

"Coming!"

"Bring my laptop while you're at it, would you? I feel like hearing some of that Bulleh Shah again."

I went into Ziad's room, the e-mails still in my hand, looking for his white MacBook. I didn't see it at first. Then I noticed a corner of it sticking out from under a pile of papers on the bed. I sifted through them quickly as I pushed them aside. The computer printout of an article containing the picture of a white-bearded old man with a turban, a *chador* draped around his shoulders, caught my eye. At first I thought it was a picture of Bulleh Shah, perhaps because I'd just heard his name.

It turned out to be part of an article entitled "A History of Spiritual Love," written by Osman Mir for *EGO,* an online magazine. The man in the picture wasn't Bulleh Shah but Jalal al-Din Rumi, one of the greatest poets and mystics in history. He was the author of the *Masnavi*—a work of such literary brilliance that it was called "the Persian Quran." That was all I knew of him. Out of curiosity I picked up the article and began skimming.

This particular piece focused on the relationship between Rumi and his teacher, Shams of Tabriz—its warmth, its intimacy, its ecstatic and celebratory subtlety. Their relationship began with a three-month period of seclusion, I read, during which the pair withdrew themselves from the rest of the world in Shams's house. They worked together for some years, until Shams heard a voice outside of his door while he and Rumi were speaking. He followed it out and was never heard from again. At that point Rumi made Shams into his poetic signature, his alter ego, and integrated him into his "I-ness." Thus wrote Rumi: "Why should I seek? I am the same as he. His essence speaks through me. I have been searching for myself."

Suddenly Ziad's voice came from the balcony. "The camel is cooked to perfection!"

Startled, I dropped the essay and the e-mails, grabbed the laptop, and ran outside. "*This* camel is coming," I called.

"Hurry up," Ziad shouted. "I'm hungry like a lion."

# 14

The burgers were so good they made me forget about the e-mails. Juice ran down my chin with each bite I took. I could feel the *shan masala* weaving through my stubble. As I chewed the tender flesh, I made muted moans of pleasure. By the time I took the next bite, one line of juice dried up and another trailed down the side of my mouth. The two lines, dry and wet, kept alternating with each bite.

"This is unlike anything I've ever had," I said appreciatively.

Ziad looked at me and smiled, nodding in agreement.

In the background Abida Parveen's voice crooned Bulleh Shah, but I was so intent on my burger that I wasn't paying much attention to it. Looking up, I noticed Ziad staring closely at me.

"Whatcha lookin' at?"

"I just thought about something I read," he said.

"What?"

"I was reading up on your Sufi poets in Punjab the other day. Did you know that one of their favorite motifs was the idea of the *bela*?"

"What's that?"

Ziad laughed. "And you call yourself a Punjabi! You know when a river changes its course? Well, the word *bela* refers to the basin it leaves behind. It's supposed to be very fertile and lush."

"Why are you thinking about that?"

"Because of the tributaries of grease on your face." He reached forward and with his index finger traced the two lines down my chin.

I dabbed with a napkin. "So what's your point?"

"Nothing," he said. "I just think it's cool that rivers change course. You wouldn't think they would. They seem so permanent. It's like they wake up one morning and go and lie down somewhere else. That's all." He shrugged and sipped his lemonade.

Ziad's reference, now lodged firmly in my head, made me listen closely to the lyrics coming from inside. I wondered if I had missed a reference to a *bela* when I'd translated the song earlier.

Suddenly I remembered the fight we'd had the last time we listened to this song together. I recalled the comment Ziad had made then—"Shut up with your reformist nonsense"—and I realized that that had been the only time he'd ever been rude to me. I decided to bring it up. "I want you to be straight with me," I said. "Fake it if you have to. Why did you get so pissed the other day when I said Bulleh Shah would be a reformist?"

"Doesn't matter. Eat your camel."

"Just tell me."

"You want answers?" he said, arching his eyebrows like Jack Nicholson in his confrontation with Tom Cruise in the film *A Few Good Men.*

"I want the truth—Colonel Jessup."

"Well, I was mad because you turned Bulleh Shah's wisdom into a weapon. I didn't like that."

"You heard the translation I did. Wasn't he clearly attacking Islamic orthodoxy and everyone else who turns religion into a series of rituals?"

"No."

"Really?" I asked, genuinely surprised. "He says, 'Prayer is for the weak.' How about that? What about, 'Only those make pilgrimages to Mecca that want to avoid daily chores.' You don't think that's a direct critique of half the Wahhabis around you?"

"Don't you think that's a direct critique of *you*?" Ziad shot back.

I was stunned. "Me?"

"I'm just saying—you have the same relationship to religion as the Wahhabis. It's all about appearance. Many of those verses apply to you: 'Until you give up idolatry you will be a stranger to the Beloved.' That's just one example."

"How does that apply to me?"

He pushed back from the little table with both hands, as if to put some distance between us. "Because you're an idolater!"

I spat out the food I was chewing and stood up in a sudden burst of anger. Now it felt like the confrontation between Tom Cruise and Jack Nicholson for real. "*What* did you say?" I demanded through gritted teeth.

"I'm sorry," he said. "Let's just drop this."

"Fuck that," I shouted. "You can't call me an idolater and not back it up. I didn't realize you were a closet fanatic. Do you support theocrats and terrorists too?"

"Forget it, Ali, Amir, whatever you are."

"No." I flung my paper plate with its remnants of food off the balcony and it spun down. "You just declared me an idolater, which is like calling me an apostate. If the Wahhabis heard you, they'd throw me in jail and execute me. I'm going to defend myself, all right? That's what *I* do. I defend Islam from people like you. People who judge other Muslims. Tell me, what's my idol? Say it. Say it to my face."

Ziad grew meek under my assault, cowering as if I'd hit him. His eyes filled with tears.

"Shit," I said, suddenly regretting my harshness. "I'm sorry!"

I moved to touch him, but he shook his head and waved me aside. He rose and stepped away from the table, standing close to the wall. He wiped his eyes with his fingers and flung the tears to the floor like he was ashamed of them. After a while he mumbled something.

"What did you say?" I asked.

"Nothing."

"You said something," I repeated softly. "You can tell me."

"Islam."

"Islam what?"

"You wanted me to identify your idol, right? You worship Islam. There's a statue in your soul to which you kneel. You call it Islam."

I furrowed my brow. I figured that Ziad was just trying to get even with me since I'd made him cry. He was just trying to say something that would hurt me. I shrugged it off, figuring that nonchalance would be more irritating to him than anger.

"You were right about one thing," I said placatingly. "Let's just drop this. You're obviously off your rocker with the idolatry stuff, though. Even when I first told you about the *mannat* at the Ka'ba you made fun of it. But it's no use trying to convince you because for a large part of my life *I* didn't buy it. I don't expect you to understand my covenant, but you could at least—"

"Screw that. I think your covenant is invalid," Ziad declared.

"Excuse me? I told you that my parents prayed in Mecca. You *do* know about Mecca, don't you? It's not that far from here. The House of God is in Mecca."

"Don't patronize me."

"You're making a mockery of yourself," I scoffed. "My covenant is 'invalid'?"

"*All* covenants are invalid. Save one."

"Oh really? Which one is that exactly?"

"It's in the Quran. Chapter 7, verse 172. 'Am I not your Lord?' God asks humanity. 'Yes!' reply the children of Adam. Do you know what I'm talking about?"

"No."

Ziad dried his eyes with his arm. His black pupils were bright and shiny. He drew closer to me and spoke softly but with feeling.

"That verse refers to the Covenant of Alast. The primordial agreement. The one that established the idea of a human 'We.' God gathered us—all of us: you, me, your ancestors, your progeny, past, present, and future—and asked us a very simple question, and we all—together, in unison with one another, as the human race—made an affirmation. He said, Am I? We said, Yes you are. We affirmed God. We gave our consent, establishing that god was God. That affirmation also established that we were We."

Ziad sat back down before continuing. "It took all of us becoming One for God to be affirmed," he said. "*Ek nuqte vich gul muqdi e.* 'It is all in One contained.' We are the one that is God. That's what Bulleh Shah was talking about. That's why I cried that night when you translated the poem—because I'd never heard it so perfectly captured. In the literature of the mystics, the affirmation of the Covenant of Alast is called the First Witness. It's primeval. It's original. There's a Second Witness too, but it occurs way later. That's when each one of us, in our own individual lives, affirms our disparate religions or ideologies or philosophies. You, my friend, place the Second Witness over and above the First. That's wrong. It's wrong because the real covenant that guides your life, the one that you *should* be obsessed with, is in the service of all humanity. It's for the 'We.' It's for God. Yet you march around the world with your covenant—that false covenant—which is in the service of Muslims only, thinking yourself to be engaged in God's work. You associate partners with God. Islam is your idol."

I stood dumbstruck, then collapsed into the chair opposite him. I had read a thousand books and debated hundreds of believers and spent my whole life in Muslim households, yet I had never encountered such thoughts. "I don't know what to say," I admitted.

"I told you before that my orientation was too simple for a great intellectual like yourself," Ziad replied.

Then, as he reached across the table and touched my hand reassuringly, Ziad started crying again. This time they were tears of reverence. I said nothing; I just looked at his dark brown face. The places where tears had run earlier had dried. New rivulets ran down his cheeks.

*Bela,* I thought to myself.

# Epilogue

I'm sitting on a bench in Monterey, California, waiting for a bus I don't intend to take. Route 3, Glenwood Circle West, means nothing to me except that it's the location of an apartment complex where Ammi lives.

Set below me, in an artificially carved armpit of the hill, is the maroon and white track of Monterey Peninsula College. Sloping above it is the interior of the gray dome that is the sky. Here and there upon its surface, light blue streaks have been sponged. In some places an angel passing by has dragged his wings and smudged together the disparate shades of gray. There's a big tree nearby around which a million moths are dancing, bursting out of the spherical clumps of leaves like laughter from little boys.

God, meanwhile, is seated beside me on the bench, today adopting the form of a lone bird, eyes cast downward. Stubborn little guy, He didn't scoot an inch when I approached to sit down. No matter. I suppose this must be because He knows that, since He is everywhere, every time I sit, I sit upon Him. I guess He realizes the Problem of Omnipresence: you can never be alone.

*Oh no,* I think, *I said too much*—because with a soft whir of His wings, God flies away. Haha, but here He returns, the Ubiquitous One. Now He has lodged Himself between the teeth of the gritting bike rider rolling quickly down the hill. Look at God! Look at Him hold onto an incisor for all His life. Too funny. I bet He now regrets having made this hill so steep.

The bus comes. The driver looks at me and I shrug. Then I get up and walk back to the apartment.

Ammi is in her bedroom, sitting at her desk, watching YouTube videos. I don't say anything; I just get into her bed and watch her from a distance. She's listening to old Punjabi love songs. The kind that lovers say are about lovers and the pious say are about God. The folk singer Reshma, with her purple lips and sorrowful eyes, is singing to an old Punjabi beat.

> *Rabba nai o lagda dil mera*
> *sajna baaj hoya hanaira*
> *O God, I'm restless*
> *Without my beloved, darkness*

Oblivious to my presence, Ammi sways for a while and sings along. The song ends and she puts on the next video. It is Noor Jahan, the graceful crooner with a flower in her hair, adorned in a supple *sari;* the same Noor Jahan that my grandfather used to listen to in the bungalow in Lahore.

> *Akh toon milain kiwayn*
> *pey gai judai kiwayn*
> *aj mera mahi challeya*
> *You don't lock gazes*
> *How we've become distant*
> *I feel so abandoned*

After listening to a few more songs Ammi wraps a gauzy scarf around her hair and goes to a prayer rug in the corner, where she performs two *rakat*s, two cycles of prayer. She finally sees me when she turns her head to give the peace offerings. She laughs out loud.

"First song, then prayer," she says in a guilty voice. "I'm such a con-tradiction, aren't I?"

I smile. "There's nothing inconsistent there."

"You should get up and pray," she says.

"Will you tell me about the *parris* afterwards?" I ask.

"You remember them?" she asks.

"They're *all* I remember," I reply.

"My little Abir. You grew up all these years," she says, touching her hands to my hair. "Just to become innocent again."

# Acknowledgments

I want to recognize my agent, Andrew Stuart, for believing in me and I want to thank my editor, Eric Brandt, for being patient, precise, and generous. I didn't expect to gain friends while writing this book.

I also want to thank all the hard-working editors, managers, and assistants at HarperCollins Publishers, especially Lisa Zuniga and Kathy Reigstad.

Finally, I must acknowledge the joy that the philosopher-alchemist gives me as well as the kindness and support that comes from the casuistically berserk bear.